THE

GRECIAN

PLATE

Compiled by

The Hellenic Ladies Society

St. Barbara Greek Orthodox Church

Durham, North Carolina

COVER

The deer on the cover is symbolic of the Island
of Rhodes. As legend has it, deer were imported
to stampede and eradicate the large number of
poisonous snakes on the island.

Printed in the United States of America
Wimmer Brothers Books
P.O. Box 18408
Memphis, Tennessee 38118-0408
"Cookbooks of Distinction"™

ACKNOWLEDGEMENTS

Our sincere gratitude and thanks to the members of our society and all our friends for their enthusiastic response to The Grecian Plate. The members of the society were most cooperative in sharing their favorite recipes and in helping to test them. We also wish to thank the local restaurateurs who generously shared their recipes with us.

To our families, we want to say thank you for your patience, love, support and understanding of many time-consuming cookbook hours that interrupted the daily family routines.

This book is a collection of nearly 300 recipes and is the second cookbook published by our society. The first book, Fasting and Feasting with the Greeks, was published in 1972, and its success has been our inspiration in writing this cookbook. Many of the original recipes are included in this collection. We regret that every recipe submitted could not be used because of space and duplication. Similar recipes were combined or varied, resulting in a more generally accepted recipe.

And finally, we express our appreciation to Erie Cocolas and A. H. Mebane, III, and the North Carolina Pharmaceutical Association for their cooperation and generous contribution of their time and invaluable services.

Joan Marinos
Lena Mousmoules
Helen Paliouras

Saint Barbara Greek Orthodox Church

HISTORY OF HELLENIC LADIES SOCIETY

On February 12, 1952, twenty women of the Greek community of Durham and Chapel Hill met to formally organize as the "Hellenic Ladies Society," an auxiliary organization of Saint Barbara Church. The Society's major concerns are the needs of the church and its members, the support of the Sunday School program, and to assist with any special projects of the church community.

Over the years, the Society has purchased necessary furnishings and equipment for the church, contributed the down payment for a new Sunday School house, and made an annual donation to the church to assist in the funding of church-related projects. The Society has been continually responsible for providing the necessary funds for materials, equipment, and special events for the Sunday School program. In addition, generous contributions to various humanitarian causes in the local community, as well as to Greek-related charities in this country and abroad have been made by the Hellenic Ladies Society.

In order to fund its many worthwhile projects, the Society relies on its bi-annual "Greek Pastry Sale"... and now endeavors to enlarge its charitable projects with the sale of this updated cookbook, The Grecian Plate.

COOKBOOK COMMITTEE

Co-Editors

Joan Marinos
Lena Mousmoules
Helen Paliouras

Cover Artist and Sketch Designs

Lena Mousmoules

Chapter Divider Artwork

Dina Lias

Typist

Erie Cocolas

Committee Members

Kally Christakos
Cadee Chronaki
Maria Costakis
Helen Dennos
Evy Glekas
Elaine Goodwin
Olimbe Holt

Sophia Livas
Cindy Paliouras
Dena Paliouras
Marian Sunas
Donna Trohanis
Helen Vassiliades

INTRODUCTION

Greece is a Mediterranean country unique in its geography and physical beauty and rich in its culture. Its many islands from the east, south and west fuse the European Greek mainland to the continents of Asia and Africa in ways that make Greece a natural bridge between western civilization and the cultures of Asia and Africa. This unique geography has influenced all expressions of Greek culture, including, of course, the Greek cuisine, but in a way that makes the final outcome distinct and refined and always characteristically Greek.

Although the natural resources of Greece are meager, the beauty of its natural landscape is superb and more than compensates for this deficiency. Greece attracts millions of tourists annually to enjoy its bright sunshine, its intensely blue sky and sea, its picturesque harbors and white-washed villages, the serenity and majestic beauty of its islands and rugged mountains, and above all the open-hearted hospitality of the native Greeks. This great influx of visitors, and the limited part of Greece that constitutes arable land have influenced greatly the Greek cuisine towards developing many practical, yet very tasty dishes that make ingenious use of seasonal vegetables and other locally available ingredients.

In **The Grecian Plate,** we endeavor to share with you this rich heritage, and we have included the unique and traditional dishes from the Greek cuisine that distinctively reflect the way of life in Greece as it is revealed through its cooking. It should be noted that religion is deeply rooted in the Greek way of life, and religious holidays, weddings, baptisms, birthdays and namedays are therefore very special occasions and are traditionally linked to the Greek cuisine. Fasting is also a part of the Orthodox Christian's life. Thus recipes are included for the Orthodox homemaker and are appropriately marked with a cross (†) beside the recipe title.

This cookbook reflects the modern approach to traditional dishes, suggesting whenever possible the use of blenders, food processors and microwave ovens. Recipes that may be prepared in advance and frozen are so designated. We have included detailed information on how to create delicious meals with the popular phyllo pastry. "On the Light Side" is a special chapter featuring timely advice for diet dishes as well as trimmed versions of traditional Greek recipes.

The authentic Greek titles of the recipes are written phonetically followed by the direct English translation. A guide to the pronunciation of all Greek terms and their definitions are listed in the glossary of the Appendix.

We are very proud of our heritage and our objective is to share it with all our friends, and we hope that **The Grecian Plate** will become your favorite collection of ethnic recipes and that it will be used frequently in your home.

TABLE OF CONTENTS

APPETIZERS

MEZETHAKIA (APPETIZERS)

After a day's work, the local taverna is a kaleidoscope of activity -- a very typical scene of Greek life where friends gather for relaxation and animated conversation. Mezethakia (appetizers) play an important role in creating a merry atmosphere for the spontaneous singing and dancing that inevitably breaks out. Tourists sampling mezethakia for the first time might be tempted to postpone dinner indefinitely for the variety is limited only by the imagination of the cook and the availability of ingredients. Simple mezethakia ranging from nuts, olives and feta cheese to the more elaborate spicy meatballs, dolmathes, fried squid and bourekakia are served with either retsina, a resin-flavored wine or ouzo, a "spirited" anise-flavored liqueur.

APPETIZERS

CANAPES

CHEESE TRIANGLES

1/2 pound feta cheese,
  crumbled
1/2 pound soft ricotta cheese

1 tablespoon minced parsley,
  dill or chives
9 slices thin sandwich bread,
  trimmed

Blend cheeses and herbs together. Spread mixture on each slice of bread. Bake at 450 degrees for 10 to 15 minutes until cheese melts. Cut each slice diagonally into 4 triangles. Serve warm. Makes 36 pieces.

CHEESE-ONION TOAST

Round cut of bread, or slices
  of rye party loaf
Butter
Onion, minced

Mayonnaise
Kasseri or Parmesan cheese,
  grated

Butter bread well; cover with onion. Spread 1 heaping teaspoon mayonnaise over onion. Sprinkle with cheese. Bake at 450 degrees until golden. Serve warm.

DIPS AND SPREADS

ARTICHOKE DIP

1 (14-oz.) can artichoke hearts,
  drained and chopped
1 cup mayonnaise

1 cup grated Parmesan cheese
Dash of garlic powder

Combine all ingredients and mix well. Place in lightly greased pyrex dish and bake at 350 degrees until bubbly. Serve with crackers. Serves 6 to 10.

EGGPLANT DIP

1 large eggplant
2 medium overripe tomatoes, chopped
2 tablespoons chopped fresh parsley
1 small onion, minced

2 cloves garlic, minced
1/2 cup unseasoned dry bread crumbs
1/2 cup olive oil
2 tablespoons red wine vinegar
Salt and pepper to taste

Pierce eggplant in several places with fork. In a microwave oven, bake at full power for 5 minutes or until soft; or bake in oven wrapped in aluminum foil at 400 degrees for 1 hour or until soft. Dip eggplant into cold water, peel quickly and chop. Place eggplant and remaining ingredients in food processor and whip for approximately 45 seconds or use a blender to puree or a mixer to blend ingredients. Chill. Serve with crackers or crusty bread. Freezes well. Thaw at room temperature and whip before serving. Makes 2 cups.

KOPANISTO TIRI
Greek Cheese Spread

1 (8-oz.) pkg. cream cheese, softened
8 ounces cottage cheese
4 ounces feta cheese

4 ounces blue cheese
1 teaspoon pepper
1/2 teaspoon oregano
1 or 2 drops olive oil

Place all ingredients in a food processor or blender. Process until smooth. Delicious with crackers, bread or raw vegetables. Makes about 2 1/2 cups.

SHRIMP DIP
A dip recipe your guests will request.

1 (8-oz.) pkg. cream cheese, softened
1 teaspoon minced onion
1 tablespoon ketchup
1/2 tablespoon Worcestershire sauce

1/8 teaspoon cayenne red pepper
Dash of salt
Dash of pepper
1/4 pound small shrimp, cooked and peeled

Halve shrimp if desired. Mix all ingredients well. Serve with raw vegetables or crackers. Makes 1 1/2 cups.

13

TARAMOSALATA†
The famous Greek caviar spread

2 or 3 slices stale white bread*
4 ounces tarama (fish roe)
1 egg (optional)*
1 1/2 cups olive or vegetable oil
  (or half of each)

5 tablespoons lemon juice
1 tablespoon grated onion
  (optional)

Remove crust from bread, moisten with water, and squeeze out excess moisture. Place in mixing bowl with tarama. Beat until well blended. Add egg. Slowly add oil and lemon juice alternately in a steady stream; beat until smooth. Store in refrigerator. Add onion just before serving. Serve with sliced bread, crackers or as a dip. Makes 2 1/2 cups.

---

* Since tarama is quite salty, more bread may be added. The egg gives this recipe a creamy consistency; may omit egg if using during Lent.

MEZETHAKIA (HORS d'OEUVRES)

SAGANAKI
Fried Cheese Squares

2 pounds kefalotiri cheese
1 cup butter

2 tablespoons lemon juice

Cut cheese into bite-size cubes. In a heavy skillet, fry cheese in hot butter quickly (a few seconds on each side) until golden. Arrange on a platter and sprinkle with lemon juice. Serve hot. Makes about 100 pieces.

DOLMATHAKIA YIALADJI[†]
Grape Leaves Stuffed with Rice

Since vineyards are plentiful throughout Greece, grape leaves provide the basic ingredient for several inexpensive but nutritious meals.

1 (16-oz.) jar grape leaves	2 tablespoons minced fresh dill
4 medium onions, chopped	2 tablespoons minced fresh mint
1/2 cup whole scallions, chopped	1 teaspoon sugar
1 cup olive oil	1/2 cup lemon juice
1 cup long grain rice	1/4 cup pignolia nuts (optional)
1/4 teaspoon salt	1/4 cup white raisins (optional)
1/4 teaspoon pepper	Water
1/2 cup minced fresh parsley (reserve stems)	

Drain brine from grape leaves, snip off stems and rinse in cold water. Drain in colander. Saute onions and scallions in 1/2 cup olive oil for 2 to 3 minutes. Add rice, salt, pepper, parsley, dill, mint, sugar, 1/4 cup lemon juice, pignolia nuts, raisins and 1 cup of water. Cover and cook for 15 to 20 minutes.

Cut any large grape leaves in half. Lay out leaf with underside up. Place 1 tablespoon filling at base of leaf, fold sides over and roll up. Line bottom of Dutch oven with any torn or coarse leaves. Interlace parsley stems over leaves. Layer dolmathes snugly seam-side down. Add remaining olive oil, lemon juice and enough water to cover dolmathes. Place an inverted heavy plate on top to prevent shifting. Cover and simmer 40 minutes, or until rice is tender. Make up 2 days prior to a party and cover loosely with waxed paper in the refrigerator. Dolmathes are best served at room temperature. Makes about 36 pieces.

Note: See Miscellaneous Chapter for additional information on grape leaves.

TIROBISKOTAKIA
Layered Cheese Squares
A real taste treat for cheese lovers.

3 tablespoons butter
3 tablespoons all-purpose flour
1 1/2 cups warm milk
3/4 teaspoon salt (less if feta
   is very salty)
1/4 teaspoon pepper
2 cups crumbled feta cheese

1 (8-oz.) cottage cheese,
   small curd
4 ounces cream cheese, softened
6 eggs, beaten
Pastry dough (below)
Olives, sliced (optional)

Melt butter in heavy saucepan. Blend in flour, stirring constantly for 2 minutes to form a paste. Add milk with salt and pepper; stir constantly until sauce thickens. Remove from heat. In a large bowl, combine cheeses with eggs; pour into cream sauce and mix well. Set aside.

Remove prepared dough from refrigerator; allow to come to room temperature. Press into bottom of 13 x 9-inch baking pan. Bake shell at 450 degrees for 10 minutes. Remove from oven; pour filling over crust. Bake at 350 degrees for 30 to 35 minutes. Let stand 15 minutes before cutting into squares. Serve warm. Freezes well. Bake directly from freezer at 300 degrees for 25 minutes to reheat through. Garnish with sliced olives, if desired.

Pastry Dough:
   4 ounces cream cheese, softened
   1/2 cup butter, softened

1 cup all-purpose flour

Combine cream cheese and butter. Cut in flour with pastry blender. Work dough with hands until it holds together. Make a ball; wrap and chill overnight.

Variation: Filling may also be used in making cheese tarts. Press dough into miniature muffin pans; fill with 1 1/2 teaspoons of filling. Bake at 450 degrees for 15 to 20 minutes or until golden brown.

Quickie appetizer: Core center of a large dill pickle or of a pared cucumber. Stuff tightly with a firm cheese mixture. Chill and slice 1/4-inch thick.

16

CHEESE AND OLIVE BALLS

1/2 cup margarine, melted
1 cup all-purpose flour
2 cups grated Cheddar cheese

Paprika to taste
Pimiento olives

Combine margarine, flour, cheese and paprika. Knead mixture well. Shape into small balls, stuffing olive in each one and covering completely with the dough. Bake at 375 degrees for 10 to 15 minutes or until lightly browned. May be frozen before baking. Bake directly from freezer at 400 degrees for 15 minutes. Makes about 25 to 35 balls.

CHEESE-SESAME ROUNDS

1/2 cup butter
1 (3-oz.) pkg. cream cheese,
 softened

1 cup all-purpose flour
3/4 teaspoon chili powder
1 tablespoon sesame seeds

Cream butter and cream cheese until light and fluffy. Combine flour and chili powder; gradually add to butter mixture. Beat well. Shape dough into a ball, wrap in waxed paper and freeze one hour or until firm. Roll dough to 1/8-inch thickness on a lightly floured surface. Cut into 2-inch rounds. Place on lightly greased cookie sheet; sprinkle with sesame seeds. Bake at 400 degrees for 10 minutes or until lightly browned. Cool. Store in air-tight containers, using waxed paper between layers. Makes about 3 dozen.

MINIATURE PARTY CHEESE WAFERS

1 cup potato flakes
3 tablespoons sharp cheese spread
2 tablespoons margarine, softened
2 tablespoons all-purpose flour

1/2 teaspoon salt
1/4 teaspoon paprika
1 tablespoon cold water

Combine all ingredients and knead mixture well. Shape into roll 10 inches long and 1 inch in diameter. Wrap in plastic wrap and refrigerate at least 2 hours. Slice thinly and bake on ungreased cookie sheet at 425 degrees for 10 minutes or until golden brown. Makes 20 to 25 slices.

APPETIZERS

SOUZOUKAKIA A LA SMYRNI
Cocktail Meatballs, Smyrna-Style

1 1/2 pounds lean ground beef, ground twice
1/2 cup dry unseasoned bread crumbs
1/2 to 1 teaspoon powdered cumin
1 to 1 1/2 teaspoons salt
1/4 teaspoon pepper

1 to 2 cloves garlic, crushed
Dash of ground cinnamon
2 teaspoons minced fresh parsley
1/4 cup water
1/2 cup butter
Sauce (below)

Combine all ingredients, except butter, in a large bowl. Knead thoroughly until mixture resembles a paste. Shape into oblong balls; brown on all sides in hot butter. Do not drain. Pour sauce over meatballs and pan drippings; simmer 30 minutes. Freezes well; reheat in a covered casserole at 350 degrees or place in microwave. Makes 20 to 25 meatballs.

Sauce:
2 cups tomato sauce
1 cup water
2 bay leaves

1 clove garlic, minced
1/2 teaspoon salt
3 tablespoons red wine

Combine all ingredients in a saucepan and bring to a boil. Reduce heat; and simmer until thickened, about 15 to 20 minutes.

MARINATED SAUSAGE MEATBALLS

1 pound bulk hot sausage
2 pounds bulk mild sausage
3 eggs, slightly beaten
1 cup herbal dry stuffing mix

3/4 teaspoon ground sage
Oil for frying
Marinade (below)

Combine first 5 ingredients and mix well. Shape into small balls, using 1 tablespoon for each meatball. Brown in hot oil; drain. Pour marinade over meatballs and simmer for 30 minutes. Serve in heated platter or chafing dish. Makes 20 to 25 meatballs.

Marinade:
3/4 cup ketchup
3/4 cup chili sauce
3 tablespoons soy sauce

6 tablespoons brown sugar
3 tablespoons red wine vinegar
1 1/2 cups water

Combine all ingredients and mix well.

LOUKANIKO A LA THRAKEE
Thrasian Sausage

1/2 cup red wine
2 teaspoons dried oregano
3 pounds ground pork (not lean)
4 to 5 whole green onions,
  finely minced

2 teaspoons salt
2 teaspoons pepper
1 orange peel, grated finely
1 teaspoon allspice
Lemon juice

Heat wine, add oregano and boil for a few minutes. Strain liquid into a large bowl onto the meat; add the remaining ingredients, except the lemon juice, and mix well. Cover bowl and refrigerate overnight. Shape into small patties and panbroil about 8 minutes on each side. Sprinkle with lemon juice the last minute of broiling. Makes about 3 1/2 dozen patties.

Variation: If you wish to stuff sausage meat into casing, obtain 2 pounds of pork casing from butcher. Run water through each casing; soak overnight in cold water. Gently parboil for 5 minutes. Using proper attachment on meat grinder for stuffing, force meat mixture into casings, tying string every 12 inches. Prick casings with fork and refrigerate, freeze, or hang up to dry in a very cold place for 1 week. When ready to use, cut into 1-inch pieces and panbroil until done.

DOMATITSES MEH KAVOURI
Crab-Stuffed Cherry Tomatoes
Takes time but worth the effort for that special occasion.

6 dozen cherry tomatoes
Salt
1/2 cup cottage cheese, small
  curd
3 teaspoons minced onion
3 teaspoons lemon juice

1 teaspoon prepared horseradish
Dash of garlic salt
1 pound fresh crabmeat, drained
  and flaked
1/2 cup minced celery
1 tablespoon chopped green pepper

Cut top off each tomato; scoop out pulp, reserving for other uses. Sprinkle inside of tomato with salt and invert on paper towels to drain. Process cottage cheese in blender until smooth; add onion, lemon juice, horseradish and garlic salt. Spoon crabmeat, celery and pepper in mixture and stir well. Fill tomatoes with crabmeat mixture. Chill. (Recipe may be halved.) Makes 72 tomatoes.

19

KALAMARAKIA TIGANITA[†]
Fried Baby Squid

2 pounds baby squid	1 cup vegetable oil
Salt and pepper	Juice of 1 lemon
1 cup all-purpose flour	

Wash squid; drain on paper towel. Cut squid into rings and tentacles into pieces. Season with salt and pepper. Place squid and flour in a plastic bag; shake to flour evenly. In a deep skillet, fry in hot oil for 7 to 10 minutes or until golden brown. Sprinkle with lemon juice. Serve hot. Serves 4.

ROLLED SHRIMP

1 pound fresh or frozen medium shrimp	2 teaspoons lemon juice
10 slices bacon	Dash of hot pepper sauce
1 1/2 ounces cream cheese with chives, softened	

Thaw shrimp, if frozen. Remove shells and devein. Cut bacon slices in half crosswise and fry in a skillet until partially done; drain on paper towel. Split shrimp in half lengthwise; spread bottom half with 1/2 teaspoon cream cheese; replace top half of shrimp. Combine lemon juice and hot pepper sauce. Brush each stuffed shrimp with lemon mixture. Wrap bacon half around each shrimp; secure with toothpick. Broil 4 to 5 inches from heat for 2 to 3 minutes. Turn; broil 2 minutes more or until shrimp are done. Serve hot. Makes 16 to 20.

TARAMOKEFTETHES[†]
Fish Roe Patties

5 medium potatoes, boiled and peeled	2 tablespoons cracker meal
	Salt and pepper
1 (7-oz.) jar tarama	Fresh parsley and mint, minced
1 small onion, minced	Vegetable oil for frying

Mash potatoes; add tarama and mix well. Add remaining ingredients and mix well. Shape into small patties or balls and roll in cracker crumbs; fry in hot oil until golden or broil in greased shallow pan. Makes about 2 dozen.

SAVORY CRESCENT MUSHROOM ROLL-UPS

2 cups chopped mushrooms (about
  1/2 pound)
1/2 cup chopped onion
1/4 teaspoon garlic powder
1/2 to 1 teaspoon dried dill

1/2 teaspoon salt
1/4 teaspoon pepper
3 tablespoons butter
1/2 cup sour cream
1 (8-oz.) can crescent rolls

Preheat oven to 425 degrees. Combine first 7 ingredients and place on lightly greased cookie sheet to brown until moisture evaporates. Remove from heat, cool for 10 minutes and stir in sour cream. Separate crescent dough into 2 rectangles. Press perforated areas together with fingers. Roll out each rectangle to a 10 x 6-inch size. Place 1/2 mushroom mixture on each rectangle; spread out evenly to cover dough. Starting with long side, roll up jellyroll fashion and seal. Refrigerate briefly to firm dough; remove and cut each roll into 10 slices. Place flat on cookie sheet. Bake at 425 degrees for 15 to 20 minutes or until golden brown. Makes 20 slices.

SPINACH TURNOVERS

2 cups all-purpose flour
Dash of salt
4 tablespoons olive oil

Water
Filling (below)
Vegetable oil for frying

Blend flour, salt and oil with fork. Add 3 or 4 tablespoons water to make a soft dough. Knead a few minutes. Separate into 8 equal balls. Chill in refrigerator for 30 minutes. Divide 1 ball into 2 parts. Roll out each part into a small circle; place 1 tablespoon prepared filling on one side of circle. Fold over, sealing edges with fork. Moisten with fingers dipped in water. Fry until golden, being careful not to brown. Makes 16 turnovers.

Filling:
  1 (10-oz.) pkg. frozen chopped spinach, cooked and drained
  1/4 pound feta cheese, crumbled
  1 egg
  Salt and pepper

Combine all ingredients and mix well.

EGG-ANCHOVY BARRELS

Eggs, hard boiled, peeled
Anchovy fillets, whole and minced
Chives, minced
Gherkins, minced

Olive oil
Dash of wine vinegar
Salt and pepper

Prepare number of eggs desired. Cut thin slices off each end of egg. Scoop out yolks; mash well. Add minced anchovy fillets, chives, gherkins, olive oil, wine vinegar, salt and pepper to taste. Stuff back into eggs. Encircle each egg with a whole anchovy fillet to resemble a barrel. Secure with a toothpick.

OUZO-STUFFED EGGS
A different, aromatic taste and very Greek.

6 eggs, hard boiled, peeled
1 tablespoon Ouzo*
1 tablespoon minced fresh parsley

1/2 teaspoon minced fresh mint
2 tablespoons mayonnaise
Watercress (optional)

Slice eggs in half lengthwise, scoop out egg yolks and blend with ouzo to make a smooth paste. Blend in remaining ingredients. Fill egg whites; sprinkle with additional fresh parsley. Garnish with watercress around eggs, if desired. Makes 12 pieces.

PICKLED EGGS

1 1/2 cups white cider vinegar
3/4 cup water
1 small onion, chopped
1/4 teaspoon whole rosemary

1/4 teaspoon salt
3 peppercorns
Few grains cayenne pepper
8 eggs, hard boiled, peeled

In a saucepan, combine all ingredients, except eggs; simmer for 10 minutes. Place eggs in quart jar. Strain mixture and pour over eggs. Seal jar and store in refrigerator for 1 week. Serve as an appetizer or in salads.

---

* See wine and liqueur section in the Appendix.

BOUREKAKIA (PHYLLO PASTRY APPETIZERS)

The perfect appetizer — small, flaky phyllo triangles filled with
a delectable filling of either cheese, spinach, meat or seafood.
Elegant to serve and delicious to eat. Keep a supply handy in the
freezer to pop into a hot oven for a quick snack. Read "How to
Work with Commercial Phyllo" in the Miscellaneous Chapter before
preparing the following recipes.

BASIC ASSEMBLY OF TRIANGLES

1 pound phyllo
1 pound butter, clarified,
 melted and warm

Filling of choice (see following
 recipes)

Gently unfold phyllo. With a sharp knife cut through stacked
phyllo lengthwise into 3 equal portions. Cover phyllo not
immediately used with plastic wrap. Lay out 1 strip of phyllo;
brush with melted butter. Fold in half lengthwise to make a strip
3 inches wide; butter again. Place a teaspoon of filling at center
bottom, 1 inch from edge. Fold one corner over to form a triangle;
continue folding over triangle to the end of the phyllo strip.
(Process is same as folding a flag; see sketch next page.) Brush
triangle with butter. Repeat until phyllo, butter and filling are
all used. Bake on ungreased baking sheet as specified in following
recipes. Makes about 60 pieces.

Freezing: Cool baked triangles; layer in plastic container, using
waxed paper between layers. Bake directly from freezer at 425
degrees for 10 minutes. To freeze unbaked triangles, place on
baking sheets lined with waxed paper. Place in freezer. When
frozen, pack triangles in plastic containers or plastic bags and
return to freezer. Bake directly from freezer on ungreased baking
sheets at 400 degrees for 25 minutes or until golden. May freeze
up to 2 months.

VARIATION ON TRIANGLES

The fillings in the following recipes can also be used for making
turnovers, using either pastry dough recipe listed in Miscellaneous
Chapter.

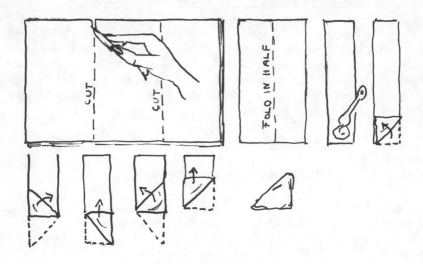

SPANAKOPITAKIA
Spinach Triangles

1 medium onion, minced
3 tablespoons olive oil
1 (10-oz.) pkg. frozen chopped
  spinach, thawed and well drained
1 teaspoon salt
1/4 pound feta cheese, crumbled

1/2 cup cottage cheese
1 egg, beaten
1 pound phyllo
1 pound clarified butter,
  melted and warm

Saute onions in hot oil until soft. Add spinach and salt; saute a few minutes. Cool slightly. Stir in cheeses and egg, blending thoroughly. Prepare triangles as directed in introduction of section. Bake at 400 degrees for 15 minutes or until golden.

TIROPITAKIA
Cheese Triangles

3 eggs
1 (8-oz.) pkg. cream cheese, softened
3/4 pound feta cheese, crumbled
2 tablespoons chopped fresh parsley

1 pound phyllo
1 pound clarified butter,
  melted and warm

Beat eggs until fluffy. Add cheeses and parsley, mixing well. Prepare triangles as directed in introduction of section. Bake at 375 degrees for 20 minutes or until golden.

TIROPITAKIA MEH FISTIKIA
Cheese Pistachio Triangles

3 (8-oz.) pkgs. cream cheese, softened
6 egg yolks
3 teaspoons lemon juice
3/4 cup pistachios, finely chopped
3/4 cup grated Parmesan cheese

1 tablespoon scallions, minced
1 tablespoon minced fresh parsley
1 pound phyllo
1 pound clarified butter, melted and warm

Beat cream cheese until fluffy. Add egg yolks and lemon juice; beat well. Stir in pistachios, cheese, scallions and parsley. Prepare triangles as directed in introduction of section. Bake at 350 degrees for 25 to 30 minutes or until golden.

KREATOPITAKIA
Meat Triangles

1 pound lean ground beef
1/8 teaspoon garlic salt
1/8 teaspoon onion salt
Dash of ground cinnamon
1 (8-oz.) can tomato sauce
1/2 cup red wine

1/4 cup grated Parmesan cheese
1 egg, beaten
1 pound phyllo
1 pound clarified butter, melted and warm

Brown meat until crumbly. Drain off excess fat. Season with garlic salt, onion salt and cinnamon. Add tomato sauce and wine. Cook over medium-high heat until most of the liquid has been absorbed. Cover and simmer 15 minutes. Cool. Blend in cheese and egg. Prepare triangles as directed in introduction of section. Bake at 375 degrees for 10 minutes or until golden.

Keftethes (meatballs) may be frozen after cooked, then heated through to defrost when needed. If served in a sauce, drop frozen in boiling sauce and heat through until defrosted.

GARITHOPITAKIA
Shrimp Triangles

2 large onions, minced
1/3 cup butter
2 to 2 1/2 pounds small shrimp,
  peeled
1/2 cup minced fresh parsley
Salt and pepper

3 eggs
1/2 cup grated kefalotiri or
  Parmesan cheese
1 pound phyllo
1 pound clarified butter,
  melted and warm

Saute onions in hot butter until tender. Add shrimp, parsley, salt
and pepper; saute until shrimp turns pink and liquid is absorbed.
Remove from heat; cool. Beat eggs and cheese together well; add to
shrimp mixture. Prepare triangles as directed in introduction of
section. Bake at 350 degrees for 20 minutes or until golden.

KAVOUROPITAKIA
Crabmeat Triangles

1 small onion, minced
5 tablespoons butter
2 tablespoons all-purpose flour
2 cups lukewarm milk
1 tablespoon minced fresh parsley
1 tablespoon dried dill
1/2 cup fresh mushrooms, chopped
2 eggs, hard boiled, finely chopped

1 teaspoon sherry (optional)
Salt to taste
1 1/2 pounds crabmeat
1/2 cup bread crumbs
1 pound phyllo
1 pound clarified butter,
  melted and warm

Saute onion in hot butter until tender. Blend in flour. Add milk
gradually, stirring constantly until creamy. Remove from heat; add
remaining ingredients, except phyllo and melted butter, and mix
well. If mixture is too thin, add more bread crumbs; if too thick,
add more milk. Prepare triangles as directed in introduction of
section. Bake at 350 degrees for 30 to 35 minutes until golden.
If baking triangles directly from freezer, increase baking time by
10 minutes.

CHICKEN ROLL-UPS
So delicious, you'll go back for more.

2 chicken breasts, boned
3 tablespoons lemon juice
2 tablespoons olive oil
1/2 teaspoon minced garlic
3/4 teaspoon dried oregano

Salt to taste
1/2 pound phyllo
1 cup clarified butter,
   melted and warm

Cut uncooked chicken into small pieces. Combine lemon juice, olive oil, garlic, oregano and salt; mix well. Add to chicken and marinate overnight. Cut phyllo into 4 equal strips crosswise. Brush one phyllo strip with butter. Place a teaspoon of filling at center bottom of strip, 1 inch from the edge. Fold sides over filling. Brush with butter and roll up loosely jellyroll fashion to the end. Brush roll and seam with butter. Repeat procedure with remaining phyllo and filling. Bake seam-side down on ungreased baking sheet at 350 degrees for 25 minutes or until golden brown. Makes 3 1/2 dozen.

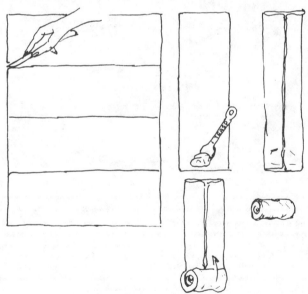

SOUPS, SALADS AND SAUCES

SOUPS, SALADS AND SAUCES

Greeks start the meal with soup to whet the appetite and stimulate the gastric juices. The most famous soup is the creamy and slightly tart avgolemono, an egg and lemon-flavored broth, that can also double as a sauce to flavor many vegetable and meat dishes. It is believed that this ancient recipe is the precursor of mayonnaise. Frequently in a Greek household, the entire meal will consist of a thick soup like fasolatha accompanied by fresh bread and black olives.

Many soup recipes are closely identified with the traditions of Greek religious holidays. For example, lentil soup, fakies, is eaten during Lent and particularly on Holy Friday. The Easter soup, mayeritsa, is customarily served after midnight services on Easter morning, along with dyed eggs, Easter bread and feta cheese to break the fast.

No table in Greece is without a salad to help balance the main meal. The traditional Greek salad is a popular favorite in America with its tangy olive oil and lemon (or vinegar) dressing. Chunks of zesty feta cheese provide the crowning ingredient.

We are indebted to the unknown Greek chef who more than 20 centuries ago created the versatile white cream sauce so widely used today. It differs from the French white sauce in that it contains grated cheese. Moussaka and pastitsio are two examples of classic dishes topped with a savory layer of white cream sauce.

SOUPS

KOTOSOUPA AVGOLEMONO
Chicken Egg–Lemon Soup
The famous egg and lemon soup

1 stewing hen (3 to 4 pounds)	1/2 cup chopped fresh parsley
2 celery stalks and leaves	2 quarts water
2 medium carrots	3/4 cup long grain rice
3 whole green onions	Salt

Cover hen and vegetables with water; bring to a boil. Skim off scum. Reduce heat and cook partially covered 1 1/2 to 2 hours, until hen is tender. Remove hen from broth; set aside for later use as desired. Strain broth into a kettle, discarding vegetables. Bring broth to a boil, add rice, stir and salt to taste. Reduce heat and cook covered until rice is tender. Blend hot soup with avgolemono sauce.

Avgolemono Sauce:
  3 eggs, separated   Juice of 1 1/2 lemons

With an electric mixer, beat egg whites until stiff but not dry. Continue beating and add yolks one at a time. Slowly add lemon juice, using a rubber spatula to scrape sides of bowl. Add a little hot broth to egg sauce. Pour egg sauce into remaining broth in kettle, stirring vigorously over very low heat until thickened. Do not boil as it will curdle. Serve hot. Serves 6 to 8.

KOTOSOUPA AVGOLEMONO APLI
Chicken Egg–Lemon Soup (Simplified)

2 (10 1/2-oz.) cans condensed chicken rice soup	1/4 cup lemon juice
1 (10 1/2-oz.) can condensed chicken broth	3 egg yolks, well beaten
3 cups water	1 tablespoon chopped fresh dill (optional)

Combine and heat first 4 items, then slowly add hot mixture to eggs, stirring constantly. Heat over low heat for 2 to 3 minutes. Garnish with dill. Serves 6.

MAYERITSA
Easter Soup

Heart, liver, lungs and
  intestines of young lamb
2 beef bouillon cubes
2 quarts water
1/2 cup butter
4 bunches whole green onions,
  finely chopped

1/4 cup minced fresh dill
1/4 cup minced fresh parsley
2 teaspoons salt
1/2 teaspoon pepper
1/3 cup long grain rice
4 eggs
Juice of 2 lemons

Wash well heart, liver and lungs. To wash intestines, use a long
pencil to turn them inside out, scrub with salt and rinse under
running water. Using a large soup kettle, dissolve bouillon cubes
in the boiling water, adding organ meats to scald. Simmer gently
about 30 minutes. Remove from heat, lift out organ meats with a
slotted spoon, strain the broth and reserve. Cut organ meats into
1-inch pieces. In same kettle, melt butter and saute chopped meat,
onions and herbs. Add salt and pepper. Simmer until onions are
tender. Add reserved broth and rice, cover and simmer about 15 to
20 minutes until rice is cooked. Remove from heat.

In medium-size bowl, beat eggs and lemon juice with a wire whisk.
Slowly add 1 cup soup broth, stirring constantly. Pour mixture
back into soup kettle, stirring vigorously until thickened. Reheat
briefly over very low heat and serve immediately. Do not boil soup
as it will curdle. Serves 6.

MAYERITSA APLI
Easter Soup (Simplified)

3 pounds lamb shoulder
2 pounds lamb bones
2 stalks celery
1 carrot
2 large onions, quartered
Salt and pepper
3 quarts water

1 1/2 bunches whole green
  onions, finely chopped
1/4 cup minced fresh dill
1/4 cup minced fresh parsley
1/2 cup long grain rice
4 eggs
Juice of 2 lemons

Simmer meat, bones, celery, carrot, onions, salt and pepper in the
water for 2 hours. Using a colander, strain broth and reserve,
discarding vegetables. Remove meat from bones and dice. Add meat,
green onions, herbs and rice to broth; simmer covered for 20
minutes. Remove from heat. Follow instructions for avgolemono
sauce from the preceding recipe. Serves 6 to 8.

31

SOUPA HRISTOUYENIATIKI
Christmas Soup

1 pound chicken backs	1/4 cup minced fresh parsley
Giblets and neck from turkey	1 1/2 teaspoons salt
2 quarts water	6 peppercorns, crushed
2 carrots, chopped	1/2 cup long grain rice
2 onions, chopped	2 tablespoons butter
3 celery stalks, chopped	2 egg yolks
1 teaspoon thyme	Juice of 2 large lemons

In a large soup kettle, place chicken and turkey parts, cover with water and bring to a boil. Skim off scum. Add chopped vegetables and seasonings. Partially cover and simmer gently for 2 hours. Remove poultry parts, dice and reserve for later use. Strain broth and return to kettle. Bring to a boil; add the rice. Reduce heat, cover and cook for 20 minutes until rice is tender. Add butter and reserved chopped poultry. In a separate bowl, beat egg yolks and lemon juice with a wire whisk. Gradually add a cup of hot broth, beating constantly. Slowly add egg mixture back into remaining broth in kettle, stirring vigorously over low heat until thickened. Serves 6 to 8.

FAKIES [†]
Lentil Soup
This soup is the only food eaten by devout Orthodox Christians on Good Friday. The vinegar is symbolic, recalling that it was given to Christ on the cross.

2 medium onions, chopped	1 cup lentils, sorted, rinsed
2 cloves garlic, minced	and drained
1/4 cup olive oil	1/2 cup tomato sauce
2 carrots, sliced	2 bay leaves
1 celery stalk, sliced	Salt and pepper
8 cups water or stock	2 tablespoons wine vinegar

In a soup kettle, saute onions and garlic in hot olive oil until tender. Add carrots and celery; cook 10 minutes over low heat. Add water or stock, lentils, tomato sauce and seasonings. Bring to a boil, reduce heat and cover. Simmer over low heat 1 to 1 1/2 hours or until soup is slightly thickened. Discard bay leaves. Add vinegar just before serving. Serves 6.

Note: For strict fast, omit olive oil and stock. Lentils contain more protein per serving than any other vegetable.

FASOLATHA [†]
Bean Soup

1 pound navy beans
1/2 cup olive or vegetable oil
1 large onion, chopped
1 large clove garlic, minced
1 (8-oz.) can tomato sauce
2 stalks celery, chopped

2 carrots, sliced
3 quarts water
1/2 teaspoon minced fresh
  parsley, dill or basil
  (optional)
Salt and pepper

Wash and sort beans; soak overnight in cold water. Drain. Combine oil, onions, garlic, tomato sauce, celery, carrots and water with drained beans in a large soup kettle. Add desired herbs. Cook over medium heat about 2 1/2 hours or until beans are tender. Add salt and pepper the last 20 minutes of cooking. Serves 8 to 10.

Note: Salt is added at the last of cooking to prevent toughening of the beans.

YIOUVARLAKIA
Meatball Soup
Good meal for a winter day.

1 pound ground beef or lamb
1 medium onion, minced
1/3 cup long grain rice
1 egg
3 tablespoons butter, softened

1 teaspoon minced fresh mint
1 teaspoon minced fresh parsley
Salt and pepper
2 (10 1/2-oz.) cans beef broth

Combine first 8 ingredients. Mix well and shape into small meatballs, about 1 1/4-inch in diameter. Drop into simmering broth. Broth should cover meatballs; if necessary, add a little water. Cook covered about 35 to 45 minutes until meat is tender and rice is cooked. Serves 6.

Variation: May serve with Avgolemono Sauce I (see Sauce section later in chapter).

Soups, such as fasolatha (bean soup) and fakies (lentil soup), may be easily frozen. Make a larger quantity than needed and freeze the extra amount. Avgolemono sauce or soup should not be frozen, however.

PSAROSOUPA
Mediterranean Seafood Soup
A flavorful soup containing four varieties of
succulent seafood.

1 large onion, finely chopped
1 clove garlic, minced
3 tablespoons olive oil
1/2 cup water
2 (16-oz.) cans whole tomatoes,
    chopped
1 cup dry white wine
1 cup water or fish stock
2 tablespoons chopped fresh
    parsley

1/2 teaspoon thyme
1 bay leaf
1 teaspoon seasoned salt
1/4 teaspoon pepper
12 large clams
1 pound raw shrimp, peeled
    and deveined
1/2 pound scallops
1 pound firm-flesh fish, cut
    into 1-inch chunks

In a large soup kettle, saute onion and garlic in hot oil until tender, adding 1/2 cup water to keep from scorching. Add tomatoes, wine, water, herbs and seasonings. Bring to a boil, then reduce heat and simmer uncovered about 15 minutes, stirring occasionally.

Meanwhile, place clams on a pan in a 300-degree oven about 5 to 8 minutes. Using an oyster knife, cut quickly into the clam, going in from the side to the back hinged part. Empty contents into strainer anchored over bowl. Strain clam juice through a cheesecloth; add to soup. Chop up clam meat; add to soup along with the shrimp, scallops and fish. Simmer gently an additional 10 to 15 minutes or until fish flakes with a fork. Serves 8 to 10.

Note: Frozen fish and canned shellfish can be substituted.

FISH STOCK

2 to 3 pounds raw fish heads
    and tails
2 quarts water
1 tablespoon salt
2 large onions, sliced

6 peppercorns
1 stalk celery
1 bay leaf
Pinch thyme

Wash fish parts under cold running water. Place fish and remaining ingredients in a large soup kettle. Bring to a boil; reduce heat and simmer for 45 minutes. Strain stock, discarding the rest. Stock will keep several days in the refrigerator or several weeks frozen.

SOUPA REVITHIA
Chick Pea Soup

6 cups chicken broth
1 (16-oz.) can chick peas,
  drained
2 medium onions, chopped
1/2 teaspoon salt
1/4 teaspoon pepper
1/4 cup olive oil

3 tablespoons minced celery
  leaves
1 tablespoon minced carrot
1 tablespoon minced fresh
  parsley
1 tablespoon lemon juice

In a large pot, bring first 8 ingredients to boil. Reduce heat; simmer for 30 minutes. When ready to serve, stir in parsley and lemon juice. Serves 6.

SPANAKORIZO SOUPA[†]
Spinach and Rice Soup

1 large onion, chopped
1/2 cup olive oil
1/3 cup vegetable oil
1 (10-oz.) pkg. frozen chopped
  spinach, thawed

3 tablespoons tomato paste
3 quarts water
Salt and pepper to taste
3/4 cup long grain rice

In a large kettle, saute onions in the olive and vegetable oil until golden. Add spinach; cook several minutes. Dilute tomato paste in a little water; add to spinach and onion mixture. Add water. Season to taste. Bring to a boil, add rice and stir. Reduce heat, cover and simmer about 1 1/2 hours. Serves 5 to 6.

SOUPA DOMATES MEH FETA TIRI
Tomato Soup with Feta Cheese

1 medium onion, coarsely chopped
2 tablespoons olive oil
2 tablespoons tomato paste
Salt and pepper

6 cups water
1/2 cup soupettes or orzo
1/2 cup crumbled feta cheese

Saute onions in hot oil until golden. Blend in tomato paste, salt and pepper. Add water and bring to a boil. Add orzo, reduce heat and cover. Cook over medium-low heat for 20 to 30 minutes, stirring occasionally. Garnish each serving with feta cheese. Serves 6 to 8.

SOUPA KREMMITHIA
Onion Soup

4 cups thinly-sliced sweet onions
1 clove garlic, minced
1/4 cup butter
5 1/2 cups water
1/2 cup dry sherry (optional)

8 beef bouillon cubes
6 slices crusty bread, 3/4-inch
  thick, buttered and toasted
6 slices Swiss cheese, cut in
  half crosswise

In a large saucepan, saute onions and garlic in butter until golden brown. Add water and sherry, bring to a boil and add bouillon cubes. Reduce heat and simmer for 30 minutes. Pour soup into six oven-proof bowls. Place slice of toast topped with cheese on soup and place under broiler until cheese melts. Serve hot. Serves 6.

SOUP STOCK

4 pounds bones from beef,
  lamb or chicken
1 large onion, quartered
2 carrots
2 stalks celery with leaves

6 whole peppercorns
1 tablespoon salt
2 bay leaves
2 quarts water

Wash bones under cold running water; combine with remaining ingredients in a large kettle. Cover and simmer about 2 to 3 hours. Using a colander, strain stock into a large bowl, cool and then refrigerate overnight. (Pieces of meat can be saved to use in stews or soups.)

The next morning remove congealed fat from top of stock. Use immediately, or cover and refrigerate up to 2 days. (Can be kept in refrigerator up to 6 days if congealed fat that forms on top is not removed; be sure to remove fat before using stock.) To freeze stock, heat enough to liquefy and pour into freezer containers, leaving a 1-inch headspace.

SALADS

PREPARING LETTUCE GREENS FOR SALAD

In a true Greek salad, one never sees the lettuce torn into bite-size pieces; it is finely sliced. Leaves should be separated, washed under cold running water, drained, wrapped in a clean kitchen towel and refrigerated. The towel absorbs the moisture clinging to the leaves, allowing the dressing later to coat them. The dressing, of course, is always added at the last possible moment just before tossing.

ELLINIKI SALATA
Greek Salad

1/2 head lettuce	Olive oil
1 cut clove garlic	1/2 cup crumbled feta cheese
1 small cucumber	Calamata or Greek black olives
2 tomatoes	Anchovies (optional)
1 small onion or 3 green onions	Fresh parsley, dill, fennel or
Green pepper	mint
Salt and pepper to taste	Dried oregano
Lemon juice or wine vinegar	

Prepare lettuce as directed in previous paragraph; place in a large salad bowl that has been rubbed with cut garlic. Cut up remaining vegetables as desired; add to lettuce. Add salt and pepper and toss. Serve with a dressing that consists of 1 part lemon juice or wine vinegar to 2 parts olive oil. Garnish with feta cheese, olives and anchovies. Sprinkle with fresh herbs or dried oregano. Serves 4.

AGOURIA MEH YIAOURTI
Cucumber and Yogurt Salad
Simple and refreshing

1 to 2 cloves garlic	4 medium cucumbers, peeled
1 teaspoon salt	and sliced
1 pint plain yogurt	1 teaspoon dried mint, crushed

Crush garlic with the salt in a mortar; add to yogurt and stir to blend in. Add cucumbers and mix well. Garnish with mint. Serves 6.

AGOURO—DOMATO—SALATA[†]
Tomato and Cucumber Salad

5 tomatoes, quartered
2 cucumbers, peeled and sliced
1 medium onion, chopped
1/4 teaspoon dried oregano

1/4 cup wine vinegar
1/3 cup olive oil
Salt and pepper to taste

Arrange tomatoes, cucumbers and onions in a large bowl. Mix all dressing ingredients in a small jar, shake well and pour over salad. Season with salt and pepper. Serves 6.

SALATA MEH PATATES[†]
Potato Salad

4 large potatoes, boiled,
   peeled and cubed
4 whole green onions, chopped
1 stalk celery, chopped
1 cup finely shredded red
   cabbage (optional)
1 carrot, minced

1/2 cup olive oil
1 tablespoon lemon juice
2 tablespoons wine vinegar
2 tablespoons minced fresh
   parsley
Salt and pepper to taste

Combine all vegetables in a large salad bowl. In a jar, combine remaining ingredients; mix well. Pour over salad and toss lightly. Serves 6 to 8.

Note: If adding red cabbage, serve immediately since cabbage will discolor potatoes if left to marinate too long.

FRESH SPINACH SALAD I

1 pound fresh spinach
1/2 cup crumbled feta cheese
1/4 cup olive oil

Juice of 1 lemon
1/2 teaspoon salt
Pepper to taste

Wash spinach several times. Drain thoroughly and tear into bite-size pieces. Place in bowl. Sprinkle with feta cheese. In a separate bowl, combine remaining ingredients and beat with fork until creamy; drizzle over spinach. Toss and serve. Serves 4.

Variation: Sliced, hard-boiled eggs may be used for garnish.

FRESH SPINACH SALAD II

2/3 cup olive or vegetable oil
1/4 cup wine vinegar with
  garlic
2 tablespoons white wine
1 teaspoon sugar

1 teaspoon dry mustard
1/2 teaspoon salt
1/2 teaspoon pepper
1 pound fresh spinach
5 slices bacon

Combine first 7 ingredients in a jar and shake well. Wash and drain spinach; tear into bite-size pieces. Place in refrigerator to keep crisp. Fry bacon until crispy; crumble and set aside. Arrange spinach in individual salad dishes or in a large bowl. Drizzle dressing over top and toss lightly. Garnish with crumbled bacon. Serves 4.

PANTZARIA FRESKA VRASTA[†]
Fresh Beet Salad

1 bunch of beets with stems and leaves
1/2 teaspoon salt
Garlic Sauce, Skorthalia (optional)

Cut stem and leaves 2 inches from beet; wash and reserve them. Cover beets with water, season and cook for 15 minutes. Add reserved stems and leaves to the cooking beets; cook an additional 20 minutes or until tender. Remove beets, cool and skin them. Slice beets, place in bowl along with cut-up leaves and stems. Flavor with an olive oil and vinegar dressing. If desired, serve with a side bowl of skorthalia (see Sauces). Serves 4.

PANTZARIA SALATA[†]
Beet Salad

2 (16-oz.) cans whole beets,
  drained and sliced
1 medium onion, thinly sliced
3 cloves garlic, minced
1/2 cup olive oil

1/2 cup wine vinegar
Salt and pepper to taste
Dash of msg.
Dash of dried oregano

Arrange beets and onions in a serving bowl. Combine remaining ingredients in a jar and shake well. Pour over vegetables and allow to marinate for a few hours before serving. Serves 6.

SALATA MEH FASOLIA[†]
Bean Salad

1/2 pound navy beans
1 large onion, chopped
Juice of 1 lemon

Salt and pepper to taste
1/2 cup olive oil
1/4 cup chopped fresh parsley

Soak beans overnight; drain. Cover with fresh water, bring to a boil and cook until tender. Drain. Place beans in a large bowl; combine remaining ingredients and mix well. Pour over beans, stirring to coat. Let stand 2 hours to allow flavors to blend. Serve at room temperature. Serves 8.

SALATA MEH AGINARES[†]
Artichoke Salad

1/3 cup olive oil
1/3 cup fresh lemon juice
1 (14-oz.) can artichoke
  hearts, drained
1 small head lettuce

2 tablespoons crushed dried mint
4 whole green onions, chopped
Calamata or Greek black olives
2 ripe tomatoes, quartered
Salt and pepper to taste

Combine olive oil and lemon juice by beating with fork to blend. Pour over artichoke hearts and marinate 2 to 3 hours. Tear lettuce into bite-size pieces; combine with mint, onions, olives and tomatoes in a large salad bowl. Arrange marinated artichoke hearts on top of the lettuce, season lightly with salt and pepper. Serves 4 to 5.

Wooden salad bowls are the most popular, one reason being that rubbing a cut garlic around the rough interior surface begins the base of a good dressing for your salad.

AGINARES MEH MANITARIA
Artichoke and Mushroom Salad

2 (9-oz.) pkgs. frozen artichoke
  hearts, or 2 (14-oz.) cans
  artichoke hearts, drained
1 large onion
2 (4-oz.) jars pimientos, drained
1 pound fresh mushrooms
1/2 cup olive or vegetable oil
3 tablespoons cider vinegar

1 tablespoon lemon juice
1 tablespoon prepared mustard
1/2 teaspoon salt
1/8 teaspoon pepper
1 small can anchovies (opt.)
Lettuce leaves
1 tablespoon minced fresh
  parsley

About 1 1/2 hours before serving, prepare frozen artichokes as label directs, omitting salt, or use drained canned artichokes. Thinly slice onion, pimientos and mushrooms. In large bowl with fork or wire whisk, mix oil, vinegar, lemon juice, mustard, salt and pepper. Add artichoke hearts, onions, pimientos, mushrooms and anchovies; toss gently to coat with dressing. Cover and refrigerate at least 1 hour, stirring occasionally. To serve, line a chilled platter with lettuce leaves. Spoon vegetables and dressing onto lettuce leaves. Sprinkle parsley on top. Serves 8.

CRACKED WHEAT AND PARSLEY SALAD [†]
Traditionally served as a meat substitute during Lenten season

3/4 cup cracked wheat (bulgur)
1 1/2 cups minced fresh parsley
3 medium tomatoes, chopped
1/3 cup finely chopped whole
  green onions

2 tablespoons minced fresh mint
1/4 cup olive oil
1/4 cup lemon juice
1 teaspoon salt
1/4 teaspoon pepper
Greek black olives (optional)

Cover cracked wheat with cold water; let stand 30 minutes. Drain, pressing out as much water as possible. Place wheat, parsley, tomatoes, green onions and mint in serving bowl. Combine remaining ingredients, except olives, in a jar; mix well. Pour over wheat mixture and toss. Cover and refrigerate at least 1 hour. Garnish with black olives, if desired. Serves 6.

Note: For a softer texture, cover cracked wheat with boiling water and let stand 1 hour.

41

GREEN PEPPER SALAD[†]
Serve as an appetizer or salad.

5 to 6 green peppers	Salt to taste
Onion salt to taste	1/2 cup olive or vegetable oil
Garlic salt to taste	1/3 cup vinegar

Remove seeds from peppers, wash and cut into quarters. Parboil until soft; cool in water and peel. Place in a bowl, sprinkle with onion salt, garlic salt and salt. Add enough oil and vinegar to barely cover. Allow to marinate a few hours or overnight before serving. Serves 4 to 6.

GARITHES SALATA[†]
Marinated Shrimp Salad
An excellent, make-ahead party salad.

fantastic !

Marinade:

1 (2 1/2-oz.) bottle capers, drained and rinsed *omit*	1 1/2 cups olive oil
3 bay leaves	1 teaspoon salt
1 1/2 cups wine vinegar	1/2 teaspoon pepper
1/2 cup water	1/2 teaspoon dried oregano

Three days before serving this dish, combine all marinade ingredients in a large jar and refrigerate.

3 pounds shrimp, cooked, peeled and deveined	3 (14-oz.) cans artichokes, drained and quartered
2 (4 1/2-oz.) cans button mushrooms, drained	2 large red onions, thinly sliced

On the second day, combine gently the shrimp, mushrooms, artichokes and onions. Pour marinade over top; refrigerate. To serve the following day, spoon salad into serving platter, using a slotted spoon to drain off excess marinade. Serves 16 to 20.

KAVOUROSALATA
Crabmeat Salad
An attractive luncheon salad.

1 (6-oz.) pkg. frozen crabmeat,
  or 1 (6 1/2-oz.) can crabmeat
1/4 cup minced fresh parsley
3/4 cup finely chopped celery
  hearts
1/3 cup finely shredded carrots
3/4 cup finely chopped lettuce
  hearts

1/8 cup finely chopped green
  onion
2 tablespoons olive or
  vegetable oil
1 teaspoon lemon juice
1 teaspoon white vinegar
1/2 cup mayonnaise
Salt and pepper to taste

Thaw and drain crabmeat, or if using canned crabmeat, remove small
shell pieces. Combine crabmeat with next 5 ingredients and mix
well. Beat oil, lemon juice and vinegar until pale in color. Add
mayonnaise, salt and pepper; mix well. Pour over crabmeat mixture
and toss gently to blend. Serve on lettuce leaves; garnish with
tomato wedges, lemon slices, hard-boiled eggs and parsley sprigs.
Serves 4.

MELITZANOSALATA[†]
Eggplant Salad

1 large eggplant
1 cut clove garlic
1 medium onion, chopped
1 medium green pepper, chopped
1 tablespoon minced fresh
  parsley
Salt and pepper to taste

1/2 cup olive oil
2 tablespoons wine vinegar
Juice of 1 lemon
3 drops hot sauce
Lettuce leaves
Tomato wedges
Greek black olives

Pierce eggplant with a fork a few times to keep it from bursting
while baking. Place in baking dish; bake at 350 degrees about 1
hour until soft; or place in microwave on full power 5 minutes.
Cool thoroughly, peel and chop. Rub a bowl with cut garlic;
discard garlic. Combine eggplant, onion, green pepper, parsley,
salt and pepper; mix well. Put oil, vinegar, lemon juice and hot
sauce in a jar; shake well. Drizzle over eggplant mixture; mix
well. Serve on a bed of lettuce, garnish with tomato wedges and
olives. Serves 4.

43

SALATA MEH KRITHARAKI
Orzo Salad

1 cup orzo or converted rice
3/4 cup crumbled feta cheese
3 tablespoons minced fresh
  parsley
3 tablespoons minced fresh
  basil or dill

1 tomato, cut into wedges
1/3 cup olive oil
1/4 cup lemon juice
1/2 teaspoon salt
1/4 teaspoon pepper

Cook orzo in a quart of salted, boiling water about 15 minutes until tender, stirring frequently to prevent sticking. Drain in colander, rinse with cold water and drain again. Add feta cheese, parsley, basil and tomato. In a jar, combine remaining ingredients and shake well. Pour over salad and toss until well coated. Refrigerate to chill and toss again before serving. Serves 6.

TURKEY AND RICE SALAD
A complete salad meal.

1 (10-oz.) pkg. frozen green
  peas
2 (10-oz.) pkgs. frozen
  asparagus spears
1 cup cooked rice, cold
1 cup diced cucumbers
1/4 cup mayonnaise
1/4 teaspoon salt
1/2 teaspoon curry powder

3 cups coarsely diced turkey
  or chicken
Dressing:
  1/2 cup vegetable oil
  1/2 cup vinegar
  2 tablespoons lemon juice
  1 teaspoon salt
  1/8 teaspoon pepper
  Dash of sugar

Combine dressing ingredients in a jar and shake well. Cook vegetables as packages direct and drain well. Pour 1/4 cup dressing over each vegetable separately; refrigerate covered for 1 hour. In medium bowl, combine rice, cucumbers, mayonnaise, salt and curry powder. Toss well with a fork; refrigerate covered for 1 hour along with vegetables. In a large bowl, layering or mixing together, arrange turkey, vegetables and rice mixture. Drizzle remaining dressing over top. Serves 6.

SALATA MEH YIAOURTI
Vegetable Salad with Yogurt
A colorful summer luncheon dish.

2 cups tiny raw cauliflowerets
2 cups raw mushrooms, thinly
   sliced
1 cup Calamata or Greek black
   olives
1 cup thinly sliced green pepper
1 cup plain yogurt
1/2 cup olive oil

1/4 cup vinegar
1/4 cup minced fresh parsley
   or dill
1 clove garlic, crushed
1/4 cup lemon juice
1 teaspoon salt
1/2 teaspoon pepper
1 small head Romaine lettuce

Combine the first 4 ingredients; toss lightly to mix. Blend
remaining ingredients, except lettuce, in a large jar; mix well.
Pour over raw vegetables. Serve salad on lettuce leaves. Serves 6.

LAHANO MEH YIAOURTI
Cabbage Salad with Yogurt
A different way to serve cabbage.

4 cups finely shredded cabbage
1 medium green pepper, finely
   chopped
2 tablespoons grated onion
1 teaspoon sugar
1/4 cup vinegar

1/2 teaspoon salt
1/4 teaspoon pepper
1 cup plain yogurt
1/2 cup mayonnaise
Green pepper rings

Combine cabbage, green pepper and onion; toss well. Add sugar,
vinegar, salt and pepper. Toss again and allow to stand for a few
minutes. Combine yogurt and mayonnaise; add to salad, mix well.
Garnish with green pepper rings. Serves 4.

To separate lettuce leaves for lining a plate, cut out core and
hold cavity under cold, running water until leaves easily separate
by the water and fingers.

BLUE CHEESE DRESSING
The Last Resort
Chapel Hill, N.C.
Customers enjoy this salad dressing as much as
their meal.

1 1/2 cups vegetable oil
3/4 cup red wine vinegar
1 clove garlic, finely minced
1 teaspoon dry mustard

1 teaspoon celery salt
1 teaspoon white pepper
3/4 cup crumbled blue cheese

Mix first 6 ingredients in a large bowl; fold in blue cheese.
Refrigerate in a large jar until needed. Makes 1 pint.

SALTSA YIAOURTI
Yogurt Dressing
Excellent on boiled vegetables or fresh salads.

1/2 cup minced fresh parsley
2 teaspoons minced onion
1/2 teaspoon minced garlic
1 tablespoon chopped anchovy
  (optional)
1 cup mayonnaise

1/2 cup plain yogurt
3 tablespoons vinegar
1 tablespoon lemon juice
1/8 teaspoon salt
1/8 teaspoon pepper
Dash of paprika

Combine all the ingredients; beat with electric mixer until smooth.
Makes about 2 cups.

OIL AND LEMON DRESSING[†]
A good, basic dressing for cold, boiled
vegetables.

1/2 cup olive oil
Juice of 2 lemons
Salt and pepper

1 teaspoon minced fresh parsley
Garlic (optional, according to
  vegetables used)

Combine all ingredients in a jar, shake well and drizzle over cold
vegetables, such as:

Artichokes
Asparagus
Beets
Cabbage
Carrots
Cauliflower

String beans
Lima beans
Peas
Potatoes
Zucchini
All leafy green vegetables

SAUCES

AVGOLEMONO SAUCE I*

3 eggs, separated
1 cup boiling broth or stock

Dash of salt
Juice of 1 lemon

Using an electric mixer, beat egg whites with dash of salt until thick but not dry. Add yolks one at a time, beating until well blended. Slowly beat in lemon juice and hot broth. Gradually stir into gravy or stew over very low heat, stirring constantly, until sauce has thickened. Do not let mixture boil as it will curdle. Makes 1 cup.

AVGOLEMONO SAUCE II*
Uses flour to thicken.

4 eggs
Juice of 1 1/2 lemons
2 tablespoons all-purpose flour

1 or 2 cups chicken broth,
   depending on thickness
   of sauce desired

In a heavy saucepan, beat eggs well with a wire whisk. Add lemon juice and flour; stir until smooth. Slowly add hot broth. Cook over very low heat, stirring constantly, until sauce has thickened. Do not boil as it will curdle.

AVGOLEMONO SAUCE III*
This sauce never fails.

5 egg yolks
1 tablespoon cornstarch
2 teaspoons salt

1 chicken bouillon cube
1 1/2 cups water
5 tablespoons lemon juice

In heavy saucepan, beat egg yolks, cornstarch and salt with a wire whisk until blended. Stir in chicken bouillon and water. Cook over medium-low heat about 10 minutes, stirring constantly, until thickened. Do not boil. Remove from heat and stir in lemon juice. Makes enough sauce to serve 6 to 8 people.

----

* Avgolemono sauce can be served over chicken, baked fish, meat-stuffed cabbage or grape leaves. Delicious served over many cold, boiled vegetables as well.

DOMATA YIAHNI
Tomato Sauce

2 medium onions, chopped
1 clove garlic, minced
4 tablespoons olive oil
3 medium tomatoes, peeled
   and quartered
1 (8-oz.) can tomato sauce

1 cup water
1/4 cup chopped fresh parsley
Salt and pepper to taste
Dash of allspice
Dash of sugar

In a deep saucepan, saute onions and garlic in hot olive oil until tender. Add remaining ingredients and simmer slowly about 45 minutes. To freeze, cool and pack in pint containers. One such pint is enough to cook 1 pound of vegetables. Makes 2 1/2 cups.

TZADZIKI SAUCE
This zesty sauce has made the "gyro" sandwich popular!

1 pint plain yogurt
1 large cucumber, peeled
   and seeded
2 cloves garlic, minced

2 tablespoons olive oil
1 tablespoon white vinegar
Salt and white pepper

Drain the yogurt overnight in the refrigerator in a strainer that has been lined with cheesecloth. Chop cucumber; let drain on paper towels. To drained yogurt, add cucumber, garlic, oil and vinegar. Salt and pepper to taste. Refrigerate at least 1 hour to allow flavors to blend well. Use as a topping on souvlakia or over meat filling in a "gyro." Also a good dip with raw vegetables or crackers. Makes 2 cups.

MAYIONEZA
Mayonnaise

2 egg yolks
1/2 teaspoon salt
4 tablespoons white vinegar
3 tablespoons sugar

1 teaspoon dry mustard
1/2 teaspoon paprika
2 cups vegetable oil

Combine all ingredients, except oil; beat well. Add oil in a slow, steady stream and beat until smooth and creamy. Refrigerate. Makes 2 1/2 cups.

SKORTHALIA I
Garlic Sauce

3 to 5 cloves garlic
Dash of salt
16 slices stale plain white
  bread
1 egg

1 cup pecans or walnuts, finely
ground
1 cup olive oil, or 1/2 cup
  each olive and vegetable oil
3/4 cup wine vinegar

In a mortar with pestle, crush garlic with the salt. Put garlic in large mixing bowl. Dip bread in water, squeeze out and add to garlic. Add egg, nuts and about 1/3 cup each of oil and vinegar to the mixture. Blend together on lowest speed of mixer. Increase mixer speed; gradually add remaining olive oil in a slow, steady stream, alternating with the remaining vinegar. Salt to taste. Beat about 10 minutes until creamy. Refrigerate until ready to use. Excellent served with fried fish, beets or fried eggplant. Makes 4 cups.

SKORTHALIA APLI
Garlic Sauce (Simplified)

2 thick slices white bread
2 1/2 cups ground walnuts
1/3 cup vinegar (adjust to taste)
2 to 3 cloves garlic

1 teaspoon salt (adjust to
  taste)
1/4 teaspoon white pepper
1 cup olive oil

Dip bread in water and squeeze out excess. Place all ingredients and 1/3 cup of the olive oil in a food processor or blender. Process until smooth, adding remaining olive oil gradually. Makes about 3 cups.

SKORTHALIA MEH PATATES
Garlic Sauce with Potatoes

4 large potatoes, cooked,
  peeled and mashed
5 to 7 cloves garlic, minced

1/2 teaspoon salt
1 cup olive oil
1/2 cup white vinegar

Mix potatoes, garlic and salt in blender or food processor until very smooth. Add olive oil in a slow, steady stream, alternating with vinegar and mix until smooth. Serve at room temperature. Makes 3 1/2 cups.

SALTSA KREMA MEH TIRI
White Sauce with Cheese

1 quart milk	1/4 teaspoon white pepper
1/4 pound unsalted butter	1/4 teaspoon nutmeg
4 tablespoons all-purpose flour	4 tablespoons grated
1 teaspoon salt	kefalotiri or Parmesan cheese

Heat milk just to boiling point; set aside. In a heavy saucepan, melt butter. Gradually blend in flour, stirring with a wire whisk about 3 to 5 minutes until smooth. Slowly add milk, stirring constantly. Cook 10 minutes over low heat until thick and creamy. Remove from heat; stir in last 4 ingredients. To freeze, cool and pack in covered containers. To reheat, place in microwave on full power 1 1/2 minutes, or place in top of double boiler over simmering water until hot, stirring occasionally. Makes 4 cups.

VOUTERO KAVOURTHISMENO
Browned Butter Sauce

1/2 cup butter	1/4 teaspoon garlic powder
1/4 cup grated kefalotiri or	1/4 teaspoon dried oregano,
Parmesan cheese	crushed

Melt butter in small frying pan until bubbly; add 2 teaspoons grated cheese. Brown slightly, stirring constantly. Remove from heat. Add remaining cheese and seasonings to butter and blend. Pour butter sauce over one pound of cooked spaghetti, noodles or orzo; serve immediately. Serves 4.

MARINATING SAUCE

1/2 cup olive oil	1/4 cup chopped onion
Juice of 3 lemons	1 teaspoon dried oregano
2 cloves garlic, crushed	1/2 teaspoon coarsely ground
1/3 cup wine vinegar	pepper
1/2 teaspoon salt	1/2 teaspoon dry mustard

Combine all ingredients in a large jar; mix well. Pour over meat, seafood or poultry to coat well. Refrigerate overnight or let stand at room temperature 2 to 3 hours, turning occasionally. Use remaining sauce to baste meat for added flavor and tenderness while broiling or grilling.

BARBECUE SAUCE
Recipe makes a summer's supply.

2 quarts cider vinegar
1/2 cup brown sugar
1/2 cup prepared mustard
3/4 cup ketchup
2 tablespoons salt

1 tablespoon pepper
2 tablespoons chili powder
1/2 teaspoon dried oregano
1/2 lemon, thinly sliced

Bring all ingredients, except lemon, to a boil. Reduce heat and simmer about 10 minutes. Add lemon slices; briefly bring to boil again. Remove from heat and cool. Store in dry, cool place up to 60 days. Makes 1/2 gallon.

SPAGHETTI SAUCE

2 small onions, chopped
3 stalks celery, chopped
2 cloves garlic, mashed
4 tablespoons olive or
vegetable oil
2 (16-oz.) cans whole tomatoes,
chopped
2 (6-oz.) cans tomato paste
1 cup water
1/2 tablespoon sugar

1 1/2 teaspoons salt
1 bay leaf
1 to 1 1/2 teaspoons dried
oregano
1/2 teaspoon pepper
1/4 teaspoon ground cinnamon
1 teaspoon dried basil
3 tablespoons chopped fresh
parsley
1 (4-oz.) can sliced mushrooms,
drained

In a large, heavy saucepan, saute onions, celery and garlic in hot oil until tender. Add remaining ingredients. Simmer uncovered for 1 hour, stirring occasionally. Remove bay leaf. Makes about 6 cups or 6 to 8 servings.

Variation: To make a meat sauce, add 1 1/2 pounds ground beef with the onions, garlic and celery and brown well. Drain excess fat from beef before adding other ingredients. Makes 7 1/2 cups.

SALTSA PSARIOU
Fish Sauce

1 clove garlic, chopped
2 medium onions, chopped
3 tablespoons olive oil
1 bay leaf
1/4 teaspoon dried oregano
1/4 cup chopped celery leaves

1/4 cup finely chopped carrots
1 tablespoon minced fresh
  parsley
1/2 cup water
1/2 cup dry white wine
Juice of 1 lemon
Salt and pepper to taste

Saute garlic and onions in hot oil until golden. Add bay leaf, oregano, celery leaves, carrots and parsley; simmer 3 to 5 minutes. Add remaining ingredients; cook over low heat for 20 minutes. Cool. Serve with grilled, broiled or fried fish. Makes 1 cup.

SEAFOOD COCKTAIL SAUCE

1 cup chili sauce or ketchup
2 tablespoons horseradish
1 tablespoon lemon juice

1 teaspoon Worcestershire sauce
Dash of hot sauce (optional)

Combine all ingredients and mix well. Serve at room temperature. Makes 1 cup.

SIKOTAKIA SALTSA
Chicken Giblet Sauce

Liver, heart and gizzard of
  1 chicken
1 1/2 cups boiling water
Salt and pepper to taste
1 medium onion, minced
1 (4-oz.) can sliced mushrooms,
  drained
2 tablespoons butter

2 tablespoons all-purpose flour
1 tablespoon minced fresh
  parsley
1 clove garlic, mashed
1/4 cup tomato paste
1 teaspoon dried oregano
Dash of msg. (optional)

Bring water, salt and pepper to a boil; add chicken parts and simmer until tender. Drain, reserving liquid. Cut meat into fine pieces. Saute onions and mushrooms in butter until golden. Blend in flour. Slowly add reserved liquid, stirring constantly until smooth and thickened. Add remaining ingredients; cook over low heat for 2 additional minutes. Serves 4.

MAYONNAISE AND WINE SAUCE

3 hard-boiled egg yolks
1 cup mayonnaise

2 tablespoons Greek white wine,
or other white wine

Finely mash egg yolks and mix into mayonnaise until very smooth.
Add wine slowly, stirring constantly.

A good topping for vegetables, salad, cold chicken and meats.
Makes about 2 cups.

When storing leftover tomato sauce, add a little oil in jar to
prevent mold from growing on top.

MEDITERRANEAN VEGETABLES

MEDITERRANEAN VEGETABLES

In Greece, garden fresh vegetables are found in abundance in the popular open-air markets. Tourists never fail to be impressed by the appealing variety displayed. The olive tree, which flourishes in the arrid, rocky terrain of Greece, provides the most essential ingredient of the Greek cuisine -- olive oil. Naturally, olive oil flavors most of the vegetable dishes from simple greens to elaborate vegetable casseroles.

Greeks truly possess a flair for vegetable cookery, especially eggplant, green beans and the queen of the vegetables, artichokes. When cooked alone, vegetables are usually prepared in one of two ways: lathera, braised in olive oil and onions, simmered until done, and served cold or lukewarm; or yiahni; braised in olive oil and onions and simmered until done in a tomato sauce base. Stuffing vegetables is one way to expand the function of simple vegetables from side dish to main dish. In any case, a simple vegetable plate served with feta cheese, crusty bread and black olives is a flavorful and satisfying meal in itself.

SELECTION AND PREPARATION

Suggested guidelines for selection and preliminary preparation of fresh vegetables are given below. Cooking directions only describe how to cook vegetables not otherwise stated in a specific recipe.

ARTICHOKES: (AGINARES)

Select heavy artichokes (French or globe) with tight clinging green leaves. Store whole, unwashed artichokes in plastic bag in the refrigerator for several days. To prepare, snap off stem, drawing with it the fibers from the heart. Trim all the outside leaves 1/4 inch. Rub cut surfaces with lemon juice to prevent discoloration. Cut off about 1 inch from the top. Scoop out prickly center and purplish leaves. Cut in half lengthwise; place in bowl of acidulated water (2 tablespoons lemon juice, 1 tablespoon flour and 4 cups water). Drain when ready to cook. Serve 1 medium artichoke per person.

BEANS,GREEN: (FASOLIA)

Select young, tender beans of good even color that snap easily. Remove ends and pull off strings. Cut diagonally into 2-inch pieces or snap into short pieces. Cook covered in small amount of boiling, salted water for 30 to 40 minutes. One pound serves 4.

BEETS: (PANTZARIA)

Select firm, small or medium size beets. Cut stem 1-inch above the beet. Scrub thoroughly. Cook covered in boiling, salted water for 40 to 50 minutes or until tender. Drain and cool slightly. Peel off skins, stems and roots by rubbing with the fingers. One pound serves 4.

BROCCOLI: (BROKOLA)

Select broccoli with compact green heads, short tender stems and few leaves. Remove outer leaves and tough part of stalk. Cut remaining stalks into 1-inch pieces, paring if tough. Leave whole or divide into flowerets. Cook covered in a small amount of boiling, salted water for 10 to 15 minutes. One pound broccoli serves 3.

CABBAGE: (LAHANO)

Select crisp, heavy, well-trimmed heads with greenish or white leaves. Remove wilted leaves; cut into 6 to 8 wedges. Cook in small amount of boiling, salted water for 10 to 15 minutes. One pound serves 4.

CAULIFLOWER: Select cauliflower heads that are compact, firm,
(KOUNOUPITHI) white or creamy white in color with bright green
leaves.   Remove leaves and some of woody stem.
Remove discolored portions of flowers.   Divide into
flowerets.   Cook covered in small amount of boiling,
salted water for 10 to 15 minutes.   One medium size
head serves 4.

EGGPLANT: Select firm, heavy eggplants with glossy deep-purple
(MELITZANA) color, free of scars or cuts.   Partially pare
lengthwise into 1/2 inch strips, leaving 1/2 inch of
skin in between.   Slice into 1/2-inch rounds or
lengthwise, according to specific recipe, unless
using whole.   Sprinkle eggplant with salt; let stand
15 minutes to remove bitter taste.   Rinse in cold
water; pat dry.   One medium eggplant serves 4.

LEEKS: Leeks are mild-flavored members of the onion family.
(PRASA) Cut off the green stems to within 2 inches of the
white part.   Cut into 1/2-inch rounds.   Wash several
times in cold water.   Cook covered in small amount of
boiling, salted water for 15 to 20 minutes.

MUSHROOMS: Select plump, unwrinkled mushrooms with no blemishes.
(MANITARIA) Wash in cold water; dry thoroughly.   Cut off tips of
stems, slice or leave whole.   One pound serves 4 to
6.

OKRA: Select tender, meaty medium-size pods that are light
(BAMIES) green in color.   Trim off stems, being careful not to
expose seeds.   Cover with water, 1/4 cup of vinegar,
and 1 teaspoon salt; let stand for 15 minutes.
Drain; rinse thoroughly in cold water.   Cook covered
in small amount of boiling, salted water for 10 to 20
minutes.   One pound serves 4 to 6.

SQUASH: Select young squash (zucchini or yellow) that are
(KOLOKITHIA) heavy for their size.   The rind should yield to
thumbnail pressure.   Scrub; cut off stems and blossom
end.   Does not require paring, but if desired, pare
lengthwise in 1/2 inch strips, leaving 1/2 inch of
skin in between.   Cut into 1-inch rounds.   Cook
covered in small amount of boiling, salted water for
15 to 20 minutes.   Two pounds serves 4.

LAHANIKA LATHERA[†]
Vegetables in Olive Oil

1 pound fresh vegetable of
  choice*
1 medium onion, chopped
1/4 cup olive oil

Juice of 1 lemon
Salt and pepper to taste
Fresh herbs and/or spices
  to complement vegetable

Wash and prepare vegetable according to instructions at beginning of chapter. In a Dutch oven, combine all ingredients in just enough boiling water to keep from scorching. Cover and simmer until tender.

* Choose one of the following with suggested herbs and/or spices to complement:

Artichokes	lemon, onion, dill	Peas	dill, basil, thyme
Beans, green	mint, marjoram		
Beets	dill, vinegar	Potatoes	oregano, dill, parsley
Cabbage	dill, bay leaf		
Carrots	onion, thyme, dill	Spinach	mint, dill
Cauliflower	dill, lemon	Zucchini	onion, oregano, basil, thyme

LAHANIKA YIAHNI[†]
Sauteed Vegetables in Tomato Sauce

1 pound fresh vegetable of
  choice*
1/3 cup olive oil
1 large onion, chopped
Salt and pepper to taste

1 (8-oz.) can tomato sauce,
  or 1 (16-oz.) can whole
  tomatoes, chopped
Herbs and/or spices to taste
  (see previous recipe)

Wash and prepare vegetable according to instructions at beginning of chapter. In a large saucepan, saute onion in hot oil until tender. Add tomato sauce or chopped tomatoes; simmer several minutes. Add vegetable, salt, pepper, herbs and enough water to cover. Simmer partially covered until tender, but not overcooked. Do not stir; shake pan occasionally to redistribute contents.

* Artichokes	Eggplant	Potatoes
Beans, green	Leeks	Spinach
Cabbage	Okra	Yellow Squash
Cauliflower	Peas	Zucchini

HORTA VRASTA[†]
Boiled Greens

1 pound fresh greens of choice*   Lemon and olive oil dressing
1 teaspooon salt

Trim off coarse stems from the leaves. Wash leaves in cold water several times. Place in a large kettle, sprinkle with salt and steam boil, partially covered, using only the water clinging to the leaves. (If necessary, add a little more water while cooking to keep from scorching.) Cook 10 to 20 minutes, depending on desired tenderness of greens. Drain. Serve hot or cold with lemon and olive oil dressing.

------

* Beet greens - (pantzarophylla)   Endive or escarole - (antithia)
  Collard greens   Mustard greens - (sinapia)
  Dandelions - (rathikia)   Spinach - (spanaki)

FAKIES MEH DOMATES[†]
Lentils with Tomatoes

1 cup lentils   1 cup water
8 cups water   1 beef or chicken bouillon
1 medium onion, chopped   cube (optional)
1 medium green pepper, chopped   Salt and pepper to taste
4 tablespoons olive oil   1/2 teaspoon seasoned salt
1 (16-oz.) can whole tomatoes,
  crushed

Sort and rinse lentils in cold water. In a large saucepan, cook lentils in boiling, salted water for 20 minutes or until tender; drain. Saute onion and green pepper in hot oil until tender. Add lentils and remaining ingredients. Cook 30 minutes, uncovered, stirring occasionally. Serve as side dish or over rice. Serves 4 to 5.

AGINARES LATHERES[†]
Artichokes with Oil

6 artichokes	Juice of 2 lemons
1/2 pound pearl onions	1 cup water
1/2 cup vegetable or olive oil	1/2 cup chopped fresh parsley
Salt and pepper to taste	

Prepare artichokes according to instructions at beginning of chapter. Spread onions in bottom of a Dutch oven. Layer artichokes on top of onions. Add oil, salt, pepper and lemon juice which has been diluted in water. Cover and simmer about 45 minutes or until tender. Sprinkle with parsley; simmer another 5 minutes. Serve warm or cold. Serves 6.

AGINARES MEH PILAFI
Artichokes with Pilaf

1 large onion, chopped	1 (8-oz.) can tomato sauce
3 tablespoons butter	Salt and pepper to taste
2 cups long grain rice	1 tablespoon dried dill
2 (14-oz.) cans artichoke	6 to 8 tablespoons butter,
hearts, drained	as desired
5 cups chicken broth (too much - could be $1^{to}4$)	

In a large saucepan, saute the onion in the 3 tablespoons butter until tender. Add rice and brown slightly, stirring constantly. Add artichokes. In a separate saucepan, bring to a boil the chicken broth and tomato sauce. Stir into the rice and artichoke mixture. Add salt, pepper and dill. Cover and simmer 20 to 25 minutes until liquid has been absorbed. Remove from heat. Melt remaining butter to sizzling point. Pour over rice. Let stand covered for 10 minutes. Serve immediately. Serves 8.

Fresh herbs such as parsley, basil, dill and mint can be dried in the microwave. Spread out on a shallow microwave dish, cover with paper towels and microwave on full power for 1 or 2 minutes. Stir herbs around and microwave a little more. When cooled, crumble herbs into a jar and store in kitchen cabinet until ready to use.

AGINARES LATHOXITHO[†]
Marinated Artichoke Hearts

3 (14-oz.) cans artichoke hearts,
  drained
1/4 cup lemon juice
1/4 cup olive oil
1/4 cup red wine vinegar
1 clove garlic, crushed
1 tablespoon minced fresh
  parsley

Dash of msg.
1/2 teaspoon dried oregano
1/2 teaspoon salt
Dash of pepper
Few sprigs of fresh mint
  (optional)
Spanish red onion, thinly
  sliced (optional)

Arrange artichokes in a shallow bowl. Combine next 10 ingredients
in a jar and shake vigorously. Pour marinade over artichokes,
stirring gently to coat. Refrigerate 4 hours, covered, stirring
occasionally. Serve, using slotted spoon to drain off excess
marinade. If desired, garnish with Spanish red onion. Serves 6
to 8.

MELITZANES PSITES
Baked Eggplant

3 large eggplants, sliced
  1/2-inch thick
5 large onions, sliced
  1/4-inch thick
2 stalks celery, sliced
  1/2-inch thick
1 green pepper, 1/4-inch cubes
1/2 teaspoon garlic powder
2 tablespoons minced fresh parsley
1/2 teaspoon minced fresh mint
1 teaspoon salt

1/8 teaspoon pepper
1/2 teaspoon sugar
1/8 teaspoon nutmeg
1/8 teaspoon ground cinnamon
3 tablespoons olive oil
1 tablespoon lemon juice
1 (8-oz.) can tomato sauce
1 teaspoon ketchup
1/2 cup water
2 fresh tomatoes, sliced
1/2 cup grated Parmesan cheese

Prepare eggplant according to instructions at beginning of chapter.
In a skillet, slightly brown eggplant slices on both sides in small
amount of oil. Drain on paper towels; set aside. Steam boil the
onions, celery and green pepper about 15 minutes until tender.
Place vegetables in a bowl and mix in next 10 ingredients.

In a 17 x 11-inch baking pan, layer eggplant and vegetable mixture,
beginning and ending with eggplant. Mix tomato sauce, ketchup and
water; pour over the vegetables. Arrange tomatoes on top; sprinkle
with Parmesan cheese. Bake at 350 degrees for 45 minutes. Serves
12 to 15.

IMAM BAILDI[†]
Stuffed Eggplant

1 large eggplant
Salt
3/4 cup olive oil
1 pound onions, thinly sliced
3 large tomatoes, peeled and sliced

3 cloves garlic, minced
3 tablespoons minced fresh
  parsley
Salt and pepper

Slice off stem end of eggplant. Pare lengthwise in 1-inch strips, leaving about 1 inch of skin in between. Slice into all pared portions about 1 inch in depth. Sprinkle eggplant with salt; let stand 10 to 15 minutes. Wash in cold water and pat dry. In a heavy saucepan, brown eggplant in 1/4 cup olive oil for 5 minutes, turning 2 or 3 times. Combine remaining ingredients and saute in 1/2 cup hot olive oil about 5 minutes. Stuff mixture into incisions in eggplant. Tie a string around eggplant in 2 or 3 places to secure. Return eggplant to pan. Add 1/2 cup water and remaining vegetable mixture. Bring to a boil, cover and simmer 40 minutes or until eggplant is tender. Cool before serving. Serves 4.

MELITZANA TIGANITI
Fried Eggplant

1 large eggplant or 2 medium
1 egg
1 tablespoon water

1 cup all-purpose flour
Oil for frying

Prepare eggplant according to instructions at beginning of chapter. Slice eggplant into 1/2-inch thick rounds. Beat egg and water well. Dip eggplant in egg mixture, then in flour. Brown in hot oil on both sides, about 3 minutes. Serve immediately. If desired, serve with a side bowl of skorthalia (see Sauces). Serves 4.

Variation: Fried zucchini is a good substitute; omit the salting process.

If you have a large crop of cherry tomatoes, wash, then freeze whole in plastic freezer bags or freezer containers. When needed, put frozen tomatoes in a small bowl and cover them with hot water for a few seconds. Drain; the skins will slip right off. Great for use in soups, casseroles and stews.

DOMATES YEMISTES MEH RIZI
Stuffed Tomatoes with Rice
A colorful, vegetable entree.

8 large, firm tomatoes
2 medium onions, minced
1/3 cup olive oil
3/4 cup long grain rice
2 tablespoons chopped fresh mint
3 tablespoons chopped fresh parsley
Salt and pepper to taste

1 tablespoon pignolia nuts,
  or white raisins
  (optional)
1/3 cup hot water
Pinch of sugar
1 tablespoon butter
Dry bread crumbs

Slice off tops of tomatoes; reserve. Scoop out pulp, chop and set aside. In a large saucepan, saute onions in hot oil until tender. Add tomato pulp; cook a few minutes. Stir in rice and next 6 ingredients. Cover, simmer 10 to 12 minutes, stirring occasionally, until rice is almost done. If rice mixture is too thick, add a little more water. Rice mixture should not be too juicy, but have enough liquid for the rice to cook. Cool slightly.

Sprinkle a pinch of sugar in bottom of each tomato shell and stuff with rice. Arrange any leftover rice mixture around the tomatoes. Place a thin pat of butter on top of each tomato and sprinkle with dry bread crumbs. Replace tomato caps; arrange in small baking pan. Combine 1/2 cup water, 1 tablespoon olive oil and 3 tablespoons tomato sauce; pour around tomatoes. Cover with aluminum foil; bake at 350 degrees for 30 minutes. Remove foil; bake an additional 20 to 30 minutes, basting occasionally. Let stand 15 minutes. Serve warm. Serves 8.

Variation: Green bell peppers can also be used. Parboil peppers 5 minutes to tenderize; then proceed with recipe as directed.

KOUKIA YIAHNI[†]
Fava Beans in Tomato Sauce

2 medium onions, chopped
1 stalk celery, chopped
1 clove garlic, minced
1/3 cup olive oil
3/4 cup tomato sauce

1/4 cup water or red wine
1 (20-oz.) can fava beans,
  rinsed and drained
Salt and pepper to taste

In a large saucepan, saute the onions, celery and garlic in hot oil until tender. Add tomato sauce and water; simmer 5 to 10 minutes. Add fava beans, salt and pepper. Heat through gently about 5 minutes. Serves 4.

LAHANIKA PLAKI[†]
Baked Vegetables

6 potatoes, thinly sliced
1 (10-oz.) pkg. frozen cut green
  beans, thawed
3 yellow squash, thinly sliced
1 (8-oz.) can tomato sauce

1/2 cup each vegetable and
  olive oil
1/2 cup water
2 tablespoons chopped fresh
  parsley
Salt and pepper to taste

Arrange the potatoes, beans, and squash in a 13 x 9-inch baking pan. Combine tomato sauce, oil and water; pour over the vegetables. Sprinkle with parsley, salt and pepper. Cover with aluminum foil; bake at 350 degrees about 1 1/2 hours. Remove foil the last 30 minutes. Serve warm. Serves 8 to 10.

MANITARIA MEH VOUTERO
Sauteed Mushrooms

4 whole green onions, chopped
1/3 cup butter
1 (12-oz.) carton fresh
  mushrooms, sliced

Seasoned salt to taste
1/8 teaspoon pepper
1/2 teaspoon dried dill
1/3 cup chopped fresh parsley

In a large skillet, saute onions in butter until tender. Add mushrooms and next 3 ingredients. Cover and cook over medium-high heat for a few minutes. Uncover, add parsley; simmer 5 to 8 minutes or until most of the juices have been absorbed, stirring frequently. Serve warm. Serves 4 to 5.

SPANAKI KROKETES
Fried Spinach Balls
A tasty way to get kids to eat spinach.

2 (10-oz.) pkgs. frozen chopped
  spinach
1 egg
1 cup dry bread crumbs
2 tablespoons grated Parmesan cheese
2 tablespoons grated mozzarella
  cheese

2 tablespoons grated onion
2 tablespoons butter, melted
1/2 teaspoon dried oregano
Salt and pepper to taste
1 egg
1 tablespoon water
Seasoned bread crumbs

Cook spinach according to package directions; drain thoroughly in a colander pressing out excess water. Combine spinach with next 8 ingredients and mix well; let stand 10 minutes. Shape into balls, about 1 1/4 inches in diameter. Beat egg and water together. Roll spinach balls in bread crumbs, then dip in egg and roll again in the bread crumbs. Fry in deep fryer until golden. Drain on paper towel. Serve immediately. Makes 15 balls.

Variation: Cooked, well-drained yellow squash, zucchini or eggplant can be chopped and prepared in the same manner.

KOLOKITHIA PLAKI[†]
Baked Squash

5 medium yellow squash, thinly
  sliced
3 large baking potatoes, thinly
  sliced
1 large onion, thinly sliced
1 (8-oz.) can tomato sauce

2/3 cup olive oil
3/4 cup water
Salt and pepper to taste
1 teaspoon dried basil
2 tablespoons minced fresh
  parsley

Arrange squash, potatoes and onions in a 13 x 9-inch baking pan. Mix the tomato sauce, oil and water; pour over the vegetables. Sprinkle with salt, pepper and basil. Cover with aluminum foil; bake at 375 degrees for 45 minutes. Then lower to 325 degrees; bake for an additional 45 minutes. Remove foil the last 30 minutes and sprinkle with parsley. Serve warm. Can be made ahead of time and refrigerated; warm through just before serving. Serves 8 to 10.

KOLOKITHIA PAPOUTSAKIA
Zucchini Stuffed with Cheese

6 medium zucchini
3/4 cup crumbled feta cheese
2/3 cup cottage cheese, small
  curd
2 eggs
1/4 cup grated Parmesan cheese

1 tablespoon minced fresh
  parsley
Dash of pepper
Fresh dill
Parmesan cheese, grated

Cut zucchini in half lengthwise. Scoop pulp out carefully with a vegetable corer; reserve pulp for later use in a soup or vegetable dish. Parboil the zucchini 5 minutes to tenderize; drain. Combine next 6 ingredients. Stuff the zucchini with cheese mixture. Bake in shallow baking pan at 425 degrees for 10 minutes. Remove from oven; sprinkle with dill and additional Parmesan cheese. Place under the broiler to brown briefly. Serve warm. Cut into bite-size pieces if serving as an appetizer. Serves 6.

MARINATED BROCCOLI AND SQUASH[†]

1 1/2 pounds zucchini or yellow
  squash
1 (16-oz.) bag frozen broccoli
  cuts
1/2 teaspoon onion powder
1/4 teaspoon garlic powder
1/2 teaspoon dried oregano
1/2 teaspoon thyme

2/3 cup olive or vegetable oil
1/4 teaspoon pepper
1/2 teaspoon dry mustard
2 tablespoons wine vinegar
3 tablespoons lemon juice
Fresh dill or parsley, chopped
Salt to taste

Prepare zucchini according to instructions at beginning of chapter. Slice zucchini into 1/4-inch thick rounds. Steam boil zucchini and broccoli separately until slightly tender, about 3 to 4 minutes. Do not overcook. Drain thoroughly; cool. Combine remaining ingredients in a jar and shake vigorously. Arrange vegetables in a salad bowl; pour marinade over the vegetables. Cover and refrigerate overnight. Can also serve individual portions on a bed of lettuce. Serves 8 to 10.

Variation: This marinade can be used with any combination of fresh vegetables.

KAROTA MARINATA[†]
Marinated Carrots

2 pounds carrots
2 medium onions, diced
1 medium bell pepper, diced
3/4 cup vinegar
1/2 cup vegetable oil

1 (10 1/2-oz.) can tomato soup
1 teaspoon salt
1 teaspoon pepper
1 teaspoon prepared mustard
1 teaspoon Worcestershire sauce

Slice pared carrots; cook covered in a small amount of boiling, salted water for 15 to 20 minutes. Drain and cool. Add the onion and pepper; mix well. Combine remaining ingredients; pour over vegetables, stirring gently to coat. Marinate covered in refrigerator overnight. Will keep for a week. Serves 6 to 8.

PATATES TOU FOURNOU[†]
Oven-Baked Potatoes

5 large potatoes, washed and
  peeled
Vegetable or olive oil

Salt and pepper to taste
Dried oregano (optional)
Juice of 1 lemon

Slice potatoes into 1/2-inch thick rounds. Place in greased 13 x 9-inch baking pan. Add enough oil to cover potatoes half way; sprinkle with salt, pepper and oregano. Bake at 450 degrees for 20 to 25 minutes or until slightly brown on top. Turn once during baking. Sprinkle with lemon juice last 5 minutes. Serves 5 to 6.

PATATES KROKETES
Potato Balls

2 large potatoes, boiled and peeled
1/2 cup grated Parmesan cheese
1 tablespoon minced fresh parsley
1 small onion, minced
1 clove garlic, crushed

2 egg yolks
Salt and pepper to taste
1 teaspoon lemon juice
2 egg whites, beaten
Dry bread crumbs

Combine the first 8 ingredients and beat until smooth. Add a little milk if mixture is dry. Shape into 1-inch balls, dip in egg whites and roll in bread crumbs. Deep fry until golden, about 30 to 45 seconds each side. Makes 1 1/2 dozen.

RIZI PILAFI
Rice Pilaf

1 cup long grain rice	Salt and pepper
1/2 cup butter	2 1/2 cups chicken broth

In medium saucepan, saute rice in hot butter for 3 minutes, stirring constantly. Add salt, pepper and broth; bring to a boil. Cover and simmer 15 to 20 minutes or until liquid is absorbed. Remove from heat; leave covered rice to stand 10 minutes. Fluff with fork and serve hot. Serves 4.

Variations: Chopped onion may be added to rice. For a tomato flavor, add 2 tablespoons tomato paste when sauteing.

RIZI KEH KRITHARAKI PILAFI
Rice and Orzo Pilaf

1/4 cup butter	1 (10-oz.) can chicken broth
1/4 cup orzo	1 3/4 cups hot water
1 cup long grain rice	1 teaspoon salt

In medium saucepan, melt butter to sizzling point. Add orzo and rice; saute in the butter until golden, stirring constantly, being careful not to scorch. Add the broth, hot water and salt. Bring to a boil. Reduce heat, cover and simmer 20 minutes or until liquid is absorbed. Remove from heat; leave covered to stand for 10 minutes. Fluff with fork and serve hot. Serves 4.

SPANAKORIZO[†]
Spinach and Rice

1 large onion, chopped	2 beef bouillon cubes
1/4 cup olive oil	(optional)
1 cup long grain rice	Salt and pepper to taste
1/4 cup tomato sauce	1 pound fresh spinach
2 cups boiling water	Juice of half lemon

In a large kettle, saute onions in hot oil until tender. Add rice; saute a few minutes, stirring constantly. Add tomato sauce, water, bouillon cubes, salt and pepper; bring to a boil. Add spinach and cover; simmer 20 minutes or until rice is tender. Let stand 15 minutes. Sprinkle lemon juice over top. Serve warm. Serves 5.

RIZI MEH LAHANO[†]
Rice with Cabbage

1 cup chopped onions
1 cup long grain rice
4 tablespoons olive or vegetable
  oil
2 1/2 cups boiling water
1 medium head cabbage, cut into
  chunks

1 teaspoon salt
1/2 teaspoon sugar
1/4 teaspoon pepper
1/3 cup slivered almonds
1/3 cup pimiento-stuffed
  olives, sliced

In a large saucepan, saute onions and rice in hot oil for 5 minutes
stirring constantly. Add 2 cups boiling water, cover and simmer
gently 10 to 15 minutes until rice is almost done. Add remaining
ingredients. Pour in the remaining 1/2 cup boiling water, cover
and cook 5 additonal minutes until cabbage has wilted. Add a
little more water if rice seems dry. Serve warm or at room
temperature. If desired, serve with a side bowl of sour cream or
yogurt. Serves 4 to 5.

RIZI MEH KOLOKITHIA[†]
Rice with Squash

5 to 6 cups yellow squash, cut
  into 1 1/2-inch pieces
3/4 cup chopped onions
4 tablespoons olive oil
2 cups boiling water
1 cup long grain rice

1 teaspoon salt
1/4 teaspoon pepper
1/3 cup slivered almonds
1/3 cup raisins
English walnuts, chopped

In a large saucepan, saute squash and onions in hot oil for 7 to 10
minutes. Stir in remaining ingredients, except walnuts. Simmer,
partially covered, for 20 minutes or until liquid is absorbed.
Remove from heat. Let stand covered for 10 minutes before serving.
Garnish with walnuts. Serves 4 to 5.

Saute means to briskly cook in a small amount of fat over medium-
high heat. In Greek cookery, oil or butter is often flavored by
adding onion or garlic and sauteing until tender or golden,
stirring frequently to prevent scorching.

SPANAKI MEH KRITHARAKI
Spinach Casserole with Orzo
An elegant vegetable entree for company.

2 (10-oz.) pkgs. frozen chopped
  spinach
1 1/2 cups orzo
2 quarts boiling, salted water
2 medium onions, chopped
3/4 cup butter

Salt and pepper to taste
3 eggs, slightly beaten
1 cup grated Parmesan cheese
  or Romano cheese
Cream sauce (below)
1 cup bread crumbs

Cook spinach according to package directions; drain thoroughly.
Boil orzo in water until tender. Drain in colander, rinse in cold
water and drain again. Set aside. Saute onions in 1/4 cup butter
until golden. Add spinach, salt and pepper; heat through. Remove
from heat, cool and stir in eggs.

Spread half of orzo in bottom of greased 13 x 9-inch pan. Sprinkle
1/3 cup cheese over orzo. Spoon spinach mixture over cheese.
Cover with remaining orzo; sprinkle with 1/3 cup cheese. Spread
cream sauce over cheese. Melt remaining butter in a frying pan
until bubbly. Remove from heat. Add bread crumbs and remaining
cheese. Sprinkle over cream sauce. Bake at 350 degrees for 30
minutes. Makes 20 to 24 pieces.

Cream Sauce:
  3 cups milk
  1 bay leaf
  1 sliced onion
  Salt
  Peppercorns

4 tablespoons butter
6 tablespoons all-purpose
  flour
2 eggs, beaten

Combine the milk, bay leaf, onion, salt and peppercorns and bring
to a boil. Remove from heat; strain. Melt butter in a saucepan.
Add flour and stir until slightly brown. Add milk gradually,
stirring constantly, until slightly thickened. Slowly add eggs;
cook over very low heat until thickened.

GLYKOPATATES
Candied Sweet Potatoes
A good side dish with ham or turkey.

6 medium sweet potatoes
1 cup orange juice
1/2 teaspoon grated orange rind
1 cup water
1/2 cup sugar

1/2 cup brown sugar
1/4 cup butter
1/2 teaspoon salt
1 1/2 tablespoons cornstarch
Ground cinnamon

Clean and boil potatoes in large saucepan until barely tender when pricked with a fork. Drain potatoes and peel while still warm.

Slice crosswise in 1/2-inch intervals. Arrange in baking dish. Combine remaining ingredients, except cinnamon, in a saucepan and boil about 5 minutes. Pour syrup over potatoes. Sprinkle with ground cinnamon. Bake at 350 degrees for 30 minutes. Baste occasionally. Can be made a day ahead and warmed just before serving. Serves 8 to 10.

ENTREES

ENTREES

    Lamb, beef, pork and poultry entrees from the Greek cuisine are widely acclaimed for the unique and interesting ways they are prepared -- from simple roasted meat, seasoned with oregano and lemon juice, to the more elaborate meat casseroles, such as the popular moussaka.

    Holidays dictate the serving of traditionally appropriate meat entrees. At Easter, spit-roasted lamb is customarily served following the long Lenten fast. A popular Christmas entree is turkey stuffed with a savory blend of ground beef, chestnuts, raisins and spices.

    "Delicacies from the sea" has always been a major source of food for this Mediterranean country. Succulent seafood dinners eaten at one of the many restaurants by the sea are memorable experiences for the tourists.

    Throughout the meat chapter is found the repetitious listing of tomatoes, onions, parsley, oregano and cinnamon. These basic ingredients are the essentials to preparing hearty and aromatic Greek meat dishes -- a welcomed relief from the typical roasts, steaks and chops.

LAMB

ARNI PSITO
Roast Leg of Lamb

1 leg of lamb (6 to 7 pounds)	1/4 teaspoon dried thyme
1/4 cup olive oil	1/4 teaspoon dried oregano
Juice of 1 lemon	Salt and pepper
3/4 teaspoon dried rosemary	Cloves garlic, minced

Preheat oven to 500 degrees. Place lamb fat-side up in shallow roasting pan. Rub lamb with olive oil and lemon juice; season with rosemary, thyme, oregano, salt, pepper and garlic. Place in oven, reduce heat to 350 degrees and roast lamb for 2 1/2 to 3 hours, or until meat thermometer registers 175 to 180 degrees. Let lamb stand 20 minutes before cutting. Serves 8 to 10.

Variation: When lamb is almost done, place 6 large potatoes, peeled and quartered, around lamb. Sprinkle with lemon juice, salt, pepper and oregano. After 20 minutes of baking, turn potatoes over to brown other side. Continue roasting until potatoes pierce easily with a fork.

ARNI TOU FOURNOU
Baked Lamb Shoulder Chops

4 lamb shoulder chops	1 teaspoon dried oregano
Salt and pepper to taste	1/2 teaspoon thyme
2 cloves garlic, crushed	1 cup tomato sauce
2 carrots, cut into thin strips	1 cup water
1 large onion, thinly sliced	1/2 cup olive oil
2 stalks celery, thinly sliced	8 medium potatoes, peeled
2 bay leaves, crushed	

Sprinkle lamb with salt and pepper and rub with garlic. Place carrots, onions, celery and bay leaves in bottom of roasting pan. Add lamb shoulder; sprinkle with oregano and thyme. Dilute tomato sauce with water and olive oil; pour over lamb. Cover and bake at 375 degrees for 1 1/2 to 2 1/2 hours, depending on thickness of lamb shoulder chops. During last 30 minutes of cooking, raise temperature to 400 degrees and uncover pan. Add potatoes and continue cooking uncovered, basting occasionally. Serve lamb surrounded by potatoes. Strain and skim fat from sauce; serve separately. Serves 4.

ARNI BOUTI YEMISTO
Stuffed Leg of Lamb with Veal

1 (7-pound) leg of lamb, boned

Marinade:
3 cups red wine	Pinch of dried rosemary,
1 cup beef broth	crumbled
1 small onion, chopped	Pinch of dried thyme

Veal Stuffing:
1/2 pound ground veal	1 tablespoon butter
1/4 cup heavy cream	1 teaspoon rosemary
1 egg, slightly beaten	1/4 teaspoon thyme
1/3 cup bread crumbs	3/4 cup minced fresh parsley
1/3 cup grated Parmesan cheese	Salt and pepper
1/4 cup minced shallots	2 tablespoons olive oil

Mix the marinade ingredients in large bowl or pan, add lamb and let marinate in refrigerator overnight. Remove lamb, pat dry and reserve marinade.

In a large bowl, combine the veal, cream and egg; blend well. Add bread crumbs and Parmesan cheese. Saute shallots in butter until tender; cool and add to veal mixture along with 1/4 teaspoon rosemary, thyme, parsley and enough salt and pepper to taste. Mix the stuffing well.

Sprinkle cavity of lamb with salt and pepper, add the veal stuffing. Close opening tightly, securing with string tied at 1-inch intervals. Place in roasting pan; rub with olive oil, remaining 3/4 teaspoon of rosemary, salt and pepper. Roast in preheated 500-degree oven for 10 minutes, reduce heat to 325 degrees and roast, 15 minutes per pound for medium rare meat, approximately 30 minutes per pound for well done. Serves 8 to 10.

Variation: Mustard topping may be added. Combine 1/2 teaspoon rosemary, 1/2 cup Dijon mustard, 1 tablespoon soy sauce and 4 tablespoons olive oil; mix well. Brush meat with topping. Reserve some of this mixture for sauce. To make sauce, add 2 tablespoons cornstarch to leftover topping and juices from pan (skim off fat from top before using). Serve separately.

ARNI MEH AGINARES AVGOLEMONO
Lamb and Artichokes with Egg-Lemon Sauce

6 fresh artichokes
1 (3-pound) lamb shoulder, cut
  into 2-inch cubes

1/2 cup butter
Hot water
Avgolemono Sauce (below)

Prepare artichokes according to instructions in beginning of Vegetable Chapter. Set aside. In a Dutch oven, brown the lamb in butter. Add hot water to cover and cook covered over medium heat about 1 hour. Add artichokes; cook 30 minutes or until artichokes are tender. (More water may be needed.) Pour avgolemono sauce over the lamb and artichokes. Shake the pan to evenly distribute sauce. Do not boil. Serve hot. Serves 4 to 6.

Avgolemono Sauce:
  3 eggs
  2 tablespoons all-purpose flour

Juice of 1 lemon
1 cup hot pan broth

With hand mixer, beat eggs until light. Gradually add flour and lemon juice, beating well after each addition. Add hot broth slowly, beating until thickened.

ARNI MEH CELINO AVGOLEMONO
Lamb and Celery with Egg-Lemon Sauce

3 bunches celery
1 (3-pound) lamb shoulder,
  cut into 2-inch chunks
1 large onion, chopped
1/4 cup butter

Salt and pepper
Dash of msg.
Hot water
Avgolemono sauce (see direc-
  tions in preceding recipe)

Separate celery stalks, rinse in cold water; cut into 2-inch lengths including tender leaves. In Dutch oven, saute meat and onions in hot butter until brown. Season with salt, pepper and msg. Add enough hot water to cover meat; bring to a boil, cover and cook over medium-low heat for 1 hour, stirring occasionally. Add celery and continue cooking until meat and celery are tender. Remove from heat. Pour avgolemono sauce over meat, shaking pan to distribute sauce. Do not boil and do not cover with lid. Serve immediately with rice or pasta. Serves 6.

ARNI YIAHNI
Lamb Stew with Vegetables

1 (3-pound) lamb shoulder,
   cut into 2-inch chunks
1/4 cup butter
1 large onion, chopped
1 clove garlic, minced
Salt and pepper

1/2 teaspoon dried oregano
   or mint
1/4 cup minced fresh parsley
1 (8-oz.) can tomato sauce
Hot water
1 1/2 to 2 pounds fresh
   vegetable of choice*

In Dutch oven, brown meat in hot butter. Add onions, garlic and seasonings; saute until tender. Add tomato sauce and enough hot water to cover meat. Simmer covered over moderate heat about 1 hour. Add vegetable of choice and continue to simmer covered until vegetable is tender and liquid has been reduced. (Do not stir; occasionally shake pot to redistribute contents and prevent scorching.) Serves 4 to 6.

---

* Vegetables: Green beans, okra, peas, zucchini, yellow squash
             or potatoes. (With potatoes, add more liquid.)

BREEZOLES MEH DOMATES
Lamb Chops with Tomatoes

4 large, thick lamb chops
   (6 to 8 ounces each)
2 tablespoons all-purpose flour
1/4 cup vegetable oil
Salt and pepper to taste
1/2 teaspoon dried oregano
2 cloves garlic, minced

1/4 cup minced fresh parsley
1 cup canned whole tomatoes,
   chopped
1/2 cup tomato sauce
3 tablespoons vinegar
1/4 cup dry white wine

Dust lamb chops with flour. In a large skillet, brown chops in oil. Season with salt, pepper and oregano. Combine remaining ingredients and pour over meat. Cover and simmer for 1 hour. Good with rice or pasta. Serves 4.

ARNI TOURLOU MEH KREMA
Lamb, Pasta and Vegetable Casserole

1 medium onion, chopped	2 (10-oz.) pkgs. frozen leaf
1 clove garlic, minced	spinach
2 tablespoons butter	1 (8-oz.) pkg. linguine
1 pound ground lamb	4 ounces grated kasseri cheese,
Salt and pepper to taste	or 3 ounces Parmesan cheese
Cinnamon to taste	Cream sauce (below)

In a large pot, saute onion and garlic in hot butter until tender. Crumble in ground lamb and brown. Add salt, pepper and cinnamon. Cook until lamb is well done. Drain off excess fat; set aside.

Cook spinach according to package directions; drain water from spinach but reserve spinach water in pot. Add additional water and salt; bring to a boil. Cook linguine until almost tender. Layer linguine in bottom of greased 9-inch square casserole. Sprinkle with cheese. Cover with all the meat. Layer spinach on top of meat. Pour cream sauce over all. Bake at 375 degrees for 35 to 40 minutes or until golden brown. Serves 6.

Cream Sauce:

2 tablespoons butter	2 cups warm milk
2 tablespoons all-purpose	2 eggs
flour	Salt and pepper to taste

Melt butter in saucepan over low heat. Blend in flour. Remove from heat and gradually stir in milk. Return to heat, stirring constantly until sauce thickens. In a large bowl, beat eggs. Add cream sauce to eggs slowly, stirring constantly. Season with salt and pepper.

The Easter Day meal is customarily a communal event in the smaller Greek villages. Shallow trenches are dug and filled with glowing embers. Young spring lambs are put on spits (a long metal rod) over the trenches and slowly rotated by hand for many hours. The lamb is sprinkled with a little salt and oregano and basted frequently with lemon juice and olive oil to keep it from drying out. Occasionally, the cavity of the lamb is stuffed with feta cheese.

SOUVLAKIA
Shish-kebab
Souvlakia are sold on street corners
throughout Greece.

1 (3-pound) leg of lamb, boned

Marinade Sauce:
1 cup olive oil	3 tablespoons minced parsley
2 tablespoons lemon juice	3 green peppers, quartered
1 teaspoon salt	1 large onion, quartered and
1 teaspoon pepper	separated into slices
2 teaspoons dried oregano	12 cherry tomatoes
3 bay leaves	Lemon juice (optional)
4 cloves garlic, crushed	Olive oil (optional)

Cut meat into 1 1/2-inch cubes. Place in a deep bowl. Combine all
marinade ingredients in a jar; shake well. Pour over lamb. Cover
and refrigerate overnight. Remove meat; reserve marinade for
basting, if desired. Skewer on a 12-inch metal rod the lamb,
pepper, onion and cherry tomatoes; repeat ending with lamb. Baste
with reserved marinade, or beat a little lemon juice and olive oil
together and brush on lamb and vegetables. Broil on broiler rack 3
inches from flame for 15 to 20 minutes or until done. Turn
frequently. Serve with rice. Serves 6.

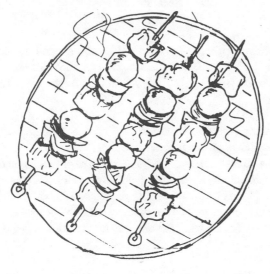

POULTRY

KOTA STIFATHO
Chicken Stew

3 to 4 pounds chicken pieces	2 tablespoons wine vinegar
2 pounds small onions, whole	Salt and pepper
3 cloves garlic, whole	1 tablespoon pickling spices
1/4 cup butter	1 spiral orange peel
3 ounces tomato paste	4 cups water or chicken broth
1 cup chicken broth	

In a large kettle, brown chicken, onions and garlic in hot butter for 10 minutes, stirring frequently. Dissolve tomato paste in the chicken broth, add vinegar and pour over chicken. Add remaining ingredients and bring to a boil. Reduce heat, cover and simmer 2 hours, or until chicken is tender and sauce has thickened. Stir occasionally. Serves 4 to 6.

KOTA MEH PILAFI
Chicken with Pilaf

2 1/2 pounds chicken pieces	4 tablespoons butter, melted
Garlic salt	2 1/2 cups boiling water
1 (8-oz.) can tomato sauce	1 cup long grain rice
Salt and pepper	

Rub chicken pieces with garlic salt. Place in a greased 13 x 9-inch baking pan and coat with tomato sauce. Sprinkle with salt and pepper. Drizzle with butter. Add 1/2 cup water; bake uncovered at 350 degrees for 30 minutes, turning chicken once. Add remaining water and rice. Lightly stir to distribute rice evenly. Cover with aluminum foil and continue baking for 30 minutes or until done. Turn oven off; leave in oven for 15 minutes. Serves 4.

KOTA MEH BAMIES
Chicken with Okra

1 1/2 pounds fresh okra
3 pounds chicken pieces
1 large onion, chopped
4 tablespoons butter
Salt and pepper to taste

1 (16-oz.) can whole tomatoes, chopped
1 cup hot water
1/4 cup chopped fresh parsley

Prepare okra according to instructions at beginning of Vegetable Chapter. In a Dutch oven, brown chicken and onion in butter until golden. Season with salt and pepper. Add tomatoes, water and parsley. Cover and cook for 30 minutes. Add okra and continue cooking until okra is tender. Do not overcook or overstir. Add more water, if needed. Serves 4 to 5.

KOTA RIGANATI
Chicken with Oregano
Chicken so tasty, you'll want seconds

3 pounds chicken pieces
1/3 cup olive oil
4 tablespoons butter, melted
1/4 cup lemon juice
2 cloves garlic, crushed

1 tablespoon dried oregano
Salt and pepper
2 large potatoes, peeled and sliced

Place chicken pieces in a large baking pan. Mix together remaining ingredients, except potatoes; pour over chicken, cover with aluminum foil and marinate overnight in the refrigerator. Bake uncovered at 425 degrees until lightly browned. Turn chicken pieces and baste. Add the potatoes, cover with aluminum foil and bake at 325 degrees for 1 to 1 1/2 hours. Serves 4 to 6.

Choosing the right kind of chicken makes for a better dish. For broiling or frying, buy fryers weighing 1 1/2 to 4 pounds. For roasting, buy a plump young chicken weighing 3 pounds or over.

KOTA MEH KARITHOSALTSA
Chicken with Walnut Sauce
Your guests will be impressed.

3 pounds chicken pieces
5 tablespoons butter
Salt and pepper
1 to 2 bunches whole green
  onions, chopped
4 tablespoons sherry

2 tablespoons lemon juice
1/4 teaspoon thyme
1 cup heavy cream
1/4 cup finely chopped walnuts
1/4 cup chopped fresh parsley

In a large skillet, brown chicken in hot butter. Season with salt
and pepper. Add onions and stir fry briefly. Add sherry, lemon
juice, thyme and cream. Cover; simmer 30 to 45 minutes or until
chicken is tender. Stir walnuts and parsley into cream sauce to
blend and heat through. Adjust seasonings if necessary. Serves 4.

KOTA MEH LEMONI
Chicken with Lemon

3/4 cup water
1/4 cup lemon juice
2 teaspoons dried oregano
1 teaspoon salt
1 teaspoon garlic powder

1/4 teaspoon pepper
3 pounds chicken pieces
1 cup flour
4 tablespoons olive oil
8 lemon slices

Combine the first 6 ingredients in a jar and mix well. Prick skin
of chicken with a fork, pour marinade over chicken, turn to coat.
Cover and refrigerate overnight.

Drain chicken, reserving marinade. Coat chicken with flour, and
brown in hot oil. Place chicken in 13 x 9-inch baking pan. Pour
reserved marinade over chicken. Top each chicken piece with a
lemon slice. Bake covered at 350 degrees for 50 minutes or until
chicken is tender. Baste occasionally. Remove cover last 15
minutes. Serves 4 to 6.

KOTOMEZETHES HRYSES
Chicken Nuggets
An excellent way to serve chicken at a buffet
dinner.

1/2 cup bread crumbs
1/4 cup grated Parmesan cheese
2 teaspoons msg.
3/4 teaspoon salt
Dash of pepper
1/4 teaspoon garlic powder

1 teaspoon dried basil leaves
1/4 teaspoon thyme
3 chicken breasts, boned, cut
 in 1 1/2-inch squares
1/2 cup butter, melted

Combine bread crumbs, cheese and seasonings. Dip chicken pieces
into melted butter, then into bread crumb mixture. Place in single
layer on foil-lined baking pans. Bake at 400 degrees for 20
minutes. Serves 4.

SIKOTAKIA KOTAS
Chicken Livers

1 pound chicken livers
1/4 cup all-purpose flour
1 teaspoon salt
1/8 teaspoon pepper
Thyme or oregano
3 tablespoons vegetable oil
3 tablespoons butter

1 cup chopped onions
2 cups fresh mushrooms, sliced
2 teaspoons cornstarch
1/4 cup water
1 cup chicken broth
1/2 cup dry vermouth or dry
 white wine

Slice livers in half. Combine flour, salt, pepper and desired
herbs. Coat livers with flour mixture. Brown in 2 tablespoons
each of oil and butter. In a saucepan, saute onions and mushrooms
in remaining oil and butter until tender. Add to livers. In a
separate saucepan, dissolve cornstarch in water. Add the chicken
broth and vermouth and cook until thickened. Pour over livers and
bring to a quick boil. Serve over rice. Serves 6.

GALOPOULA PSITI MEH YEMISI
Roast Turkey with Greek Stuffing

1 (15-pound) turkey
Salt and pepper
Oregano

Juice of 1 large lemon
1/2 cup butter, melted

Thaw turkey in refrigerator for 2 days. Simmer the neck, gizzard and heart about 1 hour in 4 cups of water with 1 teaspoon salt to make broth for gravy. Set aside. Rinse turkey in cold water; drain and pat dry. Rub skin with lemon juice and brush with butter. Sprinkle inside and out with salt, pepper and oregano. If desired, stuff and truss with string or skewers. Place turkey, breast side up, in a deep roasting pan and briefly brown under the broiler. Reduce oven to 325 degrees, top loosely with aluminum foil and bake 4 1/2 to 5 1/2 hours or until meat thermometer registers 190 degrees. Baste occasionally with remaining lemon juice and butter. Roast uncovered the last 20 minutes.

Stuffing: (An old family recipe from Eastern Thrace)

3 pounds lean ground beef
2 large onions, chopped
1 cup dry white wine
Turkey liver, chopped
1 pound chestnuts, cooked
  and quartered*
1/2 cup pignolia nuts, or
  slivered almonds

1/2 to 1 cup white raisins
1 to 2 teaspoons cinnamon
2 teaspoons sugar
Salt and pepper
1 (1-pound) sliced, white
  loaf bread, toasted, dried
  and crumbled**
1 cup butter

In a large skillet, brown beef; pour off excess grease. Add onions and saute for 2 to 3 minutes. Add wine; simmer a few more minutes. Add remaining ingredients and seasonings, except bread crumbs and butter. Simmer until liver has lost its red color. In a large saucepan, saute bread crumbs in butter until crisp and golden, stirring constantly. Add meat mixture and mix well. Adjust seasonings to taste. Stuffing may be made the day before; it may be served separately or stuffed into the turkey just before roasting. Serves 15.

---

* See Miscellaneous Chapter for "Cooking Fresh Chestnuts."

** See Miscellaneous Chapter for "Making Dry Bread Crumbs."

BEEF

STIFATHO I
Greek Beef Stew

3 pounds lean beef, cut into
  1-inch cubes
1 large onion, chopped
1 (8-oz.) can tomato sauce
1 carrot, chopped
3 stalks celery, chopped
1/2 cup minced fresh parsley

1 bay leaf
1 stick cinnamon
1 teaspoon meat tenderizer.
  (optional)
1/2 to 1 teaspoon garlic salt
1/4 teaspoon pepper
1 cup water

Combine all ingredients in a Dutch oven. Bring to a boil; reduce heat and simmer covered about 2 hours. When liquid is absorbed, stew is done. Serves 6.

STIFATHO II
Greek Beef Stew

3 pounds lean beef, cut into
  1-inch cubes
Salt and pepper
1/2 cup butter, melted
2 1/2 pounds small onions, peeled
1 (6-oz.) can tomato paste
1/3 cup red wine
2 tablespoons wine vinegar

1 tablespoon brown sugar
1 clove garlic, minced
1 bay leaf
1 small stick cinnamon
1/2 teaspoon whole cloves
  (optional)
1/4 teaspoon ground cumin
2 tablespoons raisins

Season meat with salt and pepper. In a Dutch oven, add meat and coat with butter; do not brown. Arrange onions over meat. Mix tomato paste, wine, wine vinegar, sugar and garlic; pour over meat and onions. Add remaining ingredients and gently stir. Simmer covered for 3 hours or until meat is very tender. Add water if needed to prevent scorching. Serve over rice or pasta. Serves 6.

KOUNELI STIFATHO
Rabbit Stew

Rabbit is a versatile meat that can be substituted in any chicken or beef stifatho recipe. To prepare rabbit, marinate for several hours in cold water to cover, adding 2 tablespoons vinegar and 1 to 2 tablespoons salt. Rinse and dry meat with paper towel; proceed with your favorite stifatho recipe.

85

STIFATHO MEH KARITHIA KEH FETA TIRI
Beef Stew with Walnuts and Feta Cheese
A gourmet version of the traditional stifatho.

3 pounds lean beef, cut into
  1 1/2-inch cubes
5 tablespoons butter
Salt and pepper
1 large onion, chopped
3 ounces tomato paste
1 1/2 cups water

2 tablespoons wine vinegar
1 clove garlic, crushed
1 bay leaf
2 pounds small onions, peeled
3/4 cup walnut halves
1/2 pound feta cheese, crumbled

In a Dutch oven, brown meat in butter; season lightly with salt and
pepper. Add onion; saute until soft. Mix tomato paste with 1/2
cup of water, wine vinegar and garlic; pour over the meat. Add bay
leaf; cover and simmer 1 hour. Add remaining water as needed
during cooking. Add onions, cover and simmer an additional hour or
until onions and meat are tender. Sprinkle walnuts and feta cheese
over top; simmer covered 5 minutes. Serves 6.

KREAS MEH RIZI FORMA
Meat and Rice Mold
An attractive and inexpensive entree.

2 pounds lean chuck, cut into
  1-inch cubes
6 tablespoons butter
3 medium onions, chopped
1/3 cup red wine
1 (8-oz.) can tomato sauce

1 cup boiling water
2 beef bouillon cubes
Salt and pepper to taste
Dash of ground cinnamon
  and sugar
2 cups long grain rice

In a large, heavy saucepan, brown meat in butter. Add onions and
saute until tender. Add remaining ingredients, except rice; cover
and simmer for 1 hour or until meat is tender. Add more water if
necessary. About 30 minutes before meat is ready, prepare rice
according to package directions; set aside. Place all the meat and
half the sauce in bottom of a 9 or 11-inch ring mold. Add cooked
rice and pack tightly. Turn out onto a heated, round serving
platter. Serve remaining sauce separately. Garnish with parsley.
Serves 6.

KREAS YIAHNI MEH AVGOLEMONO
Beef Stew with Egg-Lemon Sauce

3 pounds beef or veal, cubed
3 medium onions, chopped
4 to 6 celery stalks, chopped
3 tablespoons butter
3 1/2 cups boiling water
1 1/2 teaspoons salt
1/4 teaspoon pepper

2 tablespoons minced fresh dill
  or parsley
1 pound fresh vegetable of
  choice: brussel sprouts,
  string beans, broccoli, peas,
  artichokes or zucchini
Avgolemono sauce (below)

In a Dutch oven, brown meat, onions and celery in butter, stirring frequently. Add water and bring to a boil; reduce heat, cover and simmer 1 1/2 to 2 hours. Add seasonings, dill and vegetable during last 30 to 50 minutes; cook until meat and vegetables are tender. Remove meat and vegetables from pan with slotted spoon. Prepare avgolemono sauce and pour over meat and vegetables. Serve immediately. Serves 6 to 8.

Avgolemono Sauce:
  4 eggs
  Juice of 2 lemons

1 1/2 cups pan broth (may need to add
    additional water)

In a small saucepan, beat eggs with wire whisk until thick. Slowly add lemon juice, beating constantly. Add pan broth very slowly to keep eggs from curdling. Beat vigorously over <u>low</u> heat until thickened.

A short cut to preparing a Greek stew is to braise the meat as recipe specifies and then freeze. When defrosted, heat and add vegetable of choice; cook until done.

BEEF

KREAS YIAHNI MEH SALTSA DOMATAS
Pot Roast with Vegetables

3 pounds beef, pork, lamb or
  veal
3 medium onions, chopped
3 tablespoons butter
1 (8-oz.) can tomato sauce
3 1/2 cups water
3 tablespoons currants
2 bay leaves
1 1/2 teaspoons salt

1/4 teaspoon pepper
3/4 teaspoon ground cinnamon
1 spiral peel from orange
1/2 cup red wine
3 tablespoons pignolia nuts
  (optional)
1 pound fresh vegetable of
  choice (see previous recipe)

In a Dutch oven, brown meat and onions in hot butter. Add remaining ingredients, cover and bring to a boil. Reduce heat; simmer gently about 2 hours, or meat may be baked covered in oven at 350 degrees for 2 hours, basting occasionally. Add fresh vegetable of choice during the last 30 to 60 minutes; cook until meat and vegetable are tender. Serves 6 to 8.

VOTHINO MEH KRASI MADEIRA
Beef Tenderloin with Madeira

3 1/2 to 4 pounds beef tenderloin
1/4 cup vegetable oil
Thyme

Oregano
Salt and pepper
Madeira sauce (below)

Tie the meat with butcher's string at 1 1/2-inch intervals, turning the last 2 inches of meat under. The top of the meat is the side that is covered with a shiny membrane. Brush meat with vegetable oil; rub in thyme and oregano. Season with salt and pepper. Roast at 450 degrees for 30 to 40 minutes for medium rare. For a well-done roast, cover with aluminum foil to keep from drying out and roast an additional 20 to 30 minutes. If desired, serve with a Madeira sauce. Garnish with fresh mushrooms sauteed in butter. Serves 8.

Madeira Sauce:
  2 tablespoons chopped onions
  2 tablespoons butter
  1 1/2 cups canned beef gravy

2 tablespoons lemon juice
1/4 cup Madeira wine

Saute onions in butter until tender. Add beef gravy and lemon juice. Bring to a boil. Add Madeira wine and simmer for 2 minutes.

GROUND BEEF

MOUSSAKA I
Baked Eggplant and Beef Casserole I
The most famous eggplant recipe in the Near East.

3 medium eggplants
1 1/2 cups all-purpose flour
1 cup olive oil
1 cup butter
2 large onions, minced
1/4 cup butter
2 pounds lean ground beef
2 cups tomato sauce

1/2 cup red wine
Salt and pepper to taste
1/4 cup chopped fresh parsley
1/8 teaspoon ground cinnamon
Dash of sugar
6 tablespoons bread crumbs
1 cup grated Parmesan cheese
Cream sauce (below)

Prepare eggplants according to instructions in beginning of Vegetable Chapter, but slice eggplants lengthwise 1/4-inch thick. Dip into flour. In large skillet, fry eggplant slices in olive oil and 1 cup butter until golden on both sides. Drain on paper towels.

In a large skillet, saute onions in 1/4 cup butter until tender. Crumble beef into pan and brown. Add the tomato sauce, wine, salt, pepper, parsley, cinnamon and sugar; mix well. Simmer uncovered for 30 minutes or until juice is absorbed. Remove from heat; cool. Drain excess oil. Stir in 3 tablespoons bread crumbs and 1/2 cup Parmesan cheese. Sprinkle remaining bread crumbs on bottom of greased 17 x 11-inch baking pan. Place a layer of eggplant slices on the bottom; then layer of meat mixture. Repeat layers ending with eggplant. Pour cream sauce over all. Sprinkle with remaining cheese. Bake at 350 degrees for 50 minutes or until golden brown. Remove from oven; cool 15 minutes. Cut into squares. Makes 30 pieces.

Cream Sauce:
6 tablespoons butter
6 tablespoons all-purpose flour
3 cups warm milk

4 egg yolks, beaten
Salt and pepper
1/4 teaspoon nutmeg

Melt butter in top of double boiler over hot water; blend in flour, stirring constantly with wire whisk. Slowly add warm milk, stirring constantly until slightly thickened. Slowly add 1/2 cup cream mixture to egg yolks, then pour back into cream sauce. Cook over low heat until thickened, about 6 minutes. Add salt, pepper and nutmeg.

89

MOUSSAKA II
Eggplant and Ground Beef Casserole II

3 medium eggplants
Salt
1/2 cup butter, melted
2 tablespoons butter
1 cup minced onions
1 clove garlic, crushed
1 1/2 pounds lean ground beef
1/2 teaspoon dried oregano
1 teaspoon basil

1/2 teaspoon ground cinnamon
1 teaspoon salt
Dash of pepper
2 (8-oz.) cans tomato sauce
2 tablespoons dry bread crumbs
1/2 cup grated Parmesan cheese
1/2 cup grated Cheddar cheese
Cream sauce (below)

Halve unpared eggplants lengthwise; then slice crosswise 1/2-inch thick. Sprinkle lightly with salt; let stand for 15 minutes. Rinse with cold water; pat dry. Place in bottom of broiler pan and brush slices with 1/2 cup butter. Broil 4 inches from heat, 4 minutes per side.

In Dutch oven, saute onions, garlic and beef in butter until brown. Drain off fat. Add oregano, basil, cinnamon, salt, pepper and tomato sauce; bring to a boil. Reduce heat; simmer uncovered for 30 minutes. Remove from heat; cool. Stir in bread crumbs. In separate bowl, combine Parmesan and Cheddar cheese.

In bottom of greased 13 x 9-inch baking pan, layer half of eggplant slices, overlapping slightly. Sprinkle with 1/4 cup cheese mixture. Cover with meat mixture and sprinkle again with 1/4 cup cheese. Layer remaining eggplant slices; sprinkle with 1/4 cup cheese. Pour cream sauce over all and sprinkle with remaining cheese. Bake at 350 degrees for 35 to 40 minutes or until golden brown. Cool slightly, cut in squares. Serves 12.

Cream Sauce:
2 tablespoons butter
4 tablespoons all-purpose flour
1/2 teaspoon salt

Dash of pepper
2 cups warm milk
2 eggs

In medium saucepan, melt butter; blend in flour. Season with salt and pepper. Add milk gradually, stirring constantly until thickened. Remove from heat. In small bowl, beat eggs with wire whisk. Beat in 1/2 cup cream sauce; return to saucepan and mix well.

MOUSSAKAS MEH KALAMBOKI
Corn Moussaka

1 (17-oz.) can whole kernel
  corn, drained
1 1/2 pounds lean ground beef
1 tablespoon all-purpose flour
1 (8-oz.) can tomato sauce
1/2 teaspoon garlic salt
1/4 teaspoon ground cinnamon

2 eggs, beaten
1 1/2 cups cottage cheese with
  chives, drained
1/4 cup grated Parmesan cheese
1 (4-oz.) pkg. mozzarella
  cheese, shredded

Spread corn in bottom of ungreased, shallow 1 1/2 quart casserole.
Brown beef in a skillet; drain off fat. Add flour. Cook and stir
for 1 minute. Stir in tomato sauce, garlic salt and cinnamon.
Pour meat mixture over the layer of corn. Bake at 350 degrees for
15 minutes. Combine eggs and cottage cheese. Spread over meat,
top with Parmesan and mozzarella cheese. Bake an additional 10 to
15 minutes. Serves 6.

MOUSSAKAS MEH PATATES
Potatoes Moussaka

3 pounds potatoes, boiled
1/2 cup butter
1 cup milk
Salt and pepper
1 medium onion, chopped

1 1/2 pounds ground beef
1/2 cup water
3 tablespoons minced fresh
  parsley
3 eggs

Mash potatoes with 1/4 cup butter, milk, salt and pepper, set
aside. In a large saucepan, saute onions in remaining butter until
tender. Add crumbled ground beef and brown well. Add water and
parsley. Simmer uncovered for 15 minutes. Spread half of potatoes
on bottom of greased 13 x 9-inch baking pan. Cover with meat
mixture, then remaining potatoes. Beat eggs well and pour over
top. Bake at 350 degrees for 45 minutes. Serves 8 to 12.

PASTITSIO I
Macaroni and Meat Casserole I

Pastitsio is a popular dish served at family gatherings and elegant buffet dinners. The creamy sauce on top gives this recipe its uniqueness.

2 large onions, minced
3 tablespoons butter
2 pounds lean ground beef
Salt and pepper to taste
1 (8-oz.) can tomato sauce
1 cup water
1/2 teaspoon ground cinnamon
Dash of sugar

1/2 cup bread crumbs
2 1/2 cups grated Parmesan cheese
1 pound elbow macaroni
1 1/2 tablespoons olive oil
3 tablespoons melted butter
Cream sauce (below)

In a large saucepan, saute onions in butter until tender. Crumble meat into the pan and brown well. Drain off fat. Add salt, pepper, tomato sauce, water, cinnamon and sugar; simmer for 35 to 40 minutes or until liquid is absorbed. Remove from heat and cool. Add half the bread crumbs and 1 1/4 cups cheese to the meat mixture.

Cook macaroni in boiling, salted water with oil until almost done. Rinse; drain well. Butter a 17 x 11-inch baking pan; sprinkle with 2 tablespoons bread crumbs. Spread half of macaroni on bottom. Sprinkle 1/2 cup cheese over the macaroni. Cover with meat mixture. Pour half the cream sauce over the meat; then spread remaining macaroni; sprinkle with 1/2 cup cheese. Top with remaining sauce. Sprinkle with remaining bread crumbs and cheese. Bake at 350 degrees for 50 minutes or until golden brown. Let stand 20 minutes before cutting. Freezes well. To reheat, place frozen pastitsio, covered loosely with foil, in a 350-degree oven for 1 1/2 to 2 hours or until heated through completely. Makes 24 squares.

Cream Sauce:
1 cup butter
1/2 cup all-purpose flour
6 cups warm milk

Dash of nutmeg
6 eggs
1/2 cup grated Parmesan cheese

In a saucepan, melt butter and blend in flour, stirring constantly with a wire whisk. Gradually add warm milk, stirring vigorously until sauce thickens. Add nutmeg, remove from heat and cool. Beat eggs with wire whisk. Add 1/2 cup cooled sauce; then pour back into cream sauce. Stir in cheese.

PASTITSIO II
Macaroni and Meat Casserole II

1 large onion, chopped
1/2 cup butter
2 pounds lean ground beef
2 teaspoons salt
1/4 teaspoon pepper
1 tablespoon dried parsley
1 (8-oz.) can tomato sauce
1 stick cinnamon

1 pound elbow macaroni
1/2 cup butter, melted
1 (8-oz.) can grated Parmesan
    cheese, or 1 1/2 cups grated
    kefalotiri or Romano cheese
Ground cinnamon
Cream sauce (below)

In large saucepan, saute onion in hot butter until tender. Crumble
meat into the pan and brown well. Drain off fat. Add salt,
pepper, parsley, tomato sauce and cinnamon stick. Simmer for 30
minutes or until liquid is absorbed. Remove cinnamon stick.

Cook macaroni in boiling, salted water for 10 minutes. Rinse,
drain well, and mix with 1/2 cup melted butter. Sprinkle 2
tablespoons grated cheese on bottom of buttered 14 x 11-inch baking
pan. Spread half of macaroni on the bottom. Sprinkle with 2/3 cup
grated cheese and lightly with ground cinnamon. Cover with meat
mixture. Spread the remaining macaroni over the meat. Sprinkle
with 2/3 cup cheese and cinnamon. Pour cream sauce over all.
Sprinkle with remaining cheese.

Bake at 350 degrees for 50 minutes or until golden brown on top.
To freeze, cook and cool completely; wrap in aluminum foil. Thaw
at room temperature and reheat at 350 degrees for 20 to 30 minutes.
Serves 15.

Cream Sauce:
1/2 cup butter
1/2 cup all-purpose flour
4 cups warm milk
5 egg yolks, slightly beaten

1 teaspoon salt
1/4 teaspoon pepper
1/4 teaspoon nutmeg

Melt butter in top of double boiler over hot water. Blend in flour
with wire whisk. Gradually add milk, stirring constantly until
slightly thickened. Slowly add egg yolks and cook until thickened,
stirring constantly. Add salt, pepper and nutmeg.

DOLMATHES
Meat-Stuffed Grape Leaves with Egg-Lemon Sauce
Delicious and so typically Greek.

1 (16-oz.) jar grape leaves
1 1/2 pounds lean ground beef
1/2 cup long grain rice
3 large onions, minced
3 tablespoons olive oil
Salt and pepper

1/2 tablespoon minced fresh mint
1/2 tablespoon minced fresh dill
1/2 cup water
6 tablespoons butter, melted
1 cup beef stock
Avgolemono sauce (below)

Drain brine from grape leaves, snip off stems and rinse under cold water. Drain in colander. Mix well the ground beef, rice, onions, oil, salt, pepper, mint, dill and water. Spread any torn leaves on bottom of greased Dutch oven. With stem end facing up, place 1 tablespoon of meat mixture on the base of the leaf. Fold sides over and roll up. (See sketch in Appetizers under Dolmathakia Yialadji.) Do not roll too tightly as the rice will expand during cooking.

Layer in circular fashion in Dutch oven seam-side down. As each layer is completed, dot with butter. Shape any remaining meat mixture into meatballs and place on top. Add beef stock and enough water to cover the dolmathes. Place an inverted heavy plate on top to prevent shifting. Bring to a boil, reduce heat and simmer covered for 50 minutes. Shake pan occasionally to prevent sticking. Place dolmathes in large serving dish; pour avgolemono sauce over dolmathes. Makes 50 to 60.

Avgolemono Sauce with Yogurt:
1/2 cup plain yogurt
1 cup pan broth from dolmathes
1 1/4 tablespoons cornstarch
2 tablespoons cold water

4 eggs, beaten
5 tablespoons lemon juice
Dash of salt
Dash of white pepper

Combine yogurt and pan broth; set aside. In a medium saucepan, dilute cornstarch in water, add eggs and beat well. Add lemon juice, salt and pepper while beating. Fold in yogurt mixture. Place over low heat; continue beating until sauce thickens to consistency of heavy cream. Do not boil as eggs will curdle.

DOMATES KEH PIPERIES YEMISTES
Stuffed Tomatoes and Peppers

6 large tomatoes
6 green peppers
Sugar
Salt and pepper
3 large onions, chopped
6 tablespoons olive oil
1 1/2 pounds lean ground beef
6 tablespoons tomato paste
1/2 cup long grain rice
1/2 cup minced fresh parsley

1/2 cup chopped fresh dill
1 tablespoon minced fresh mint
1 teaspoon salt
Freshly ground pepper
1/4 teaspoon ground cinnamon
2 tablespoons white raisins
   (optional)
2 tablespoons pignolia nuts
   (optional)
1/2 cup beef broth

Cut thin slice from top of each tomato and reserve. Scoop out pulp; chop and reserve. Cut tops off peppers and reserve. Remove seeds and wash out. Sprinkle inside of tomatoes and peppers with pinch each of sugar, salt and pepper.

Saute onions in 3 tablespoons of oil. Crumble meat into the pan and brown. Drain off fat. Add 2 tablespoons tomato paste, rice, parsley, dill, mint, salt, pepper, cinnamon and all but 3 tablespoons of the reserved tomato pulp. Simmer 20 to 30 minutes or until juices are absorbed. Stir in raisins and pignolia nuts. Stuff tomatoes and peppers with meat mixture. Replace reserved tops. Place in greased baking pan. Combine remaining tomato pulp, olive oil, tomato paste and beef broth; pour around the tomatoes and peppers. Bake covered at 350 degrees for 45 minutes; uncover and return to oven for 15 more minutes. Serves 8 to 10.

KREAS ROLO TOU FOURNOU
Meat Loaf I

9 slices bread
1/2 cup milk
3 pounds lean ground beef
1 1/2 cups chopped onions
3 eggs, beaten
1 1/2 teapoons salt
1 teaspoon pepper

Pinch of dried oregano
1 clove garlic, crushed
1/4 cup Worcestershire sauce
3 tablespoons minced fresh
   parsley
1/2 teaspoon msg.

In a large bowl, soak bread in milk. Add remaining ingredients and mix well. Loosely shape into 2 or 3 standard-size loaf pans. Bake at 350 degrees for 1 to 1 1/2 hours or until done. One loaf serves 4 to 6.

MEAT LOAF II

9 slices bread
3 pounds lean ground beef
1 3/4 cups ketchup
1 large Spanish onion, finely
  chopped

3 eggs, beaten
1 green pepper, chopped
2 to 3 teaspoons salt
1 teaspoon pepper

Dip bread in water and press out excess. Combine all ingredients and mix well. Loosely shape into 4 (9 x 5-inch) loaf pans and bake at 350 degrees for 1 hour to 1 1/2 hours or until done. One loaf serves 6 to 8.

MELITZANA PAPOUTSAKIA
Stuffed Eggplant

4 medium eggplants
1 large onion, chopped
1/4 cup butter
1 1/2 pounds lean ground beef
2 cloves garlic, minced
1/4 cup chopped fresh parsley
1/2 cup tomato puree

Salt and pepper
3 eggs
1/2 cup grated kefalotiri,
  or Romano cheese
Bread crumbs
1/2 cup water

Prepare eggplant according to instructions in beginning of Vegetable Chapter. Slice eggplant in half lengthwise, scoop out pulp, chop and set aside. Saute onion in hot butter. Add crumbled beef and brown. Drain off excess fat. Add garlic, parsley, tomato puree, salt, pepper and reserved eggplant pulp. Simmer over moderate heat for 25 minutes or until liquid is absorbed. Remove from heat; cool.

In separate bowl, beat eggs and cheese together; fold into meat mixture. Stuff eggplant shells with meat mixture. Sprinkle top with bread crumbs. Place in a shallow baking pan with water. Bake at 400 degrees for 45 minutes. Serves 4 to 6.

Sliced green peppers, spearmint and parsley can be frozen; wash and store in small plastic containers.

PIPERIES YEMISTES
Stuffed Peppers

4 large green peppers
1 medium onion, chopped
2 teaspoons butter
1 pound lean ground beef
1 (8-oz.) can tomato sauce
1 (8 3/4-oz.) can whole kernel
  corn, drained

1 to 2 teaspoons chili powder
1/2 teaspoon salt
1/2 teaspoon garlic powder
1/2 teaspoon dried oregano
1/2 teaspoon thyme
1/2 cup shredded Cheddar cheese

Cut off tops of peppers, remove seeds and discard. Parboil peppers in boiling water for 5 minutes; drain and set aside. In a large saucepan, saute onion in hot butter until tender. Crumble ground beef into the pan and brown well. Drain off fat. Add the next 7 ingredients and mix well. Stuff peppers with meat mixture. Place in small baking dish with a little water. Bake at 350 degrees for 15 minutes. Sprinkle tops of peppers with shredded cheese; return to oven and bake 5 more minutes. Serves 4.

LAHANO—DOLMATHES
Stuffed Cabbage Leaves

2 medium cabbages, cored
1 pound lean ground beef
2 medium onions, chopped
3 tablespoons butter
Salt and pepper to taste
2 tablespoons tomato paste
1/2 teaspoon ground cinnamon
1 cup boiling water
1/4 cup long grain rice

2 tablespoons currants or
  white raisins (optional)
2 tablespoons pignolia nuts
  (optional)
2 tablespoons chopped fresh
  dill or parsley
1/2 cup tomato sauce
Water
Lemon slices

Parboil cabbage leaves for 5 minutes. Drain in colander. In large saucepan, saute beef and onions in hot butter. Add the next 8 ingredients and simmer until rice is partially done. Carefully remove center vein from each large cabbage leaf and cut in half. Place 1 heaping tablespoon of meat mixture near cut end of leaf; fold over. Fold edges in toward center and roll up. Chop any leftover cabbage leaves and place in bottom of Dutch oven. Layer cabbage rolls. Cover with an inverted heavy plate to act as a weight. Add tomato sauce with enough water to cover rim of plate. Cover and simmer about 1 to 1 1/2 hours or until rice is done. Garnish with lemon slices. Serves 6.

KEFTETHES MEH RIZI AVGOLEMONO
Meatballs with Rice and Egg-Lemon Sauce

2 slices stale white bread
4 cups chicken broth
2 pounds lean ground beef
1 egg, slightly beaten
1 medium onion, grated
1/2 cup chopped fresh parsley
1 to 2 cloves garlic, crushed
1/2 teaspoon chopped dried mint

3/4 teaspoon dried oregano
1/2 teaspoon cumin
Salt and pepper
3 tablespoons butter
1 cup long grain rice
3 egg yolks
Juice of 1 lemon
1/4 cup pan broth

Soak bread in 1/2 cup chicken broth; squeeze out excess. Add next 10 ingredients and mix well. Shape into balls about 2 inches in diameter. In a Dutch oven, brown meatballs in hot butter. Add remaining chicken broth and bring to a boil. Stir in rice, cover and simmer for 20 minutes or until rice is done. In a small bowl, beat egg yolks until light and fluffy; slowly beat in lemon juice. Gradually beat in hot pan broth. Pour sauce over meatballs and rice. Remove from heat; let stand 5 minutes. Sprinkle with additional parsley. Serves 6.

KEFTETHES MEH DOMATA SALTSA
Meatballs with Tomato Sauce

1 medium onion, chopped
1 clove garlic, minced
4 slices stale white bread
1 pound lean ground beef
1 egg, slightly beaten

1 teaspoon dried oregano
Salt and pepper
All-purpose flour
Oil for frying
Tomato sauce (below)

Cook onion and garlic in small amount of water until tender. Soften bread in a little water; squeeze out excess. In a large bowl, combine onion, garlic, bread and ground beef. Add egg, oregano, salt and pepper; mix well. Shape into small balls. Dust with flour and brown in hot oil. Drain. Proceed with following:

Tomato Sauce:

1 (16-oz.) can whole tomatoes, chopped
1 (15-oz.) can tomato sauce
2 to 3 tablespoons red wine

1 tablespoon butter
Salt and pepper to taste
1 teaspoon sugar
1/2 cup water

Combine all ingredients in saucepan and simmer for 5 minutes. Add meatballs and cook partially covered for 1 hour. Serve with spaghetti, rice or noodles. Makes 25 to 30 meatballs.

PORK

HIRINO PSITO
Roast Pork

1 (3 to 4 pound) pork loin roast,
  boned, rolled and tied
4 whole cloves garlic

Salt and pepper to taste
Thyme or oregano
1 cup chicken broth

Cut slits in roast and insert slivers of garlic; season with salt and pepper and desired herbs. Roast uncovered fat side down in a shallow pan at 350 degrees for 2 1/2 to 3 hours, or until meat thermometer registers 170 degrees. During the last hour of baking, pour the chicken broth over the meat. Baste frequently. Serve with spaghetti or linguine. Flavor pasta with pan drippings. Serves 6 to 8.

HIRINO MEH LAHANO
Pork with Cabbage

2 pounds pork (country ribs or
  cubed lean pork)
Salt and pepper to taste
1 medium onion, chopped
2 tablespoons butter

1 (16-oz.) can whole tomatoes,
  chopped
2 cups water
1 medium head cabbage, cut in
  wedges

Salt and pepper meat. In a heavy kettle, brown meat and onions in hot butter. Add tomatoes and water. Cook covered about 1 hour or until meat is fully cooked. Remove meat and add cabbage wedges; place meat on top of cabbage. Cover and cook about 15 minutes or until cabbage is tender, but not overdone. Serves 4.

Pork recipes from Greece are limited, even though pork is considered a great delicacy. For centuries, the Moslem Turks forbade the eating of pork. In some parts of Greece, to this day, a pig is only slaughtered for special occasions.

HIRINO MEH PRASA
Pork with Leeks
The leeks make that flavorful difference.

3 pounds leeks (1 bunch)
3 pounds pork, cut into 2-inch cubes
Salt and pepper to taste

2 medium onions, chopped
1/2 cup butter
3 tablespoons tomato paste
3 cups water

Prepare leeks according to instructions in beginning of Vegetable Chapter. Cut white part of leeks into 2-inch pieces. Parboil a few minutes and drain.

Season meat with salt and pepper. In a heavy kettle, lightly brown meat and onions in hot butter. Add tomato paste diluted with the water. Cover and simmer for 1 hour. Add leeks; cook until meat and vegetables are tender. Serves 6 to 8.

Variation: Lamb or beef can be substituted.

HIRINO MEH REVITHIA
Minted Pork and Chick Peas

2 pounds lean, boneless pork slices, 1/4-inch thick
1/4 cup olive oil
Salt and pepper
1 large onion, minced
1 to 2 cloves garlic, minced

2 (20-oz.) cans chick peas, drained
2 large tomatoes, coarsely chopped
2 tablespoons minced fresh mint
Lemon wedges

In a large skillet, lightly brown pork slices in hot oil until cooked. Season with salt and pepper. Add onions and saute until tender. Add garlic, chick peas, tomatoes and mint. Cover and simmer 15 to 20 minutes. Garnish with lemon wedges. Serves 6.

A pinch of baking soda added to dry beans while cooking decreases the amount of gas produced by the beans during digestion.

HIRINO MEH PRASINES ELIES
Pork with Green Olives

2 pounds pork tenderloin, cubed	1/2 pound sliced fresh
2 tablespoons butter	mushrooms (optional)
1 clove garlic, crushed	1 cup dry white wine
2 tablespoons pignolia nuts	1 tablespoon chopped fresh
(optional)	mint
1 1/2 teaspoons salt	2 tablespoons chopped fresh
1/4 teaspoon pepper	parsley
1 cup sliced onions	12 tsakistes olives, pitted*

Brown pork in hot butter with garlic and pignolia nuts. Season with salt and pepper. Add onions and mushrooms; saute until tender. Add wine, mint and parsley; cover and simmer for 30 minutes or until liquid is absorbed. Garnish with olives. Serves 6.

---

* Tsakistes olives are green, cracked olives marinated in herbs and brine, found in specialty stores (see Shopper's Guide).

LOUKANIKO MEH FASOLIA
Sausage and Butter Beans

1 1/2 cups large, dried butter	1 clove garlic, mashed
beans	2 (8-oz.) cans tomato sauce
Water	1/2 cup chopped fresh parsley
Salt	2 pounds loukaniko, or link
3 tablespoons olive oil	sausage*
1 large onion, chopped	Salt and pepper
1 cup chopped celery	

Soak beans overnight in water to cover. (For quick soaking, bring beans to a boil in water to cover, remove from heat and let stand 1 hour.) Drain, rinse, cover with fresh salted water, bring to a boil and simmer until almost tender, about 45 minutes; drain. Heat olive oil in a large skillet; add onion and celery and saute until heated through. Add garlic, tomato sauce and parsley; heat through. Add cooked loukaniko and beans. Cover and simmer 30 minutes; season vegetables with salt and pepper. Garnish with additional fresh parsley. Serves 6.

---

* Recipe for homemade loukaniko in Appetizers Chapter.

SEAFOOD

PSARI PLAKI A LA SPETSES
Baked Fish a la Spetses Island
Nick Triantafillis, Burlington, N.C.
The most popular way of serving fish in
Greece.

2 to 3 pounds whole fish, cleaned (red snapper, blue fish, pompano or sea bass)	1/2 cup dry white wine
	1/2 cup water
	3 medium tomatoes, chopped
Salt and pepper	3/4 cup chopped fresh parsley
6 to 8 whole green onions, chopped	3 tablespoons minced fresh dill
	Bread crumbs
2 cloves garlic, crushed	Lemon slices
1/2 cup olive oil	

Salt and pepper fish, set aside. Saute onions and garlic in hot
oil until tender. Add wine, water, tomatoes, parsley and dill;
saute until liquid is absorbed. Place fish in large greased baking
pan. Score flesh of fish to the bone at 2-inch intervals. Pour
sauteed vegetables over top. Sprinkle with bread crumbs; garnish
with lemon slices. Add 3/4 cup water to pan; bake at 350 degrees
for 45 to 60 minutes, or until fish flakes with a fork. Baste
often. Serves 4.

Variation: For more tomato flavor, add 1 (8-oz.) can tomato sauce
to sauteed vegetables.

FLOUNDER FILLET

2 pounds flounder fillets	Salt and pepper
1 small onion, thinly sliced	1 cup dry white wine
1 carrot, coarsely chopped	1/2 cup fresh mushrooms, sliced
2 tablespoons olive oil	1/4 cup chopped fresh parsley

In a rectangular baking dish, layer flounder, onion, carrot, olive
oil, salt and pepper. Bake at 350 degrees for 10 minutes. Combine
wine, mushrooms and parsley; pour over flounder. Bake 10 more
minutes, or until fish flakes with a fork. Remove from oven.
Spoon or suction out liquid in pan; boil down until thick. Pour
over flounder and serve hot. Serves 4 to 5.

SOLE DUGLERE
Raleigh Powell
Raleigh's Restaurant, Chapel Hill, N.C.
A popular item on Raleigh's famous menu.

8 fillets of sole
1/2 cup butter
20 shallots, minced
6 large tomatoes, peeled,
  seeded and chopped
1 cup chopped fresh parsley
Salt and pepper

2 cups dry white wine
5 tablespoons butter
4 tablespoons all-purpose flour
1 cup creme fraiche (below)
3 egg yolks, beaten
3 tablespoons cognac

In a large skillet, saute shallots in 1/2 cup hot butter until lightly browned. Remove from heat; place half the shallots in bottom of a baking pan large enough to hold fillets. Roll fillets up, skin-side in and stand them on end atop shallots. Combine tomatoes with 1/2 cup parsley, salt, pepper and remaining shallots; sprinkle over and around rolled fish. Add wine, cover and bring to a boil on top of stove. Remove from heat; carefully remove two-thirds of the pan liquid; set aside.

In a saucepan, combine remaining butter with flour. Add 3/4 cup creme fraiche; blend well. Slowly add reserved pan liquid. Cook, stirring constantly, over medium heat for 10 minutes or until slightly thickened. In a bowl, mix remaining creme fraiche with egg yolks, remaining parsley and cognac. Gently combine with cooked sauce. Pour sauce over fillets. Bake at 400 degrees covered for 10 minutes. Serve immediately. Garnish with additional parsley. Serves 4.

Creme Fraiche: Combine 1 cup whipping cream and 1 tablespoon buttermilk or yogurt in a jar, cover and shake for 1 minute. Loosen lid; let stand at room temperature for 18 to 24 hours or until very thick. Refrigerate. Makes 1 cup.

GARITHES BAKATSIAS
Shrimp Bakatsias
George Bakatsias
Bakatsias Cuisine, Durham, N.C.
A delicious gourmet meal by one of the
Triangle area's best-known chef.

3 pounds fresh spinach, trimmed
and washed
5 ounces fine noodles, cooked
and drained

6 tablespoons butter, melted
Shrimp-Tomato sauce (below)
Romano cheese, grated

Blanch spinach in boiling, salted water; drain well. Briefly saute
spinach in 3 tablespoons hot butter. In another pan, saute cooked
noodles briefly in remaining butter. Spread spinach in a circle on
a plate. Place a mound of noodles in the center; top with shrimp-
tomato sauce. Sprinkle top with Romano cheese. Serves 4.

Shrimp-Tomato Sauce:

6 to 8 whole green onions,
chopped
1/2 cup butter
1 ripe tomato, finely chopped
1/2 cup chopped fresh parsley
2 ounces dry white wine
1/2 ounce brandy
1 cup chicken stock

1/2 teaspoon dried basil
Juice of 1/2 lemon
Salt and pepper
1/2 pound medium shrimp,
peeled and deveined
2 cloves garlic, minced
4 ounces feta cheese,
crumbled

Saute onions in 1/4 cup hot butter until tender. Add the next 8
ingredients and cook down (uncovered) over medium-high heat for 15
to 20 minutes or until sauce thickens. In another pan, saute
shrimp and garlic in remaining butter for 2 minutes; season lightly
with salt and pepper. Drain. Add shrimp and feta cheese to tomato
mixture; simmer 1 minute. Pour sauce over spinach and noodles.

GARITHES MEH FETA TIRI
Shrimp with Feta Cheese

1 pound large shrimp, peeled
   and deveined
1/4 cup butter
Juice of 1 lemon
1 large onion, chopped
1 clove garlic, minced
1/4 cup olive oil

3 ripe tomatoes, peeled and
   chopped
1/4 cup chopped fresh parsley
1/2 teaspoon dried basil
Salt and pepper
1/4 cup dry white wine
1 cup crumbled feta cheese
1 cup long grain rice

Saute shrimp in butter and lemon juice over medium-high heat until shrimp turns pink. Drain; set aside. In a large skillet, saute onions and garlic in hot oil until tender. Add tomatoes, parsley, basil, salt, pepper and wine; saute 15 to 20 minutes, stirring occasionally. Stir in feta cheese; saute until cheese softens. Add shrimp and briefly heat through. Remove from heat. Cook rice according to package directions. Pack rice into 4 large, rounded coffee cups. Unmold in center of plate. Ladle shrimp sauce over top. Garnish with parsley sprigs. Serves 4.

GARITHES KEH KTENIA SOUVLAKI [†]
Shrimp and Scallops on Skewers

1/2 cup olive oil
1/4 cup lemon or lime juice
2 tablespoons dry white wine
1/4 teaspoon each dried oregano,
   thyme and garlic powder

Salt and pepper
2 pounds scallops, drained
2 pounds shrimp, peeled and
   deveined

To make marinade, combine all ingredients, except scallops and shrimp, in a jar and shake well. Marinate seafood at room temperature for 2 to 3 hours. Alternate shrimp and scallops on skewer. Broil over charcoal or under broiler for 10 minutes, turning once. Delicious served with rice pilafi or pasta. Serves 6 to 8.

SALMON-SCALLOP SUPREME
An elegant entree for company.

4 salmon fillets (4 to 6 ounces each)
Dry white wine
1 pound scallops, drained
6 tablespoons butter, melted
6 tablespoons all-purpose flour
1 cup heavy cream
2 teaspoons lemon juice

1 teaspoon Dijon mustard
3 tablespoons capers
Salt and pepper
Hot buttered rice
Lemon slices and parsley
  for garnish

Place salmon in skillet and barely cover with wine. Simmer uncovered until just tender and flaky. Remove salmon with slotted spatula to a heated platter; place in warm oven. Add scallops to wine in skillet; simmer 3 to 5 minutes or until tender. Place on top of fillets. Cook wine down to approximately 1 cup. Blend butter and flour together; stir into reduced wine and simmer until thickened, stirring constantly. Lower heat; blend in cream, lemon juice, mustard and capers, stirring until thickened. Season with salt and pepper. Spoon sauce over fish. Garnish with lemon slices and parsley. Serve with rice. Serves 4.

BAKALIAROS TIGANITOS
Fried Codfish
Traditionally served on Palm Sunday.

1 dried codfish
1 cup all-purpose flour
1 cup ice water
1/2 teaspoon garlic salt

1 egg
1/2 teaspoon baking powder
Oil for frying (1/2 olive oil
  and 1/2 vegetable oil)

Cover dried codfish with cold water and soak 36 to 48 hours in refrigerator, changing water occasionally. Combine flour, ice water, garlic salt, egg and baking powder. Blend well until consistency of pancake batter. Cut codfish into small serving pieces; pat dry. Dip into batter, allowing excess batter to drain. Fry in hot oil until golden brown, about 7 to 10 minutes on each side. Serve with Garlic Sauce (see Sauces). Serves 6 to 8.

ASTAKOS A LA SKYROS
Lobster a la Skyros Island
A spectacular entree for a special dinner party.

Tomato Sauce:

1 cup chopped onions
2 cloves garlic, crushed
1/4 cup olive oil
1 (28-oz.) can Italian plum
  tomatoes, chopped
2 to 3 tablespoons dry white wine
1/2 cup chopped fresh parsley

1/2 teaspoon dried oregano
1/2 teaspoon salt
1/4 teaspoon sugar
1/8 teaspoon red pepper
1/8 teaspoon black pepper
1 spiral lemon peel
1/4 cup crumbled feta cheese

In a heavy saucepan, saute onions and garlic in hot oil until tender, about 10 minutes. Drain tomatoes, reserving 3/4 cup juice. Add tomatoes and reserved juice; saute 2 minutes. Add remaining ingredients, except feta cheese. Bring to a boil; reduce heat and simmer uncovered for 30 minutes or until thickened. Add feta cheese; cool. (Sauce can be made ahead of time and refrigerated.)

* * * * * * * * *

4 (8-oz.) frozen lobster tails, thawed   1/4 cup butter
1/4 cup all-purpose flour

With kitchen shears, cut away shell membrane on underside of lobster; discard. Remove black vein. Pull out lobster meat and cut into bite-size pieces. Rinse and refrigerate shells. Coat lobster with flour and saute in hot butter, stirring frequently, for 8 minutes or until fully cooked. Combine with tomato sauce.

Arrange lobster shells in shallow baking pan. Spoon in lobster. Cover tightly with aluminum foil. Spoon any remaining lobster into small baking dish. Bake covered at 400 degrees for 20 to 25 minutes. To serve, arrange stuffed lobster shells on a bed of rice pilafi. Garnish with sprigs of parsley. Serves 4.

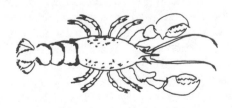

CLEANING SQUID

Cleaning whole squid is relatively simple. Purchase about 1/3 more uncleaned squid than you will need.

1. Holding the squid's body in one hand, grasp the head just behind the eyes with other hand and pull separating into 2 parts. The squid's viscera and ink sac will come out attached to the head.

2. Using a sharp knife, cut tentacles off head. Discard viscera and ink sac.

3. Squeeze small bony beak out of tentacles.

4. Push out from body the long, thin plastic-like sword.

5. Under cold running water, peel the purplish translucent skin from body. Rinse body inside and out.

Note: See Appetizers Chapter for "Fried Baby Squid" recipe.

KALAMARIA YEMISTA[†]
Stuffed Squid

2 pounds medium squid
1 large onion, finely chopped
3/4 cup olive oil
1 cup water
1/2 cup minced fresh parsley
1 tablespoon tomato paste
Salt and pepper

1/2 cup long grain rice
2 tablespoons pignolia nuts
 (optional)
1/4 cup white raisins
 (optional)
Juice of 1 lemon

Prepare squid according to instructions in preceding paragraph. Cut tentacles into very small pieces. In a skillet, saute onions and tentacles in 1/2 cup olive oil until tender. Add water, parsley, tomato paste, salt and pepper; cook covered for 15 minutes over low heat. Add the rice, pignolia nuts and raisins; cook until water is absorbed. Stuff squid with rice mixture, being careful not to overstuff. Secure ends with toothpicks. Arrange stuffed squid snugly in a pot, add remaining olive oil, lemon juice and 1 cup water. Cover; cook gently until squid is tender and rice is cooked, about 20 to 25 minutes. Serves 4 to 6.

OKTAPOTHI KRASATO[†]
Octopus in Red Wine
The most traditional way octopus is served in
Greece.

2 pounds fresh octopus
Tenderizer (optional)
2 large onions, minced
1/2 cup olive oil
Salt and pepper

1 bay leaf
1 cup red wine
1 tablespoon tomato paste
1 cup water

Purchase clean and well-pounded octopus. Sprinkle with tenderizer, if desired. Wash octopus carefully. Cut into bite-size pieces. Saute onions in hot oil until tender. Add octopus, salt, pepper and bay leaf; saute about 15 minutes. Slowly pour in wine and enough water to cover and bring to a boil. Reduce heat and simmer 1 1/2 to 2 hours or until octopus is very tender. If necessary, add a little more water during cooking to prevent scorching. Serve hot over rice pilafi. Serves 4.

TUNA FISH WITH CHICK PEAS
A simple, easy dish to prepare for a summer
luncheon.

1 (7-oz.) can tuna, drained
1 (20-oz.) can chick peas, drained
1 (10 1/2-oz.) pkg. frozen garden
  peas, cooked and drained
4 whole green onions, minced
1/2 cup minced celery
2 tablespoons minced fresh parsley

Dressing:
1/2 cup olive oil
1/4 cup lemon juice
1 clove garlic, crushed
1/2 tablespoon oregano
1/2 tablespoon marjoram
Salt and pepper to taste

Mix together tuna and vegetables. Combine all dressing ingredients in a jar and shake well. Pour dressing over tuna and vegetables. Serve on lettuce leaves or stuff into an open tomato. Serves 6.

PHYLLO ENTREES (PITES)

PHYLLO ENTREES (PITES)

Savory pites (pies) are certainly the most popular and frequently prepared dishes of Greece. Crispy buttered layers of phyllo pastry enveloping a vegetable, cheese, meat or poultry filling make an excellent entree for a family gathering or party buffet.

Phyllo pastry is a glamorous cover-up for many leftovers -- chicken salad, egg salad, seafood salad, meat stew, meat loaf slices, chopped cooked vegetables -- providing a wealth of possibilities for the imaginative cook. Bake a layered pita in a large baking pan for 45 to 60 minutes.

For more detailed information on "How to Work with Commercial Phyllo," see Miscellaneous Chapter and the Shopper's Guide in the Appendix for listings of where to purchase phyllo.

BASIC ASSEMBLY OF PITA

Prepare filling according to recipe; set aside. Take phyllo out of plastic bag and carefully unfold. Line buttered pan with half of phyllo sheets, making sure to overlap and drape phyllo over sides of pan (see sketch 1). Brush each sheet generously with melted butter. Spread prepared filling evenly over phyllo. Fold overhanging phyllo over filling and brush with butter. Top with remaining phyllo, buttering each sheet. Trim phyllo sheets used for top 1 inch beyond pan size. Tuck phyllo down the sides with edge of pastry brush to seal. Sprinkle a few drops of water over top of pita to keep phyllo from curling during baking. Score through top layer of phyllo with a sharp knife, making 4 equal rows lengthwise in a 13 x 9-inch pan (see sketch 2), 5 rows lengthwise in a 14 x 11-inch pan (see sketch 3) and 5 rows lengthwise in a 17 x 11-inch pan (see sketch 4). Recipes calling for 1 pound of phyllo will use 10 phyllo sheets on the bottom and 10 sheets on the top. Recipes using 1/2 pound of phyllo will use 5 sheets on bottom and 5 sheets on the top. The filling should not be too juicy as the bottom layers of phyllo will become soggy.

Bake pita as specified in recipe. Remove from oven; let stand 15 minutes before cutting into squares. Serve warm for best flavor. Refrigerate leftovers. To heat, place in 300-degree oven for 10 to 15 minutes.

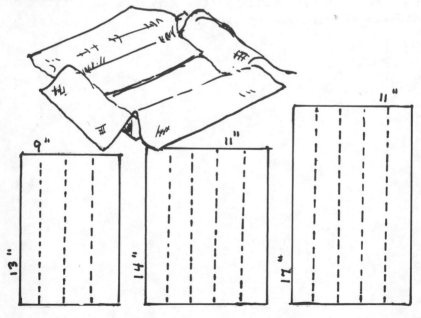

TIROPITA
Cheese Pita

3 tablespoons cream of wheat
1/3 cup milk
1/3 cup water
Dash of salt
2 1/2 cups crumbled feta cheese
1 cup cottage cheese
1/4 cup grated Parmesan cheese

6 eggs, beaten
2 tablespoons minced fresh
  parsley
1 pound phyllo
1 to 1 1/4 cups butter,
  melted and warm

In a small saucepan, cook cream of wheat in milk and water over medium-low heat for 2 1/2 minutes or until thickened. Stir in salt; cool. Combine cheeses and eggs in a large bowl. Add cream of wheat and beat until smooth. Set aside. Assemble pita as directed at beginning of chapter. Bake in a greased 17 x 11-inch baking pan at 350 degrees for 50 to 60 minutes or until golden brown. Makes 35 pieces.

SPANAKOPITA
Spinach Pita
- The most popular pita in Greece -

3 (10-oz.) pkgs. frozen chopped
  spinach, thawed
4 medium onions, chopped
6 whole green onions, chopped
1/4 cup olive oil
1/4 cup water
1 teaspoon salt
1/4 teaspoon pepper
1/4 cup minced fresh parsley

1/4 cup minced fresh dill
  (optional)
1 teaspoon cream of wheat
5 eggs, beaten
1 cup cottage cheese
1 1/2 cups crumbled feta
  cheese
1 pound phyllo
1 to 1 1/4 cups butter,
  melted and warm

Drain spinach thoroughly in colander, squeezing out excess moisture. In a large skillet, saute onions in olive oil over medium heat until tender, stirring constantly. Add spinach, water, seasonings and herbs; cook until liquid is absorbed. Sprinkle cream of wheat over top; cool. In a large bowl, combine eggs and cheeses; stir in spinach mixture, blending well. Set aside. Assemble pita as directed at beginning of chapter. Bake in greased 17 x 11-inch baking pan at 350 degrees for 55 to 60 minutes, or until golden brown. Makes 35 pieces.

KOLOKITHOPITA
Zucchini and Cheese Pita
A tasty combination of zucchini, onions and
cheese.

5 medium zucchini, grated
6 to 8 whole green onions, minced
6 tablespoons butter
1 cup crumbled feta cheese
1 cup cottage cheese, small curd
1/2 cup grated Parmesan cheese

1 cup grated kasseri or Swiss
  cheese
1/4 cup minced fresh parsley
5 eggs, beaten
1 pound phyllo
1 to 1 1/4 cups butter,
  melted and warm

Drain zucchini in colander for 1 hour, squeezing out excess
moisture. In a large skillet, saute zucchini and onions in 6
tablespoons butter until liquid is absorbed. In a large bowl,
combine all the cheeses, parsley and eggs; beat until well blended.
Add zucchini mixture; mixing well. Set aside. Assemble pita as
directed at beginning of chapter. Bake in greased 14.x 11-inch
baking pan at 350 degrees for 45 to 55 minutes or until golden
brown. Makes 30 pieces.

PRASOPITA
Leek Pita

7 to 8 leeks
6 to 8 whole green onions, chopped
1 tablespoon minced fresh dill
Salt and pepper
1/2 cup butter
1 (16-oz.) can whole tomatoes,
  drained and chopped
1/4 cup dry white wine

4 eggs, beaten
1 (12-oz.) cottage cheese,
  small curd
1 cup crumbled feta cheese
1/2 cup grated Parmesan cheese
1 pound phyllo
1 to 1 1/4 cups butter,
  melted and warm

Prepare leeks according to instructions in beginning of Vegetable
Chapter. In a large skillet, saute leeks, onions, dill, salt and
pepper in hot butter until tender. Add tomatoes and wine; simmer
until liquid is absorbed. Let cool. Combine eggs and cheeses; add
to leek mixture. Set aside. Assemble pita as directed at
beginning of chapter. Bake in greased 14 x 11-inch baking pan at
350 degrees for 40 to 50 minutes, or until golden brown. Makes 30
pieces.

PRASOPITA MEH KEMA
Leek and Meat Pita
A creamy, rich filling that melts in your mouth.

4 to 5 leeks (1 bunch)
3 tablespoons butter
1/4 cup water
1 pound lean ground beef
1/4 cup dry white wine
Salt and pepper

Dash of nutmeg
Cream sauce (below)
6 eggs, well beaten
1 pound phyllo
1 to 1 1/4 cups butter,
  melted and warm

Slice only white, bulbous part of leeks into chunky pieces; wash
well in cold water. Drain. Chop finely; or place in food
processor on intermittent speed 10 to 15 seconds. In a large
skillet, saute leeks in 3 tablespoons butter and 1/4 cup water
until tender. Remove leeks to a dish; set aside. Brown ground
beef, draining off excess fat. Add wine, salt, pepper, nutmeg and
leeks. Simmer 15 to 20 minutes or until wine has evaporated;
remove from heat. Make cream sauce; fold in eggs. Add meat and
leek mixture; mix well. Set aside.

Assemble pita as directed at beginning of chapter. Bake in greased
17 x 11-inch baking pan at 350 degrees for 50 to 60 minutes. Makes
35 pieces.

Cream Sauce:
  1 quart milk
  1/2 cup unsalted butter
  4 tablespoons all-purpose flour
  1 teaspoon salt

1/4 teaspoon white pepper
1/4 teaspoon nutmeg
3/4 cup grated Parmesan
  cheese

Heat milk just to boiling; set aside. Melt butter in heavy
saucepan. Gradually add flour, stirring constantly for 3 to 5
minutes. Add milk slowly, stirring vigorously. Cook over low heat
10 minutes. Remove from heat; stir in remaining ingredients.

Pites should be assembled and then frozen unbaked. When needed,
bake directly from freezer.

KREATOPITA
Meat Pita
A complete meal in itself.

2 pounds boned leg of lamb or veal (4 cups)
2/3 cup vegetable or olive oil
2 medium potatoes, finely diced
1 medium onion, chopped
1 teaspoon minced garlic
2 to 3 tablespoons tomato paste
2 to 2 1/2 cups water
Salt and pepper
Dash of ground cinnamon
Dash of ground clove
1 cup converted rice
3 eggs, well beaten
3 tablespoons minced fresh parsley
3 tablespoons grated Parmesan cheese
1 pound phyllo
1 to 1 1/4 cups butter, melted and warm

Dice meat into very small pieces. In a large skillet, brown meat in hot oil over medium-high heat for 5 minutes. Add potatoes, onions and garlic; cook for 10 minutes. Add tomato paste diluted in water, salt, pepper, cinnamon and ground clove. Simmer partially covered over medium heat for 10 minutes. Stir in rice, cover and cook over low heat for 7 minutes, stirring occasionally. Add more water if necessary to keep from scorching. Rice should be barely tender. Remove from heat; leave covered and cool slightly. Blend in eggs, parsley and Parmesan cheese; set aside.

Assemble pita as directed at beginning of chapter. Bake in greased 14 x 11-inch baking pan at 350 degrees for 45 minutes. Reduce oven to 325 degrees and bake 30 to 45 minutes more. Cover pan loosely with aluminum foil first 30 minutes of baking. Makes 30 pieces.

Note: This pita's flavor is really enhanced if homemade phyllo is used (see Miscellaneous Chapter).

On the Island of Kefallinia in the Ionian Sea, the Feast Day of Analipseos (Ascension Day) is celebrated with the traditional kreatopita. This spicy pita also ushers in the beginning of the Lenten season on the day of Apokreas.

KOTOPITA A LA KERKIRA
Corfu-Style Chicken Pita

1 cup chopped onions	1/2 teaspoon nutmeg
1 clove garlic, minced	1/4 cup minced fresh parsley
6 tablespoons butter	Salt and pepper
3 cups finely-diced cooked	Cheese sauce (below)
chicken or turkey	1/2 pound phyllo
1/8 cup dry white wine	1 cup butter, melted and warm

In a large skillet, saute onions and garlic in hot butter until golden. Add chicken; saute 2 minutes. Add wine, nutmeg, parsley, salt and pepper. Simmer briefly, stirring constantly. Remove from heat. Stir in cheese sauce, mixing well. Set aside. Assemble pita as directed at beginning of chapter. Bake in greased 13 x 9-inch baking pan at 350 degrees for 45 to 55 minutes or until golden brown. Makes 24 pieces.

Cheese Sauce:

1/4 cup butter	1/2 teaspoon white pepper
4 tablespoons all-purpose flour	1 1/2 to 2 cups grated Parmesan
2 cups warm milk	cheese (according to taste)
1 1/2 teaspoons salt	4 eggs, beaten

Melt butter in heavy medium saucepan. Blend in flour, stirring for 2 minutes with wire whisk. Remove from heat; stir in milk. Cook over medium heat for 5 minutes, stirring constantly. Add salt, pepper and cheese; stir until melted. Remove from heat; cool for 5 minutes. Add eggs, stirring vigorously for 2 minutes.

KOLOKITHOPITA APLI
Zucchini Squares

1/4 cup vegetable oil	5 whole green onions, minced
1 cup Bisquick	2 tablespoons minced fresh
4 eggs	parsley
4 medium zucchini, grated	1/2 teaspoon dried dill
1/2 cup grated Parmesan cheese	1/2 teaspoon salt

Combine oil, bisquick, and eggs; beat for 1 minute. Add remaining ingredients and mix well. Bake in a greased 13 x 9-inch baking pan at 350 degrees for 30 minutes. Place under broiler 1 or 2 minutes to brown top. Cut into squares and serve. Freezes well. Warm in oven or microwave. Makes 24 pieces.

SPANAKI MEH KREMA
Spinach Quiche
An attractive dish for a company luncheon.

1 (11-oz.) pkg. pie crust mix	1 1/2 cups warm milk
2 (10-oz.) pkgs. frozen chopped spinach	1/2 teaspoon salt
	1/4 teaspoon pepper
5 to 6 whole green onions, minced	Dash of nutmeg
1 clove garlic, minced	6 eggs
5 tablespoons butter	1 cup crumbled feta cheese
1 teaspoon dried dill	
3 tablespoons all-purpose flour	

Prepare pie crust mix as directed on package. On floured surface, roll dough into a circle large enough to line bottom and sides of an ungreased 10-inch pie plate. Flute a high edge.

Cook spinach; drain, pressing out all moisture. In skillet, saute onions and garlic in 2 tablepoons melted butter until golden. Stir in spinach and dill; set aside. In saucepan, melt remaining 3 tablespoons butter, blend in flour, stirring constantly for 2 minutes. Gradually add milk. Cook over low heat, stirring constantly until sauce bubbles and thickens. Remove from heat. Stir in salt, pepper, nutmeg and spinach mixture.

In a large bowl, beat eggs well and stir in cheese. Blend in spinach and sauce mixture. Pour into pie shell. Bake at 350 degrees for 40 to 45 minutes or until center is firm to the touch. Serve warm. Freezes well up to 4 weeks. Thaw and reheat. Serves 8 to 12.

Variation I: For a milder cheese taste, use 1/2 cup feta cheese and 1/2 cup cottage cheese.

Variation II: Substitute 2 (10-oz.) packages of chopped broccoli for the spinach.

ZIMAROPITA
Spinach Squares

1 medium onion, chopped
6 whole green onions, chopped
3 tablespoons olive oil
1 (10-oz.) pkg. frozen chopped
   spinach, thawed and drained
4 eggs, beaten
1 (12-oz.) cottage cheese,
   small curd

1/2 cup crumbled feta cheese
1/3 cup yellow or white cornmeal
1/3 cup self-rising flour
2 teaspoons sugar
1 teaspoon baking powder
1/2 cup butter, melted
2 eggs

In a skillet, saute onions in hot oil until tender. Add spinach; cook over medium heat until water is absorbed. Remove from heat; place in large bowl. Add eggs, cottage cheese and feta cheese. Mix well. Combine cornmeal, flour, sugar and baking powder; add to spinach mixture, blending well. Pour into greased 13 x 9-inch baking pan. Beat melted butter and 2 eggs with wire whisk. Spread evenly over top of spinach mixture. Bake at 350 degrees for 40 to 45 minutes. Cool slightly before slicing. Makes 24 pieces.

MAKARONIA KEH TIRI MEH PHYLLO
Meatless Pastitsio with Phyllo

1 pound elbow macaroni
3/4 cup butter
1 cup grated Romano or Parmesan
   cheese
1 cup mizithra, ricotta, or
   cottage cheese
1 cup crumbled feta cheese

6 eggs, beaten
2 cups milk
1/2 teaspoon white pepper
8 phyllo sheets
1/2 cup butter, melted
   and warm

Cook macaroni in boiling, salted water until almost tender. Drain in colander, rinse in cold water and drain again. Heat 3/4 cup butter until sizzling; stir into macaroni. Combine cheeses, eggs, milk and white pepper; add to macaroni, stirring well to blend. Spread macaroni mixture evenly in greased 13 x 9-inch baking pan. Top with 8 buttered phyllo sheets. Score through top 4 sheets with sharp knife, making 4 equal rows lengthwise. Bake at 350 degrees for 15 minutes; reduce oven to 300 degrees and bake for 35 minutes. Cool for 15 minutes, cut into squares and serve warm. Makes 24 pieces.

PASTITSIO MEH PHYLLO
Meat Pastitsio with Phyllo
A gourmet variation of the traditional pastitsio.

2 pounds lean ground beef
2 medium onions, finely chopped
3/4 cup butter
1 teaspoon dried oregano
Dash of garlic powder
Dash of ground cinnamon
2 teaspoons salt
1/4 teaspoon pepper
1/2 cup red wine (optional)

2 tablespoons tomato paste
1 cup water
1 1/4 pounds elbow macaroni
1/2 pound phyllo
1 cup butter, melted and warm
3 cups grated Parmesan cheese
12 eggs
1 quart milk

Crumble ground beef in a large skillet and brown well. Drain off fat. Add onions and 4 tablespoons butter; saute until onions are tender. Add seasonings, wine, tomato paste and water. Simmer uncovered about 40 minutes until liquid is absorbed. Meanwhile, cook macaroni in boiling, salted water until almost done. Drain in colander, rinse in cold water and drain again. Heat remaining 1/2 cup butter until sizzling and stir into macaroni.

Place 5 phyllo sheets in greased 14 x 11-inch baking pan, brushing each with butter. Place half of macaroni over phyllo; sprinkle with 1 cup Parmesan cheese. Spread meat mixture evenly over macaroni. Sprinkle 1 cup Parmesan cheese over meat; cover with remaining macaroni. Sprinkle with remaining cheese. Beat eggs until light and fluffy; stir in milk. Pour evenly over macaroni. Top with 5 buttered phyllo sheets. Score through top layer of phyllo with a sharp knife, making 5 equal rows lengthwise. Bake at 350 degrees for 40 to 50 minutes or until golden. Cool for 15 minutes, cut into squares. Makes 30 pieces.

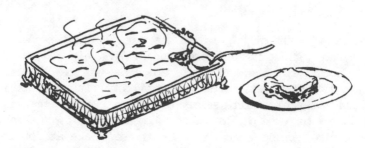

ZUCCHINI QUICHE

4 cups thinly-sliced unpeeled
zucchini
1 cup coarsely chopped onion
1/3 to 1/2 cup butter (as desired)
1/2 cup chopped fresh parsley
1/2 teaspoon salt
1/2 teaspoon black pepper
1/4 teaspoon garlic powder
1/4 teaspoon crushed dried basil

1/4 teaspoon crushed dried
oregano
2 eggs, well beaten
8 ounces shredded
mozzarella cheese
1 (8-oz.) can refrigerated
crescent dinner rolls
2 teaspoons prepared
mustard

In a large skillet, cook zucchini, onion, butter, parsley and
seasonings over medium heat about 10 minutes; set aside. In a
large bowl, blend eggs and cheese. Stir in vegetable mixture.

Separate dough into triangles and place over bottom and up sides of
an ungreased 10-inch pie pan or quiche plate to form crust. Spread
mustard over crust. Pour in vegetable mixture. Bake at 375
degrees for 18 to 20 minutes. Let stand 10 minutes before serving.
Serves 6.

BREADS

BREADS

Of all foods prepared and eaten by man today, bread still remains one of the most satisfying sustenances. Everyone, especially a Greek, loves homemade bread! It was the ancient Hellenes who discovered the secret of cultivating yeast and refining the flour that makes our present day breads so light and soft. Whether it is of the crusty plain or the decorated sweet variety, bread is always present on the "Grecian Plate."

BREADMAKING TECHNIQUES

There is not a perfect recipe with precise measurements in breadmaking. Taking your time and keeping in mind the following techniques will help assure success for the novice breadmaker:

YEAST: In the following recipes, packaged dry yeast is used. Dissolve yeast in warm water (110 degrees). (Hot water will kill yeast; cold water retards growth.) Let stand covered 5 to 10 minutes. Yeast is active when a distinct light, bubbly layer appears on top. Any ingredients added to yeast such as milk, eggs, butter and water should be at room temperature.

FLOUR: All-purpose flour is generally used in the following recipes and should be added gradually to the bread batter. Add last 4 to 5 cups of flour, 1 cup at a time, until dough is soft and comes cleanly away from sides of bowl. Do not add more flour than dough can absorb.

KNEADING: When kneading, add as little flour as possible, except to flour hands and working area. Use a folding-pushing motion, rotating dough a quarter turn each time. If dough is too sticky, let dough rest covered for 10 minutes. Wash hands, dry thoroughly and lightly dust with flour before kneading again. If dough is too dry, add a little oil. Ten minutes are required for the first kneading. Dough is ready when it is smooth and elastic and non-sticky. After the dough is punched down, the second kneading requires only 2 minutes.

RISING: Place dough in greased bowl, turning once to grease the top. Cover with clean cloth to prevent crust from forming. Let rise in a warm place (80 to 85 degrees) until double in bulk. When properly risen, dough will look rounded and full and will retain a dent when pressed lightly.

RESTING: After first rising, punch down dough, place on lightly-floured surface, cover and let rest for 10 to 12 minutes. Dough will be easier to handle and keep desired shape.

BAKING: Bake bread in center of oven. Place pans about 2 inches apart allowing heat to circulate around bread. If tops are browning too fast, cover loaves loosely with aluminum foil. Bread is done when well browned on top and when top or bottom sounds hollow when tapped with fingertips.

STORAGE: To keep bread fresh, wrap cooled loaves in aluminum foil or seal in plastic bags. Store in cool, dry place or freeze. Thaw at room temperature or place in microwave for 2 minutes on defrost cycle.

HOLIDAY BREADS

Breadmaking is an art, and the baking of holiday breads is the ultimate in the art of breadmaking. Tsoureki is the general name for the sweet and delightfully fragrant bread that Greeks bake for holidays or any festive occasion. New Year's Day is ushered in with the ceremonial cutting of the Vasilopita (a bread made in honor of St. Basil, whose feast day is January 1). At midnight, the family gathers around the table. The head of the household makes the sign of the cross over the bread and offers the first slice to the church. Slices are then cut for the family in order of age. A foil-wrapped coin is baked into the bread, and the custom is that whoever finds the coin will have good luck in the coming year.

The Greek word for Easter is Lambri and for bread, psomi; Lambropsomo is a combination of both words. Traditionally, the bread is braided and decorated with dyed red eggs. Christopsomo or "Christ's bread" is made at Christmas and decorated with a "Byzantine" cross.

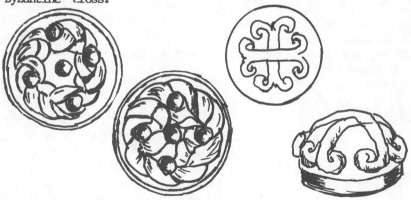

TSOUREKI I
Braided Holiday Bread
A delicious bread that can be used for any
occasion.

5 pkgs. active dry yeast
3/4 cup warm water (110 degrees)
2 cups milk
4 cups sugar
1 1/2 teaspoons mastiha,
  finely ground
40 seeds mahlepi, finely ground

2 pounds butter, room
  temperature
7 to 8 pounds all-purpose
  flour (28 to 32 cups)
18 eggs, room temperature,
  well beaten

Dissolve yeast in water; let stand covered 10 minutes. Heat milk and sugar until sugar dissolves. Cool to lukewarm; stir in mastiha and mahlepi. (Grind spices together with mortar and pestle.) Partially melt the softened butter in a separate saucepan or place 30 seconds in microwave on full power. In a very large mixing bowl, place 5 pounds of flour. Make well in center; pour in yeast liquid. Knead briefly. Gradually add butter, milk mixture and eggs alternately with the remaining flour, kneading thoroughly after each addition. Knead for 10 minutes or until dough is smooth and elastic and comes cleanly away from sides of bowl. Cover with cloth; place on wire rack over a large pan partially filled with hot water in a draft-free place. Let rise for 3 1/2 hours or until double in bulk.

Punch down, cover and let dough rest for 10 minutes. Pinch off 3 balls of dough, about the size of an orange. Roll each ball into a long smooth rope about 10 inches long (see sketches below). Place ropes 1 inch apart, press together at one end, leaving middle end on top. Braid loosely, press together at the end and tuck under. Place loaves in greased 9 x 5-inch loaf pans, cover and let rise again for 2 hours. Brush tops gently with 1 egg white beaten with 1 tablespoon milk. Sprinkle generously with sesame seeds. Bake at 325 degrees about 30 minutes or until nicely browned. Freezes well. Makes 9 to 10 loaves.

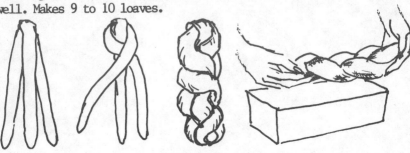

TSOUREKI II

5 pkgs. active dry yeast
1/2 cup warm water (110 degrees)
1 tablespoon sugar
3 pounds all-purpose flour
  (12 cups), sifted
3/4 pound butter, melted

7 eggs, room temperature
1 3/4 cups sugar
1/2 teaspoon ground mastiha
1/2 teaspoon ground mahlepi
1 teaspoon salt
1 1/2 cups warm milk

Glaze:
  1 egg
  1 teaspoon sugar

1 teaspoon water
Sesame seeds

Dissolve yeast in water, adding sugar and a little flour to make a soft dough. Let rise covered in a warm place about 15 minutes or longer.

Place butter in large mixing bowl. Separately beat eggs, adding sugar gradually; add to butter along with mastiha, mahlepi and salt. Mix well. Add milk, yeast mixture and remaining flour, 1 cup at a time. Knead 5 to 10 minutes in bowl until dough is not sticky and comes away cleanly from sides of pan. Cover bowl tightly with aluminum foil and place in an unheated oven to rise. (A pan of hot water can be placed in oven to bring temperature up to 80 degrees.)

Let rise about 1 1/2 hours, or until doubled in bulk. Punch down, remove from bowl, knead lightly, and let rest a few minutes. If dough is sticky, grease fingers with vegetable oil. Shape dough into individual small twists, or roll small portions of dough into long ropes, braiding 3 ropes together, sealing ends firmly. Place on greased baking sheets (not more than 2 braids per sheet). Let rise again until double in bulk in a warm place.

To glaze, beat egg, sugar and water together and brush lightly on bread. Sprinkle with sesame seeds. Bake at 350 degrees for 25 to 30 minutes or until golden brown. Size of twists determines quantity.

VASILOPITA
New Year's Bread

3 pkgs. active dry yeast
3/4 cup warm water (110 degrees)
1 stick cinnamon
2 bay leaves
1 tablespoon anise seed
1/2 cup water
9 eggs
4 cups sugar

12 cups all-purpose flour
1 teaspoon salt
1 1/2 cups butter, melted
1 1/2 cups warm milk
1 egg yolk, beaten
Sesame seeds
Blanched almonds

Dissolve yeast in water; let stand covered 10 minutes. Gently boil cinnamon stick, bay leaves and anise seed in water for 10 minutes; strain and reserve. Beat eggs and sugar until light-colored. In a large bowl, sift flour and salt into butter. Work ingredients well with fingers. Make well in center of flour; pour in yeast, egg mixture and reserved spice liquid, mixing well after each addition. Add warm milk gradually, kneading until all is used. Dough should be soft but not sticky. Cover bowl with waxed paper, then with a clean towel. Let rise in a draft-free warm place for 3 hours, or until double in bulk. Punch down, knead lightly and shape into 4 smooth, round loaves and place in 4 greased 9-inch round cake pans. Conceal a foil-wrapped clean silver coin in the dough, if desired. Cover; let rise again for 1 hour. Brush tops with beaten egg yolk or evaporated milk. Decorate with sesame seeds or blanched almonds, or reserve enough dough to write out the number of the year on top. Bake at 350 degrees for 25 minutes or until golden. Makes 4 round breads.

Variation: For a different flavoring, substitute this spice liquid, following directions as stated in recipe above:

1 orange rind, grated
1 teaspoon anise seed

1/2 stick cinnamon
1/2 cup water

A Liquid Substitute for Mahlepi

In a saucepan, combine 3 cloves, 1 bay leaf, 1/2 stick cinnamon and 3/4 cup of water. Simmer covered over low heat for 20 minutes. Strain and use, substituting about 2 tablespoons of liquid for 1 tablespoon ground mahlepi.

CHURCH BREADS

The role of bread in the Greek Orthodox Church has always been important. Prosphoron (Bread of Oblation) is distributed to the congregation after each Liturgy as well as to those receiving Holy Communion.

The Prosphoron Seal is a hand-carved wooden press made by monks in a Greek monastery. The design on the bread appears as follows.

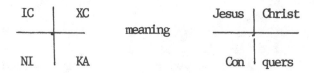

PROSPHORON
Bread of Oblation

Made to resemble the bread eaten at the Last Supper – no shortening, milk or eggs are permitted.

1 pkg. active dry yeast
2 1/2 cups warm water
1 teaspoon salt

6 cups all-purpose flour, sifted
1 Prosphoron Seal

Dissolve the yeast in 1/2 cup water, cover and let stand for several minutes. In a large bowl, combine the remaining water, salt and yeast mixture. Add a cup of flour at a time, kneading well after each addition. Use as much flour or water as necessary to make dough very pliable. Knead 10 to 15 minutes until no longer sticky. Dust hands with flour when needed. Cover with a cloth; let rise in a draft-free, warm place for 1 1/2 hours or until double in bulk. Punch down and knead slightly. Divide dough into 2 balls. Pinch off 1/4 of dough from each ball. Shape the 2 larger portions of dough to fit a floured 9-inch round cake pan. Shape smaller portions of dough in round mounds on a floured surface. Dip the Prosphoron Seal in flour and press it down very firmly in the center of each mound. Place mounds on top of dough in pans, moistening dough with a little water so the 2 layers will adhere. Cover and let rise about 45 minutes. Bake at 350 degrees for 1 hour. Remove from oven and cover with a cloth. Gently remove cooled loaves from pans, tapping excess flour off the bottom. Cover bread with a cloth. Makes 2 Prosphora.

"ARTOCLASIA"
The ceremony of blessing and breaking the
Five Holy Loaves of Bread.

4 sticks cinnamon
1 cup water
5 pkgs. active dry yeast
3 cups lukewarm milk
1 1/2 cups butter, melted
6 eggs, beaten
3 cups sugar

1 teaspoon mastiha, ground
1 teaspoon salt
1/2 cup vegetable oil
4 to 5 pounds all-purpose
   flour, sifted
1 Prosphoron Seal

Boil cinnamon sticks in water until liquid is reduced to 1/2 cup; strain and reserve. In a large bowl, dissolve yeast in milk; let stand a few minutes. Add reserved cinnamon water and remaining ingredients, except flour. Blend well by hand. Add enough flour to form a soft dough; knead well. Cover with a cloth; let rise in a warm place for 3 to 3 1/2 hours or until double in bulk. Punch down, knead slightly, and shape into 6 smooth round loaves. Place in greased 9-inch round cake pans. Stamp center of each loaf firmly with floured Prosphoron Seal. Let rise again for 1 1/2 hours. Brush with beaten egg. Bake at 325 degrees for 35 to 45 minutes or until golden brown. Remove from pans; cool on cake rack. Select 5 best loaves for "Artoclasia".

VARIETY BREADS

PSOMI [t]
A hearty Greek white bread well worth the
time and effort.

3 pkgs. active dry yeast	1 cup whole wheat flour (optional)
7 to 7 1/2 cups warm water	3 tablespoons salt
(110 degrees)	3 tablespoons sugar
5 pounds bread flour	2/3 cup olive or vegetable oil

Dissolve yeast in water; let stand covered for 10 minutes. Combine dry ingredients in a very large bowl. Make a well in center of flour and pour in yeast liquid. Knead mixture to combine ingredients. Add oil slowly to dough. Knead 10 minutes or until dough comes cleanly away from sides of bowl. If dough feels very sticky, lightly dust with flour; if dough feels too hard, add a little oil. Place bowl on wire rack over a large pan partially filled with hot water in a draft-free place. Cover with cloth; let rise for 1 1/2 to 1 3/4 hours. Punch down, knead for 2 minutes, cover and let dough rest for 10 minutes. Divide dough into 9 equal portions. Shape and place in greased 9 x 5-inch loaf pans. Cover and let rise again for 1 hour. Bake at 350 degrees for 55 to 60 minutes. Immediately after baking, remove from pans; wrap loaves in towel and place on cake rack to cool. When cooled, wrap in aluminum foil or seal in pastic bags. Can refrigerate up to 10 days, or can freeze for several months. Thaw out naturally or defrost in microwave for 2 minutes on defrost cycle. Makes 9 loaves.

ZIMAROPITA
Squash Corn Bread

1 (19-oz.) box Ballard's corn	3/4 cup butter, melted
bread mix	1 (12-oz.) cottage cheese,
2 to 3 yellow squash, grated	small curd
4 eggs	3/4 cup crumbled feta cheese
1/2 teaspoon salt	1 egg, beaten

Combine all ingredients, except beaten egg, and mix well. Spread batter into a greased 17 x 11-inch baking pan. Brush top with beaten egg. Bake at 350 degrees for 45 to 60 minutes, or until golden. Freezes well. Makes 40 to 48 pieces.

ELIOPSOMAKIA
Olive Muffins

1 cup pitted Greek black
  olives, chopped
2 cups all-purpose flour
1 small onion, grated
1/2 cup vegetable oil
1/4 cup olive oil

3/4 cup water
1 1/2 tablespoons minced fresh
  mint
1 tablespoon sugar
1 heaping tablespoon baking
  powder

Combine all ingredients; mix well. Bake in greased, floured muffin
tins at 350 degrees for 40 to 45 minutes. Makes 1 1/2 dozen.

KOLOKITHOPSOMO
Zucchini Bread

3 eggs
2 cups sugar
3 tablespoons vanilla
1 cup vegetable oil
2 cups zucchini, peeled and grated
3 cups all-purpose flour

1/2 teaspoon baking powder
1 teaspoon salt
2 teaspoons baking soda
3 teaspoons ground cinnamon
1 cup chopped nuts

Combine eggs, sugar, vanilla and oil. Mix well. Add zucchini.
Sift dry ingredients together and add to batter. Fold in nuts.
Bake in 2 greased and floured 9 x 5-inch loaf pans at 350 degrees
for 1 hour. Freezes well wrapped tightly in aluminum foil or
sealed in plastic bags. Makes 2 loaves.

APPLESAUCE NUT BREAD

2 cups all-purpose flour
3/4 cup sugar
3 teaspoons baking powder
1/2 teaspoon ground cinnamon
1/2 teaspoon salt
1/2 teaspoon baking soda

1 cup chopped nuts
1 egg
1 cup applesauce
2 tablespoons vegetable
  shortening, melted

Sift dry ingredients together; add nuts. In a large bowl, beat egg
well; add applesauce and shortening. Mix thoroughly. Blend in
flour mixture. Bake in greased 9 x 5-inch loaf pan at 350 degrees
for 1 hour or until done. Cool in pan for 10 minutes before
removing. Completely cool before slicing. Makes 1 loaf.

BANANA BREAD

2/3 cup vegetable shortening
1 1/3 cups sugar
4 eggs
3 1/2 cups all-purpose flour
4 teaspoons baking powder

1/2 teaspoon baking soda
1 teaspoon salt
2 cups mashed ripe bananas
1 cup chopped nuts
(optional)

Beat shortening and sugar on medium speed of electric mixer. Add eggs and beat until light and fluffy, about 4 minutes. Sift flour, baking powder, baking soda and salt together and add to batter alternately with bananas; beat until smooth. Stir in nuts. Bake in 2 greased 9 x 5-inch loaf pans at 350 degrees for 1 hour or until done. Cool in pans for 10 minutes before removing. Completely cool before slicing. Makes 2 loaves.

PITA BREAD
The bread used for the "gyro."

5 to 6 cups all-purpose flour
1 tablespoon sugar
2 teaspoons salt

1 pkg. active dry yeast
2 cups warm water (120 to
130 degrees)

In a large bowl, mix 2 cups flour, sugar, salt and undissolved yeast. Slowly add water; beat 2 minutes on medium speed of electric mixer, scraping bowl occasionally. Add 3/4 cup flour; beat at high speed 2 minutes. Stir in enough remaining flour to make a soft dough. Turn out on lightly-floured surface. Knead for 10 minutes or until smooth and elastic. Place in greased bowl, turning once to grease top. Cover, let rise in draft-free warm place for 1 hour or until double in bulk. Punch down dough, place on lightly floured surface, cover and let rest for 30 minutes. Divide dough into 6 equal portions and shape each into a ball. Roll each ball into 8-inch circle, place on lightly-floured baking sheets. Bake on lowest rack of a preheated 450-degree oven for 5 minutes, or until lightly browned and centers puff up. Remove from baking sheet, wrap each in aluminum foil. When loaves are unwrapped, the top will have fallen and there will be a pocket of air in the center. If desired, bread may be slit on 1 side and the pocket filled with sandwich filling (see recipe following). Makes 6 pitas.

"GYRO" SANDWICHES
The Greek equivalent of the taco.

Tomatoes, coarsely chopped
Onions, coarsely chopped
Shredded lettuce
Shredded Cheddar cheese
Crumbled feta cheese

Meat filling (below)
Tzadziki sauce (see Sauces
    Chapter), or plain yogurt
12 Pita breads

To serve, put out the tomatoes, onions, lettuce, cheeses, tzadziki sauce and pita breads in separate dishes. Each person slits opening in pita bread and fills pocket with meat and choice of cheeses and vegetables, topped with tzadziki sauce.

Meat Filling:
  1 large onion, chopped
  1 clove garlic, minced
  2 tablespoons olive oil
  2 pounds ground beef

6 tablespoons ketchup
5 tablespoons water
1 teaspoon allspice
Salt and pepper

In a large skillet, saute onions and garlic in hot oil until tender. Add crumbled meat and brown. Drain off excess fat. Mix in remaining ingredients and simmer uncovered for 5 to 10 minutes over moderate heat.

The "gyro" sandwich originated in the Middle East; it spread to Greece, and consequently was introduced to the United States by industrious Greek immigrants. The true recipe requires that spiced lamb meat be roasted to a flavorful crispness on a vertical spit, turned electrically gyro keh gyro (round and round) — thus the term "gyro" is derived. The above recipe is an adaptation of this tasty snack.

PAXEMATHIA APLA[†]
Toasted Biscuits

2 1/2 pounds all-purpose flour
2 1/2 pounds whole wheat flour
2 pkgs. active dry yeast
4 1/2 to 5 cups warm water (110 degrees)

1 teaspoon sugar
2 teaspoons salt
1/2 cup vegetable oil

Combine all the flour in a large mixing bowl; set aside, reserving one cup. Dissolve yeast in 1 cup warm water, add sugar and reserved cup of flour; blending well. Cover and let rise in a warm place for 1 hour. Make a well in center of remaining flour; pour in yeast mixture. Dissolve salt in remaining water and add to flour. Knead slightly. Gradually add oil to dough. Knead 10 minutes, or until dough comes cleanly away from sides of bowl. If dough is sticky, dust lightly with flour; if dough is too hard, add a little oil.

Shape into 4 long loaves, 15 inches long and 3 inches in diameter. Place on greased baking sheets. With sharp knife, score loaves deeply at 1-inch intervals. Cover and let rise for 1 hour. Bake at 350 degrees for 1 hour. Cool loaves and slice through. Turn slices on their sides, return to oven and continue baking for 30 minutes or until golden brown. Put all paxemathia together in a deep pan and place in oven at 150 degrees for 4 to 5 hours to crisp thoroughly. Paxemathia will keep for weeks stored in an air-tight container. Makes about 5 dozen.

Note: If doubling recipe, increase dry yeast to 3 packages and double remaining ingredients.

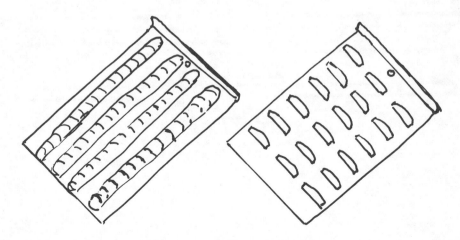

DESSERTS

DESSERTS

One of the more delightful experiences in Greece today is a visit to the zaharoplastion (pastry shop). Greeks and tourists alike congregate at the tiny sidewalk tables in front of the shop enjoying a delicious pastry as they sip their Greek coffee.

The glyka (sweets) are temptingly displayed — the favorites being baklava, kataife, galaktoboureko, finikia and kourambiethes. These traditional desserts, popular since antiquity, are each unique in taste and texture.

This chapter is divided into six sections, beginning with the popular phyllo pastry desserts, followed by cakes, cookies, fried pastries, puddings and spoon preserves. In baking it goes without saying that the oven should always be preheated. The term "clarified butter" is used throughout the chapter and is defined in the Miscellaneous Chapter. Special ingredients can be found in area specialty stores listed in the Shopper's Guide of the Appendix. It is recommended that you read "How to Work with Commercial Phyllo" in the Miscellaneous Chapter before preparing phyllo pastries.

PHYLLO PASTRY

SYRUPS

Syrups are widely used for Greek pastries, cakes, cookies and fruit preserves. Recipes are self-explanatory but it is helpful to know the basics.

Use a heavy saucepan and dissolve sugar in water over medium heat, stirring occasionally. When all the sugar crystals have been dissolved, reduce heat to gently boil. For best results, do not stir once syrup starts boiling as the syrup will become cloudy. If using a candy thermometer, be certain that at least two inches of the thermometer stem is in the liquid. Lemon juice is added at the onset to prevent crystallization; if honey is added, it is stirred in at the last. A general cooking guide follows:

<u>Thin Syrup</u>:

Used for: Most cakes, such as revani, pantespani, karithopita; also for dipping finikia cookies and loukoumathes.

Temperature on Candy Thermometer: 215 degrees F.

What to look for: Depending on proportions of sugar to water and whether gas or electric heat is used, syrup should boil about 10 minutes for use on light-textured sponge cakes and 15 minutes for heavier-textured cakes.

<u>Thick Syrup</u>:

Used for: Most phyllo pastries such as baklava, kataife, saragli; also in making fruit preserves.

Temperature on Candy Thermometer: 230 degrees F.

What to look for: As syrup boils, bubbles become smaller and the sound of the bubbling changes; the sides of the pan become peppered with minute drops of syrup. A drop of syrup on a cold plate will not spread. Syrup usually takes about 20 to 25 minutes.

138

PHYLLO PASTRY DESSERTS

BAKLAVA
Baklava is the most celebrated of all Greek pastries.

1 pound walnuts or pecans,
 finely chopped
1/3 cup sugar
1 teaspoon ground cinnamon
1/2 teaspoon ground cloves
1/2 teaspoon nutmeg

1 pound phyllo
1 pound butter, clarified,
 melted and warm
Whole cloves (optional)
Syrup (below)

Combine nuts, sugar and spices. Trim phyllo to pan size. Place 6 phyllo sheets in a buttered 13 x 9-inch baking pan, brushing each sheet generously with butter. Sprinkle a thin layer of nut mixture evenly over the phyllo. Cover with 4 buttered phyllo sheets. Continue alternating phyllo, butter and nut mixture until all nuts are used. Top with 8 buttered phyllo sheets. Cut into diamonds or squares (see sketch following page). If desired, stud each piece with a whole clove.

Bake at 325 degrees for 30 minutes, lower oven to 300 degrees and bake 30 minutes longer or until golden brown. Pour warm syrup over hot baklava. Let stand for several hours or overnight. Store in air-tight containers in a cool place; it will keep for several weeks. Freezes well; thaw to room temperature and serve. Serves 24.

Syrup:
 3 cups sugar
 2 cups water
 1 stick cinnamon

Juice of 1/2 lemon
2 to 3 tablespoons honey
 (optional)

Combine sugar, water, cinnamon stick and lemon juice and gently boil for 20 minutes or until candy thermometer reaches 230 degrees. Remove from heat; if desired, stir in honey.

BAKLAVAS MEH MELA
Baklava with Apples
A new and delicious way to make baklava.

3 cups apples, peeled and
  shredded
1 1/2 cups chopped walnuts
1 cup chopped almonds, toasted
1 cup sugar
1/2 cup raisins
2 teaspoons grated lemon peel

2 tablespoons lemon juice
2 teaspoons ground cinnamon
1 pound phyllo
1 pound butter, clarified,
  melted and warm
1/2 cup honey

In a large bowl, combine apples, walnuts, almonds, sugar, raisins,
lemon peel, lemon juice and cinnamon; mix well. Trim phyllo to pan
size. Place 8 sheets of phyllo in a buttered 15 x 10-inch baking
pan, brushing each sheet generously with butter. Cover evenly with
half of the apple and nut mixture. Add 6 more buttered phyllo
sheets. Spread remaining mixture. Top with 8 buttered phyllo
sheets. Cut into diamonds or squares. Bake at 350 degrees for 40
minutes or until golden brown. Warm honey and drizzle over hot
baklava. Cool. Serves 30.

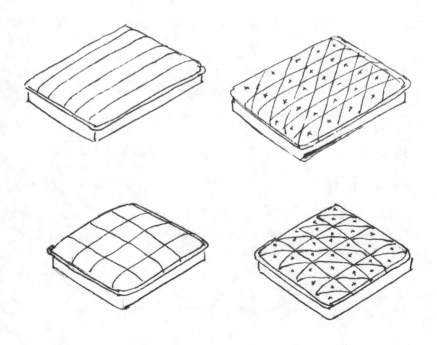

BAKLAVAS MEH FISTIKIA
Pistachio Baklava
Baklava shaped like a rosette and topped with pistachios.

1 pound walnuts, chopped	1 cup coarsely chopped
4 zwieback toasts, crumbled	pistachio nuts
1/3 cup sugar	17 phyllo sheets
1 orange rind, grated	1 cup butter, clarified,
1 teaspoon ground cinnamon	melted and warm
1/2 teaspoon ground cloves	Syrup (below)
1/2 teaspoon nutmeg	

Combine walnuts, zwieback, sugar, orange rind and spices in a bowl. Stack phyllo sheets; cut through center lengthwise making 2 stacks. Stack again and trim length to measure 15 inches. Working with 1 phyllo sheet at a time, place on a flat surface. (Keep remaining phyllo covered.) Spoon about 2 tablespoons of nut mixture in a narrow line along the length side to within 1/2 inch of the edges. Fold in edges. Fold bottom over nuts and roll jellyroll fashion. Coil half the roll in a "S", using thumb as a guide (see sketch). Finish out the coil by wrapping the remainder of roll clockwise around the "S". Coil should be about 3 inches in diameter.

Place on ungreased baking sheets. When possible, place open end of coil against the sides of the pan. Brush top and sides with butter. Bake at 325 degrees for 30 to 35 minutes or until golden brown. Drizzle cooled syrup over hot pastry. Sprinkle 1 tablespoon pistachio nuts over top. Leave pastries on baking sheet overnight to absorb the syrup. Pastry will keep 3 to 4 weeks tightly covered in the refrigerator. Makes 34 pieces.

Syrup:

3 cups sugar	Juice of half lemon
1 1/2 cups water	2 tablespoons honey

Combine sugar, water and lemon juice and gently boil for 20 minutes. Remove from heat; stir in honey.

SARAGLI
A crispy, rolled version of baklava.

3/4 pound chopped walnuts
1/4 cup sugar
1 1/2 teaspoons ground cinnamon
1 1/2 teaspoons ground cloves

1 pound phyllo
1 pound butter, clarified,
  melted and warm
Syrup (below)

Combine the walnuts, sugar and spices in a large bowl. Place 2 sheets of phyllo on a flat surface, generously brushing each with butter. Spread 1/2 cup nuts evenly over phyllo. Add another buttered phyllo sheet; spread 1/4 cup of nuts on phyllo. Top with one more buttered phyllo sheet. Lengthwise, roll tightly in jellyroll fashion. Brush seam and entire roll with butter. Continue rolling remaining phyllo, butter and nut mixture in the same manner.

Cut each roll in 1 1/2-inch intervals. Place nut-side up on a greased cookie sheet. Bake at 325 degrees for 30 minutes, invert pieces and bake an additional 30 minutes or until golden brown. Remove from oven; place saragli in a pan. Drizzle warm syrup over warm saragli. Let stand in pan 10 to 15 minutes. Saragli should be made a day or two before serving. Store in air-tight containers in a cool place. Freezes well; thaw to room temperature. Serve in foil baking cups. Makes 60 to 65.

Syrup:
  3 cups sugar
  3 cups water

1 stick cinnamon
Juice of 1 lemon

Combine sugar, water, cinnamon stick and lemon juice; boil for 20 minutes, or until candy thermometer reaches 230 degrees.

CUT ROLL

142

POURA
Nut Fingers

6 eggs, separated	3 teaspoons cocoa
1 cup sugar	1 1/2 pounds phyllo
2 cups ground almonds	1 1/2 pounds butter, clarified,
2 cups ground walnuts	melted and warm
1 teaspoon ground cinnamon	Syrup (below)

Beat egg yolks and sugar until creamy. In a separate bowl, beat egg whites until stiff; fold into egg yolk mixture. Stir in nuts, cinnamon and cocoa. Stack phyllo sheets on a cutting board. Cut in half lengthwise and crosswise making 4 rectangles, each approximately 11 x 7-inches (see sketch). Keep remaining phyllo covered. Stack 2 sheets, brushing each with butter. Spread a heaping teaspoon of nut mixture at bottom edge of short end. Fold sides over 1/2 inch, then roll in jellyroll fashion. Brush seam and top with butter. Place seam side down on ungreased baking sheet. Roll remaining phyllo and nuts in same fashion.

Bake at 350 degrees for 20 minutes or until light golden brown. With a toothpick, punch 2 small holes in bottom of each pouro and dip into warm syrup for 2 minutes, turning once. Store in air-tight containers in a cool place. Makes 50 to 60.

Syrup:
3 cups sugar	2 tablespoons lemon juice
3 cups water	

Combine all ingredients and gently boil for 20 minutes, or until candy thermometer reaches 230 degrees.

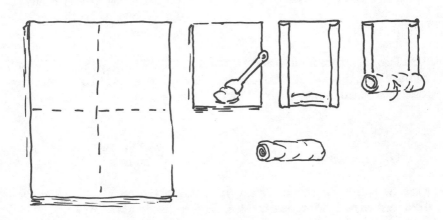

KATAIFE I

1 pound chopped walnuts or pecans	1 teaspoon nutmeg
2/3 cup sugar	1 pound kataife dough
5 zwieback toasts, ground	1 1/4 cups butter, clarified,
2 orange rinds, grated	melted and warm
1 tablespoon ground cinnamon	Syrup (below)
1 teaspoon ground cloves	

In a large bowl, combine nuts, sugar, zwieback, orange rind and spices. Cut block of kataife dough in half with a sharp knife. Separate dough to loosen and fluff. Spread half of dough in a buttered 17 x 11-inch pan; drizzle half the melted butter over it. Spread nut filling evenly over dough. Top with remaining dough and butter. Sprinkle a few drops of cold water over the top. Bake at 350 degrees for 35 to 45 minutes until golden brown and pastry shrinks from sides of pan. Spoon half of cooled syrup over hot pastry. Let stand covered for 10 minutes. Spoon remaining syrup over kataife; cover tightly to steam. Serve the next day. Can keep up to 3 weeks in an air-tight container in the refrigerator or up to 4 months in the freezer. Makes 35 to 40 pieces.

Syrup:

4 1/2 cups sugar	2 tablespoons lemon juice
3 cups water	2 tablespoons honey

Combine sugar, water and lemon juice; bring to a boil. Reduce heat, simmer 15 minutes. Remove from heat; stir in honey.

KATAIFE II (SIMPLIFIED)

5 cups crushed shredded wheat biscuits	1 1/2 teaspoons ground cinnamon
	2 cups chopped walnuts
1 cup butter, melted	Syrup (below)

Combine all ingredients and mix well. Put in a greased 9-inch square pan; bake at 300 degrees for 45 minutes. Pour hot syrup over hot kataife and cover tightly to steam.

Syrup:

3 cups sugar	2 tablespoons lemon juice
1 1/2 cups water	3 tablespoons honey

Combine sugar, water and lemon juice and bring to a boil. Reduce heat and simmer 15 minutes. Remove from heat; stir in honey.

KOPENHAGHI
Copenhagen
A truly exquisite dessert created in 1863 to honor
King George I of Greece and named for his native
Copenhagen.

Pastry:
2/3 cup butter	1 ounce brandy
1/3 cup sugar	2 cups all-purpose flour
1 egg, beaten	3/4 teaspoon baking powder
1 teaspoon almond extract	

Filling:
12 eggs, separated	1 teaspoon ground cinnamon
3/4 cup sugar	1 teaspoon vanilla extract
1 1/2 teaspoons baking powder	1 1/2 ounces brandy
3 1/2 cups blanched almonds, finely chopped and toasted	

1 (16-oz.) jar apricot preserves	1/2 cup butter, clarified,
1/2 pound phyllo	melted and warm
Syrup (next page)	

Cream butter and sugar until light and fluffy. Add eggs, almond
extract and brandy; beat well. Combine flour and baking powder;
add to batter. Knead slightly. Press soft dough evenly into
buttered 14 x 11-inch baking pan. Bake at 350 degrees for 15
minutes. Remove from oven; cool. Spread apricot preserves over
cooled pastry.

In a large bowl, beat egg yolks until thick and creamy. Add sugar
and baking powder; beat for 3 minutes. Stir in almonds, cinnamon,
vanilla and brandy. In a large bowl, beat egg whites until stiff,
but not dry. Fold gently into batter. Pour batter on top of
preserves and pastry crust. Trim phyllo to pan size. Layer phyllo
sheets lightly on top of filling, brushing each sheet with butter.
With a sharp knife, score only through top phyllo layers, making 5
equal rows lengthwise. Sprinkle a few drops of cold water over
top. Bake at 350 degrees for 40 to 45 minutes. Pastry is done
when an inserted toothpick comes out clean. Cool cake. Slowly
spoon hot syrup over cooled pastry, allowing time for cake to
absorb the syrup (see following page). Cool; cut into diamonds or
squares. Makes 30 to 35 pieces.

PHYLLO PASTRY

Syrup:
3 cups sugar	8 whole cloves
3 1/2 cups water	4 thin lemon slices
1 stick cinnamon	1 teaspoon lemon juice

Combine all ingredients in a saucepan and bring to a boil. Reduce heat and simmer for 10 minutes.

GALAKTOBOUREKO
A delicious custard baked in phyllo.

4 cups milk	1 teaspoon lemon rind, grated,
3/4 cup semolina	or 1 teaspoon vanilla
5 eggs	3/4 pound phyllo
1 cup sugar	Syrup (below)
1 cup butter, clarified, melted and warm	

In a deep saucepan, heat milk and semolina, stirring constantly until it reaches the boiling point. Remove from heat; cool 5 minutes. In a bowl, beat eggs and sugar until fluffy; add to semolina mixture. Add 1/2 cup melted butter and lemon rind; blend well.

Place 8 phyllo sheets in a buttered 13 x 9-inch baking pan, brushing each sheet generously with butter. Allow phyllo to extend up sides of pan. Spread filling evenly over phyllo; fold overhanging phyllo over the filling and brush with butter. Cover with 8 buttered phyllo sheets, which have been trimmed to fit pan. With a sharp knife, score only through the top phyllo layers making 4 equal rows lengthwise. Sprinkle a few drops of cold water over top. Bake at 350 degrees for 45 minutes. Drizzle cold syrup over hot pastry. Return to oven for 5 minutes; let stand 2 hours before serving. Cut into diamonds or squares. Galaktoboureko is best served the day it is made. Refrigerate any leftovers. Makes 24 pieces.

Syrup:
2 1/2 cups sugar	3 thin lemon slices
1 1/2 cups water	1 stick cinnamon

Combine all ingredients and bring to a boil. Reduce heat; simmer for 10 minutes.

CAKES

REVANI I

1 cup butter	1 cup quick-cooking cream of
1/2 cup sugar	wheat
5 eggs, beaten	1 teaspoon grated lemon rind
1/2 cup all-purpose flour	Whipped cream (optional)
3 teaspoons baking powder	Syrup (below)

Cream butter and sugar until light and fluffy. Gradually add the beaten eggs. Sift dry ingredients together and add to the batter with lemon rind. Bake in a greased 9-inch square baking pan at 350 degrees for 30 to 35 minutes or until firm and golden on top. Pour cooled syrup over hot cake. When cold, cut into squares and serve with whipped cream. Serves 12.

Syrup:

2 cups sugar	Strip of lemon peel
2 cups water	1 tablespoon brandy

Combine sugar, water and lemon peel and gently boil 10 minutes. Add brandy. Cool slightly.

REVANI II
An easy, make-ahead dessert for a crowd.

15 eggs, separated	2 teaspoons baking powder
2 1/2 cups sugar	2 1/2 cups farina
2 teaspoons vanilla	Syrup (below)
2 ounces whiskey	

Beat egg yolks and sugar together until thick and creamy. Add vanilla and whiskey. Combine baking powder and farina; add to the batter. In a large bowl, beat egg whites until stiff and fold gently into batter. Bake in a greased 17 x 11-inch baking pan at 350 degrees for 45 minutes or until golden brown. Pour warm syrup slowly over hot cake. Cool; cut into diamonds. Makes 40 pieces.

Syrup:

4 cups sugar	4 cups water	1 tablespoon lemon juice

Combine all ingredients and gently boil 10 minutes.

CAKES

REVANI MEH AMIGTHALA
Almond Revani

1 cup butter
3/4 cup sugar
6 eggs, separated
3/4 cup all-purpose flour

3/4 cup quick-cooking cream
of wheat
1 1/4 teaspoons baking powder
1/2 cup ground almonds

Cream butter and sugar until light and fluffy. Add egg yolks and beat well. Sift together flour, cream of wheat and baking powder; add to batter. Stir in nuts. In separate bowl, beat egg whites until stiff and fold gently into batter. Bake in greased 13 x 9-inch pan at 350 degrees for 25 to 30 minutes. Cool slightly. Slowly spoon syrup over hot cake. Cover tightly to steam for several hours. Serves 24.

Syrup:
2 cups sugar   2 cups water   Juice of 1/2 lemon

Combine all ingredients and gently boil 10 minutes.

PANTESPANI
Lemon Sponge Cake
A light melt-in-your-mouth cake.

5 eggs, separated
1 cup sugar
1 cup cake flour
1 1/4 teaspoons baking powder

1 lemon rind, grated
1 teaspoon vanilla
1/2 cup butter, melted

Beat egg yolks and sugar several minutes until light and creamy. Sift dry ingredients together and gradually add to batter. Add lemon rind and vanilla. Beat egg whites until stiff and fold gently into batter. Pour into greased and floured 13 x 9-inch pan. Spoon melted butter evenly over top. Bake at 350 degrees for 25 to 30 minutes. Slowly spoon cooled syrup over hot cake. Serves 24.

Syrup:
1 1/2 cups sugar   1 1/4 cups water   Juice of 1 lemon

Combine all ingredients and gently boil for 5 to 7 minutes, or until candy thermometer reaches 205 degrees.

HALSEMA
Yogurt Cake
Johnny Mariakakis
Mariakakis' Restaurant, Chapel Hill, N. C.
Their most requested dessert recipe.

2 eggs
1 1/2 cups quick-cooking
  cream of wheat
1 1/2 cups sugar
1/2 cup butter, melted

1 (16-oz.) carton plain yogurt
  or sour cream
Juice of 1/2 lemon
1/2 teaspoon baking soda
Syrup (below)

In a large bowl, beat eggs well. Combine the cream of wheat and sugar; add to eggs along with the butter, beating well. Reduce mixer speed and gradually add yogurt. Combine lemon juice and baking soda; add to batter. Bake in a greased 13 x 9-inch baking pan at 375 degrees for 25 to 30 minutes, or until golden brown. Drizzle cooled syrup over warm cake. Cover tightly to steam about 1 hour. Delicious served the same day topped with whipped cream and sliced strawberries, peaches or blueberries. Serves 24.

Syrup:
  1 1/2 cups sugar
  1 1/4 cups water

Juice of 1/2 lemon (boil lemon
  rind with syrup, discard)

Combine all ingredients and gently boil 10 minutes.

KARITHOPITA
Nut Cake

12 eggs, separated
1 cup sugar
1 teaspoon baking powder
1 (6-oz.) box zwieback, finely
  ground
1 teaspoon ground cinnamon

1 teaspoon vanilla
1 jigger whiskey
Rind of 1 navel orange, grated
2 cups chopped walnuts
Syrup (next page)

Beat egg yolks and sugar until light and creamy. Combine baking powder, zwieback and cinnamon; add to batter. Add vanilla, whiskey, orange rind and nuts. Beat well. In a large bowl, beat egg whites until stiff; fold gently into batter. Bake in greased 14 x 11-inch pan at 350 degrees for 35 to 40 minutes, or until toothpick inserted in center comes out clean. Pour warm syrup (see following page) over hot cake. Cut into diamonds. Serves 30.

Syrup:
  2 1/2 cups sugar   2 cups water   1 tablespoon lemon juice

Combine all ingredients and gently boil 10 minutes.

HALVA I (BAKED)
A simple, exotic dessert that dates back to
the travels of Alexander the Great.

3/4 cup butter	1 teaspoon ground cinnamon
1 cup sugar	Syrup (below)
4 eggs	Whipped cream
2 cups semolina	Cherries soaked in Kirsch
1 cup chopped almonds	brandy

Cream butter and sugar until light and fluffy. Add eggs one at a time, beating well after each addition. Add semolina; beat well. Stir in nuts and cinnamon. Bake in greased 13 x 9-inch pan at 375 degrees for 35 to 40 minutes. Pour hot syrup over hot cake. Cool and cut. When ready to serve, top with whipped cream and cherries.

Syrup:
  2 cups sugar   4 cups water   1 stick cinnamon

Combine all ingredients, gently boil for 20 to 25 minutes. Add brandy.

HALVA II

3 cups water	2 1/2 cups quick-cooking cream
3 cups milk	of wheat
2 cups sugar	1/2 cup pignolia nuts or
1 stick cinnamon	slivered almonds
1/2 cup butter	Ground cinnamon (optional)

In a large saucepan, bring water, milk, sugar and cinnamon stick to a slow boil; cook for 3 minutes, stirring frequently. Remove cinnamon stick and discard. In a separate saucepan, melt butter; blend in cream of wheat and cook until golden brown, stirring constantly. Stir in nuts; reduce heat. Slowly pour hot milk mixture over cream of wheat, stirring until halva is slightly thickened. Remove from heat. Cover; let stand 10 minutes. Stir well. Shape in individual molds or spoon into dishes for serving. Sprinkle top with ground cinnamon, if desired. Serves 12 to 16.

BUNDER NUSS TORTE
Slugs at the Pines
Chapel Hill, North Carolina

Sugar Dough:
1/3 cup butter	1 cup sifted cake flour
1/3 cup sugar	1 cup sifted all-purpose flour
1/4 cup shortening	1/4 teaspoon baking powder
1 egg	1/8 teaspoon salt
1/4 teaspoon lemon flavoring	

Cream butter and sugar together until smooth, add shortening and continue mixing at moderate speed until well blended. Add egg and lemon flavoring and mix well. Sift dry ingredients together and add to batter. Mix at moderate speed until it forms a smooth paste. Chill in refrigerator before using.

Frangipane Cream:
1 (7-oz.) pkg. almond paste	1 tablespoon and 1 teaspoon
2/3 cup sugar	Jamaica rum
2/3 cup butter	1 (21-oz.) can cherry pie
3 extra large eggs	filling (optional)
1 cup sifted bread flour	

Blend almond paste, sugar and butter until free of all lumps. Add eggs one at a time beating well after each addition. Add flour and rum. Blend well. Set aside. Remove sugar dough from refrigerator and roll dough between 2 pieces of waxed paper until 1/8-inch thick and large enough to line a greased 10 x 3-inch round cake pan. If desired, layer dough with cherry pie filling, spreading to within 1 inch from sides of pan. Pour in prepared frangipane cream and bake at 400 degrees for 40 to 50 minutes or until firm. Cool and unmold.

Topping:
3/4 cup brown sugar	1/4 cup heavy cream scalded
3 tablespoons white corn syrup	(180 degrees)
3 ounces butter	3/4 cup walnuts or pecans, halved

Combine sugar and corn syrup in saucepan and blend well. Remove from heat. Stir in butter and return to low heat for 1 minute or until butter is completely melted. Remove from heat, add cream and nuts. Blend all ingredients well. Cool to lukewarm. Spread topping over baked and cooled frangipane cream. Chill for 30 minutes before serving. Serves 8 to 10.

CAKES

ALMOND TORTE

12 eggs, separated
1 1/2 cups sugar
1 1/2 cups blanched almonds,
  finely chopped
1 (6-oz.) box zwieback toast,
  finely ground

1 teaspoon almond or vanilla
  extract
1 cup butter
Syrup (below)

In a large bowl, beat egg yolks until lemon-colored. Gradually add sugar; beat until light and fluffy. Add almonds, zwieback and almond extract. In a separate large bowl, beat egg whites until stiff; fold gently into batter. Melt butter until sizzling and fold gently into batter. Bake in a buttered 14 x 11-inch baking pan at 325 degrees for 40 to 45 minutes. When done, inserted toothpick in center of cake should come out clean. Drizzle hot syrup over hot torte. Cut into diamonds. Makes 32.

Syrup:
2 1/2 cups sugar
3 cups water

1 stick cinnamon
Peeling and juice of 1/2 lemon

Combine all ingredients and gently boil 10 minutes. Discard cinnamon stick and lemon peeling.

WALNUT AND HONEY CAKE LOAF

1 1/3 cups honey
3/4 cup butter
2 eggs
1/2 cup milk
2 tablespoons lemon juice
3 1/2 cups all-purpose flour

1/4 teaspoon soda
1/4 teaspoon salt
1 teaspoon ground cloves
1 cup chopped walnuts
1 (4-oz.) pkg. candied orange
  peel, diced

Combine honey, butter, eggs, milk and lemon juice; beat until well blended. Sift dry ingredients together and add to batter, beating until light and creamy. Add nuts and orange peel. Bake in a greased and floured 9 x 5-inch loaf pan at 350 degrees for 1 1/2 hours or until golden brown. Tastes better warm. Serves 12.

CAKES

CHOCOLATE AMARETTO TORTE
A delight for chocolate lovers.

6 tablespoons butter
15 ounces semi-sweet chocolate morsels
1 1/2 squares unsweetened baking chocolate (optional)
9 eggs
1 1/4 cups sugar
1/2 cup all-purpose flour
1/4 cup rum
2 cups chopped almonds
Filling and Glaze (below)

Melt butter and chocolate in top of double boiler, or place in microwave 60 to 90 seconds on full power. Cool. In large bowl, beat eggs and gradually add sugar. Add chocolate mixture and mix well. Add flour, rum and almonds. Pour batter into 2 greased 9-inch round cake pans. Bake at 350 degrees for 25 to 30 minutes. Cake should be set but still very fudgy. Cool in pans 10 minutes, remove and cool completely before assembling.

Spread filling between layers. Slowly coat top of torte with glaze, letting excess drizzle down sides. Sprinkle top with additional ground almonds. For a truly elegant finish, pipe an additional standard semi-sweet chocolate frosting or a whipped cream frosting around sides of torte. Leave top decorated only with glaze and almonds. Serves 16.

Filling:
1 (7-oz.) pkg. almond paste
1 egg white
1/4 cup Amaretto
1/2 cup ground almonds

Thin paste with egg white, blending well. Add Amaretto and nuts and mix well.

Glaze:
5 tablespoons water
3 tablespoons sugar
3 ounces semi-sweet chocolate morsels
1 teaspoon Greek coffee (powdered)
1 tablespoon Amaretto

Simmer water and sugar together to dissolve. Add chocolate, coffee, Amaretto and simmer, stirring constantly to blend.

153

APPLE CAKE

3 eggs
2 cups sugar
1 1/2 cups vegetable oil
2 cups all-purpose flour
1 1/2 teaspoons baking soda
1/2 teaspoon salt

2 to 3 tablespoons ground
cinnamon
4 cups minced cooking apples
1 cup chopped nuts (optional)
1 1/2 teaspoons vanilla

Beat eggs and sugar until light and creamy. Add oil and beat well.
Combine dry ingredients and add to batter. Stir in apples, nuts
and vanilla. Mix well. Bake in greased and floured Bundt pan at
350 degrees for 1 hour and 10 minutes. Cool 15 minutes before
removing from pan.

BANANA PINEAPPLE CAKE

1 1/2 cups vegetable oil
2 cups sugar
3 eggs
3 cups all-purpose flour
1 teaspoon baking soda
1 teaspoon salt

1 teaspoon ground cinnamon
1 (8-oz.) can crushed pineapple
1 1/2 teaspoons vanilla
2 cups diced bananas
Cream cheese frosting (below)

Beat oil and sugar together until creamy. Add eggs; beat well.
Combine dry ingredients and add alternately to batter with the
pineapple. Stir in vanilla and bananas. Bake in greased 9-inch
tube pan at 350 degrees for 1 hour and 20 minutes. Cool cake in
pan for 15 minutes. Remove and cool completely; frost.
Refrigerate.

Cream Cheese Frosting:
  1/2 cup butter
  1 (8-oz.) pkg. cream cheese

1 (16-oz.) box powdered sugar
1 teaspoon vanilla

Cream butter and cream cheese. Add sugar and vanilla; beat until
of spreading consistency.

To prevent nuts and fruits from sinking to bottom of batter, warm
them a little in the oven or microwave and lightly dust with flour
before mixing them into the batter.

CHOCOLATE POUND CAKE

1 cup butter
1/2 cup vegetable shortening
3 cups sugar
5 eggs
3 cups cake flour
1/2 teaspoon salt

1 teaspoon baking powder
4 tablespoons cocoa
1 cup milk
1 tablespoon vanilla
Chocolate frosting (optional,
   see recipe below)

Cream butter, shortening and sugar until light and fluffy. Add eggs and mix well. Sift dry ingredients together and add alternately with milk. Beat well. Add vanilla. Bake in a greased and floured 10-inch tube pan at 350 degrees for 1 1/2 hours. Cool cake in pan for 15 minutes. Remove; cool completely before frosting.

Chocolate Frosting:
  1/2 cup butter
  1 (16-oz.) box powdered sugar
  4 tablespoons cocoa

1/3 cup warm milk
2 teaspoons vanilla

Cream butter, sugar and cocoa. Gradually add warm milk and beat until fluffy. Add vanilla.

"FLAVORFUL" POUND CAKE

1 1/2 cups margarine
1/2 cup vegetable oil
3 cups sugar
5 eggs
3 cups all-purpose flour
1/2 teaspoon salt

1 teaspoon baking powder
1 cup evaporated milk
1 teaspoon each of following
  extracts: Sherry, rum, lemon,
  brandy, vanilla, almond,
  pineapple and butter

Cream margarine and oil. Add sugar gradually and beat until light and fluffy. Add eggs one at a time, beating well after each addition. Sift dry ingredients together and add to batter alternately with milk. Beat until smooth. Add all extracts and mix well. Bake in greased and floured 10-inch tube pan at 350 degrees for 1 1/2 hours. Cool in pan for 15 minutes before removing.

RUM CAKE

1/2 cup butter
1/2 cup vegetable shortening
2 cups sugar
4 eggs
1 teaspoon vanilla
3 cups all-purpose flour
1/3 teaspoon salt

1/2 teaspoon baking powder
1/2 teaspoon baking soda
1 cup buttermilk
Red and green cherries
 (optional)
Syrup (below)

Cream butter, oil and sugar until light and fluffy. Add eggs one at a time; beat well. Add vanilla. Sift dry ingredients together and add to batter alternately with buttermilk. Grease and flour Bundt pan and decorate bottom with cherries. Pour batter over cherries and bake at 350 degrees for 1 hour. Cool cake 10 to 15 minutes and remove from pan. Brush all the syrup on cake with pastry brush. Serves 16.

Syrup:
 2 cups sugar   1 1/2 cups water   2 tablespoons rum flavoring

Combine all ingredients, mix well and bring to a boil. Reduce heat and simmer for 7 minutes. Cool slightly.

SOUR CREAM COFFEE CAKE

1 cup butter
1 1/4 cups sugar
1 cup sour cream
2 eggs, beaten
1 teaspoon vanilla

2 cups all-purpose flour
1 teaspoon baking powder
1/4 teaspoon salt
1/2 teaspoon baking soda
Nut mixture (below)

Cream butter, sugar and sour cream. Add eggs and vanilla; beat well. Sift dry ingredients together and add to batter. Mix well. Sprinkle half of nut mixture in bottom of 10-inch tube pan that has been greased with vegetable oil. Pour half of batter over nuts; add remaining nut mixture and then remaining batter. Bake at 350 degrees for 40 to 45 minutes. Cool 15 minutes before removing from pan.

Nut Mixture:
 1 cup chopped nuts
 2 teaspoons ground cinnamon

1 tablespoon sugar
1/2 cup brown sugar

Combine all ingredients and mix well.

CHEESECAKE

1 pound cream cheese	4 eggs, separated
1 teaspoon vanilla	1 tablespoon lemon juice
4 tablespoons sugar	1 cup sour cream
1/4 cup all-purpose flour	1/2 cup sugar
1/4 teaspoon salt	Graham cracker crust (below)

Blend cream cheese and vanilla. Add 4 tablespoons sugar and blend well. Add flour and salt; cream until light and fluffy. Add egg yolks and mix well. Stir in lemon juice and sour cream. In separate bowl, beat egg whites with 1/2 cup sugar until stiff. Fold into cream cheese mixture. Pour into prepared springform pan; bake at 325 degrees for 1 hour or until set. Turn off oven, open door and leave in oven to cool for 1 hour. Refrigerate. If desired, top with fruit pie filling 2 hours before serving. Serves 12.

Graham Cracker Crust:
1 1/2 cups graham cracker crumbs	1/4 cup sugar
6 tablespoons melted butter	

Combine all ingredients and press evenly into bottom of 9-inch springform pan.

ICE CREAM COOKIE DESSERT

28 Oreo cookies	Chocolate sauce (below)
1/4 cup butter, melted	1 (12-oz.) carton whipped topping
1/2 gallon chocolate chip ice cream	1 cup chopped nuts

Crush cookies in food processor. Combine with butter and spread in bottom of 13 x 9-inch pan. Freeze. Soften ice cream, spread over cookie mixture; freeze. Make chocolate sauce, spread over ice cream; freeze. Top with whipped topping; sprinkle with nuts. Cover tightly and freeze. Remove 5 minutes before serving.

Chocolate Sauce:
1 cup sugar	4 semi-sweet chocolate squares
1 small can evaporated milk	6 tablespoons butter
1 teaspoon vanilla	

Bring the sugar and evaporated milk to a boil. Add vanilla, chocolate and butter. Melt and boil for 1 minute. Cool and pour over ice cream.

COOKIES

KOURAMBIETHES

Kourambiethes, shortbread cookies dusted with powdered sugar, are popular in Greece and are served at all festive occasions. These cookies can be shaped into crescents, circles, fingers or balls. They can be made several days in advance and stored in air-tight containers in a cool place. To freeze, place cooled cookies, lightly powdered with sugar, on a baking sheet 1/4-inch apart. When frozen hard, stack in plastic, sealable containers and return to freezer. Thaw to room temperature, dust liberally with powdered sugar and serve in baking cups.

KOURAMBIETHES I

1 pound butter, clarified and chilled
1/2 cup powdered sugar
1 egg yolk
1 ounce bourbon

1/2 cup blanched almonds, chopped
6 cups sifted all-purpose flour
1 (16-oz.) box powdered sugar
1/2 ounce rosewater (optional)

Beat butter with electric mixer until light and fluffy. Add 1/2 cup sugar and beat well. Add egg yolk and bourbon. Mix almonds with 1 tablespoon flour and add to mixture. Add flour gradually; knead for 15 minutes or until dough is soft. Pat out small portion of dough about 1/2 inch thick; cut with cookie cutters into desired shapes. Place on ungreased baking sheets and bake at 350 degrees for 15 to 20 minutes, or until cookie is set, but not brown. Remove from oven, sprinkle with rosewater and place on brown paper that has been sprinkled with powdered sugar. Sprinkle cookies generously with sifted powdered sugar. Cool. Makes 30 large or 55 to 60 small cookies.

A slice of bread in the cookie jar will help keep cookies moist.

KOURAMBIETHES II

1 1/2 pounds butter, clarified
   and chilled
1/2 cup sugar
1/2 teaspoon baking soda
1 tablespoon fresh lemon juice
1/2 teaspoon vanilla

1/4 cup cognac or bourbon
2 cups chopped almonds, toasted
6 cups sifted all-purpose flour
Rosewater
1 1/2 to 2 pounds powdered
   sugar

Beat butter with electric mixer until light and fluffy. Add 1/2
cup sugar and beat well. Dissolve baking soda in lemon juice; add
to butter mixture. Add vanilla, cognac and almonds. Gradually add
the flour; knead until soft about 15 minutes. Pinch off small
amount of dough and shape as desired about 1/2 inch thick. Place
on ungreased cookie sheet and bake at 350 degrees for 15 to 20
minutes or until very lightly browned. Remove from oven; sprinkle
with rosewater. While still warm, dip each cookie into a bowl
filled with sifted powdered sugar. Press the sugar all around with
fingers. Place on brown paper and sprinkle tops generously with
additional sifted powdered sugar. Makes 30 large or 50 small
cookies.

FINIKIA
Melomakarona
These semi-soft, honey-dipped cookies, sprinkled
with nuts, originated in Phoenicia and date back to
the 14th century.

1 pound unsalted butter
4 tablespoons vegetable
   shortening
1 1/3 cups vegetable oil
5 eggs
1/2 cup sugar
2/3 cup orange juice
1 teaspoon vanilla
1 ounce bourbon

8 1/2 cups sifted all-purpose
   flour
4 teaspoons baking powder
1 teaspoon ground cinnamon
1/2 teaspoon nutmeg
3/4 cup finely chopped
   walnuts (optional)
Syrup and Nut topping (below)

Cream butter and shortening together. Slowly add oil. Add eggs
and beat thoroughly. Add sugar, orange juice, vanilla and bourbon,
beating well after each addition. Sift together flour, baking
powder and spices; slowly add to batter along with walnuts, if
desired. Knead slightly. Pinch off pieces of dough and shape into
rounds or ovals about 1/2 inch thick.

Bake on greased baking sheet at 350 degrees for 25 to 30 minutes,
or until lightly browned on the bottom. Cool slightly. With a
slotted spoon, dip cooled cookie into hot syrup until well
saturated; sprinkle with nut topping. Makes 8 to 9 dozen.

Syrup:
   3 cups sugar   1 1/2 cups water   1/2 cup honey

Boil sugar and water for 5 minutes; stir in honey. Simmer gently
about 15 minutes.

Nut Topping:
   1 cup ground walnuts   1/2 cup powdered sugar
   1/2 teaspoon ground cinnamon

Combine all ingredients and mix well.

160

KOULOURAKIA I
A crisp, semi-sweet cookie that goes well
with coffee or tea.

1 cup butter	1/4 teaspoon baking soda
1/2 cup vegetable oil	1/2 cup orange juice
1/2 cup vegetable shortening	2 tablespoons baking powder
2 cups sugar	8 to 9 cups all-purpose flour
4 eggs	1 egg for glaze
2 teaspoons vanilla	1 tablespoon water

Cream together butter, oil, shortening and sugar. Add eggs and
vanilla and beat well. Dissolve baking soda in orange juice; add
to batter, beating well. Sift baking powder and flour together and
add gradually to batter. Knead well.

On a floured surface, roll about one tablespoon of dough into a 4-
inch long length. Shape cookies (see sketch on following page) and
place on greased cookie sheet. Beat egg with water and brush on
cookies. Bake at 350 degrees for 15 to 20 minutes or until lightly
browned. Makes 8 to 9 dozen.

KOULOURAKIA II
Sesame Twists

3 tablespoons sesame seeds	2 teaspoons baking powder
1/2 cup butter	1/4 teaspoon ground cinnamon
1/4 cup vegetable shortening	1/4 teaspoon nutmeg
1/2 cup sugar	1/4 cup heavy cream or undiluted
1 egg	canned evaporated milk
3 cups all-purpose flour	1 egg for glaze

Toast the sesame seeds on an ungreased baking sheet at 350 degrees
for 5 to 10 minutes and set aside. Cream butter and shortening.
Gradually add the sugar and cream well. Add the egg and beat well.
Sift dry ingredients together and add alternately with cream or
canned milk, blending thoroughly after each addition.

Roll dough, a tablespoon at a time, between hands to form rolls 6
inches long. Fold in half and twist together. Place on greased
cookie sheet, brush with beaten egg and sprinkle with sesame seeds.
Bake at 350 degrees for 15 to 20 minutes or until golden brown.
Makes about 3 dozen cookies.

KOULOURAKIA LEMONATA
Lemon Koulourakia

4 eggs
1 1/2 cups sugar
1 cup vegetable oil
2 tablespoons lemon extract

5 cups sifted all-purpose flour
2 1/2 teaspoons baking powder
1/2 teaspoon baking soda
Evaporated milk for glaze

Beat eggs until fluffy, add sugar and continue beating for 5 minutes. Slowly add oil and lemon extract; continue beating for 10 minutes. Sift dry ingredients together; add gradually to egg mixture, blending thoroughly. Knead well.

Pinch off small pieces of dough and roll in strips about 5 inches long and 1/2-inch thick. Shape as desired (see sketch). Place on greased cookie sheet about 1 inch apart, brush with evaporated milk, and bake at 350 degrees about 15 minutes or until lightly browned. Makes 6 1/2 to 7 dozen.

KOULOURAKIA NISTISIMA[†]
Lenten Koulourakia

1/2 cup vegetable oil
1/2 cup orange juice
1 ounce whiskey
1 cup sugar

3 teaspoons baking powder
1/2 teaspoon ground cinnamon
2 1/2 to 3 cups all-purpose
   flour

Blend together the oil, orange juice and whiskey. Combine the dry ingredients and gradually add to batter. Knead until dough is soft. Shape as desired, place on a greased cookie sheet and bake at 375 degrees for 15 minutes or until golden brown. Makes 3 dozen.

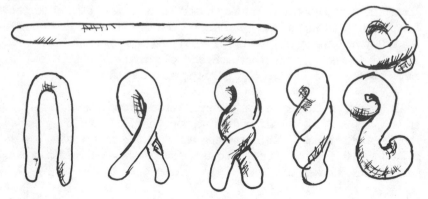

PAXEMATHIA

Paxemathia is similar to zwieback meaning
twice baked.

1/2 cup butter
1 1/4 cups sugar
1/2 cup vegetable oil
3 eggs
2 teaspoons vanilla extract
4 cups all-purpose flour

3 teaspoons baking powder
1/2 teaspoon baking soda
1/4 teaspoon salt
1 egg
1/2 teaspoon sugar
1 teaspoon water

Cream butter and sugar, gradually add oil and beat for 10 minutes.
Add eggs one at a time, beating well after each addition. Add
vanilla. Sift 3 cups flour with the baking powder, soda and salt;
add to batter. Add remaining flour. If dough is sticky, add a
little more flour and knead lightly.

Divide dough into six portions. Roll into six loaves, 10 inches
long; place loaves on shallow baking pans. Beat egg, sugar and
water together and brush loaves. Bake at 350 degrees for 20
minutes or until lightly browned. Remove from oven; cut loaves
diagonally into 1/2-inch thick slices. Turn slices on their sides,
return to oven and continue baking at 250 degrees for 40 minutes.
Turn off oven and leave in oven to cool. Makes 7 to 8 dozen.

PAXEMATHIA MEH KARITHIA

Paxemathia with Walnuts

1 cup butter, clarified and
   chilled
1 cup sugar
3 eggs
1 teaspoon vanilla
3 1/2 cups sifted all-purpose flour

1 teaspoon baking powder
1 cup ground walnuts
1 1/2 teaspoons ground
   cinnamon
1/2 cup sugar

Cream butter with one cup sugar until light and fluffy. Add eggs
one at a time, beating well after each addition. Add vanilla.
Sift flour and baking powder together; add gradually to batter.
Mix well. Stir in walnuts. Form dough into three loaves about 15
inches long. Place on a cookie sheet and bake at 350 degrees for
15 minutes. Remove from oven; cut loaves in 1/2-inch slices. Dip
each slice into a mixture of 1 1/2 teaspoons cinnamon and 1/2 cup
sugar. Return to cookie sheet and bake at 250 degrees for 40 to 45
minutes. Makes about 5 1/2 dozen.

PAXEMATHIA MEH AMIGTHALA
Paxemathia with Almonds

3/4 cup butter
3/4 cup sugar
3 eggs, beaten
1/2 cup finely chopped almonds

2 1/2 cups all-purpose flour
1/2 tablespoon baking powder
1 teaspoon baking soda
1 tablespoon vegetable oil

Cream butter and gradually beat in sugar. Add eggs and almonds. Sift dry ingredients together and mix into batter. Add vegetable oil. Form into three loaves about 1 inch thick. Place on ungreased baking sheet and bake at 350 degrees for 30 minutes. Remove from oven; cut loaves into 1/2-inch thick slices. Turn slices on their sides, return to oven and continue baking 30 minutes longer at 250 degrees. Makes about 2 1/2 dozen.

PASTA FLORA I
A simple, shortbread cookie.

1/2 cup butter
1/4 cup sugar

1 egg
1 1/2 cups all-purpose flour

Cream butter and sugar until light and fluffy. Add egg and beat well. Gradually add flour, knead slightly and shape into a ball. Place dough in a cookie press and make desired designs on ungreased cookie sheet. Bake at 350 degrees for 10 minutes or until lightly browned. Makes 2 1/2 to 3 dozen.

PASTA FLORA II

1 cup butter
1/2 cup sugar
2 eggs, beaten
1 teaspoon almond extract
1/4 cup brandy

3 cups all-purpose flour
1 teaspoon baking powder
1 (16-oz.) jar apricot, peach,
   or strawberry jam
1 egg white, slightly beaten

Cream butter and sugar until light and fluffy. Add eggs, almond extract and brandy; beat well. Combine flour and baking powder; gradually add to mixture. Knead slightly. Pinch off 1/3 of dough and set aside. Press remaining dough into bottom of ungreased 13 x 9-inch baking pan. Spread jam on top. Cover with strips of reserved dough in lattice fashion. Brush top with egg white. Bake at 375 degrees for 15 to 20 minutes. Makes 24 pieces.

SKALTSOUNIA KRITIKA
Cretan Turnovers

Pastry Dough:
- 1 cup butter
- 1 (8-oz.) pkg. cream cheese
- 2 cups all-purpose flour

1 egg for glaze
Sesame seeds

Filling:
- 1 (8-oz.) pkg. cream cheese
- 1 cup sugar
- 1/4 cup all-purpose flour
- 1 egg, beaten
- Fresh or dried mint to taste

Cream butter and cream cheese; cut in flour with pastry blender. Shape into ball and refrigerate several hours or overnight. (If overnight, take out 2 hours before using.) Roll pastry, 1 rounded tablespoon at a time, into 3 or 4-inch circles. Combine all filling ingredients and mix well. Put 1 tablespoon of filling in center of each circle. Fold over, press edges of dough together with fork. Place on greased cookie sheet, brush tops with beaten egg; sprinkle with sesame seeds. Bake at 425 degrees for 15 minutes or until golden brown. Makes 3 dozen.

SKALTSOUNIA MEH FROUTA
Candied Fruit Turnovers

Pastry Dough:
- 1 cup butter
- 1 (8-oz.) pkg. cream cheese
- 2 cups all-purpose flour
- Dash of ground cinnamon
- 1 tablespoon apricot brandy

Filling:
- 1/2 cup golden raisins
- 1/2 cup chopped candied fruit
- 1 cup chopped nuts
- 1 cup apricot marmalade

Topping:
- Rosewater
- Powdered Sugar

Cream butter and cream cheese; cut in flour with pastry blender. Add cinnamon and enough brandy to hold dough together. Roll into ball and refrigerate several hours. Roll out a small portion of dough into a 3 or 4-inch circle. Combine raisins, candied fruit, nuts and marmalade for filling. Place 1 tablespoon of filling on round of dough. Wet edges with water and fold over to form a half moon. Press edges with fork to seal. Place on greased baking sheet and bake at 375 degrees for 20 minutes or until lightly browned. Sprinkle with rosewater and roll in powdered sugar. Makes 3 dozen.

FRUIT TARTS

1 cup butter	2 1/2 cups all-purpose flour
3/4 cup sugar	1 teaspoon baking soda
2 eggs	1/2 teaspoon salt
1 teaspoon lemon rind, grated	Strawberry or Apricot Jam
1 teaspoon vanilla extract	Topping (below)

Cream butter and sugar. Blend in eggs, rind and vanilla. Sift dry ingredients together and gradually add to batter. Knead dough until smooth. Pinch off small pieces of dough, shape into ball and press into small muffin tins. Fill with 1 1/2 teaspoons of jam. Add prepared topping and bake at 350 degrees for 30 to 35 minutes. Makes 3 1/2 to 4 dozen.

Topping:

4 eggs, separated	1 teaspoon lemon rind, grated
1 cup sugar	1 teaspoon brandy
1 cup ground almonds	

Beat egg whites until stiff. Add yolks, sugar, almonds and rind; mix well. Add brandy slowly.

PECAN TARTS

1/2 cup butter	1 cup all-purpose flour
1 (3-oz.) pkg. cream cheese	Filling (below)

Cream butter and cream cheese. Stir in flour. Shape into ball. Chill in refrigerator an hour or longer. Pinch off small pieces of dough, shape into ball and press into small muffin tins. Fill pastry shells with 1 teaspoon prepared filling. Bake at 325 degrees for 20 to 30 minutes. Makes 2 dozen.

Filling:

1 egg	Dash salt
3/4 cup brown sugar	1 teaspoon vanilla
1 teaspoon butter	2/3 cup chopped pecans

Beat egg slightly; add sugar and butter; mix well. Add remaining ingredients and blend well.

ALMOND MERINGUES

4 egg whites
1 cup sugar
1/2 cup chopped almonds

1 teaspoon vanilla or
   almond extract

In a large bowl, beat egg whites, gradually adding sugar; beat until stiff. Add remaining ingredients and mix well. Place 1 heaping teaspoon of mixture onto baking sheet lined with waxed paper. Bake at 200 degrees for 1 hour or until golden on top. Makes 2 1/2 to 3 dozen.

CHOCOLATE OATMEAL COOKIES

1 1/2 cups butter
2 cups dark brown sugar
2 eggs
1/2 cup water
2 teaspoons vanilla
6 cups uncooked oats

2 cups all-purpose flour
1 teaspoon baking soda
1 cup chopped walnuts
1 cup chopped dates
1 cup raisins
1 cup chocolate chips

Cream butter and sugar until light and fluffy. Add eggs, water and vanilla; mix well. Add oats, flour and soda; beat well. Stir in remaining ingredients. Drop by spoonfuls onto a greased cookie sheet. Bake at 350 degrees for 12 minutes. Cool on cookie sheet until set, about 1 minute. Remove to wire rack to cool completely. Makes 8 to 9 dozen.

CHOCOLATE-MARSHMALLOW SLICES
Easy to make and displays attractively.

1/2 cup butter
1 (12-oz.) pkg. semi-sweet
   chocolate chips

1 (10 1/2-oz.) pkg. miniature
   marshmallows
1/2 cup chopped nuts

Melt butter and chocolate chips over low heat in large pan or place in microwave for 60 seconds on full power. Stir to blend. Cool. Fold in marshmallows and nuts; stir to cover with chocolate mixture. Spoon half of mixture on waxed paper about 2 feet long. Without touching with hands, mold with paper into a roll about 1 1/2 inches in diameter. Repeat with remaining mixture. Refrigerate until firm. Slice with sharp knife as needed. Makes about 5 dozen.

FRIED PASTRIES

THIPLES
Delicate, deep-fried pastry strips sprinkled
with nuts.

4 eggs, room temperature
2 tablespoons vegetable oil
1/2 teaspoon vanilla
2 1/4 cups plus 2 tablespoons
  all-purpose flour
1 teaspoon baking powder

Syrup (next page)
2 cups finely grated walnuts
  or pecans
1/4 cup sugar
1/2 teaspoon ground cinnamon

Beat eggs well with wire whisk. Add oil and vanilla, beating well.
Sift flour and baking powder together; gradually add to batter.
Knead lightly until dough is soft and not sticky. (If using mixer
with dough hook, knead about 4 minutes.) Divide dough into 4 balls
and refrigerate overnight. Take out 2 hours before using.

Dust dough and rolling pin with cornstarch; roll out 1 ball of
dough at a time until paper thin. To make rosettes, cut dough into
strips 16 x 2 inches. Pierce one end of dough strip with fork;
immerse in hot oil (360 degrees) in deep-fat fryer or in large
heavy saucepan and start twirling fork (see sketch next page).
With another fork, mold loose end of strip around first fork to
form a rosette. Pastry will bubble while frying. After rosette
shape is set, remove forks; fry until golden brown on both sides,
about a minute on each side. Remove gently with slotted spoon;
drain on paper towels. (During frying, skim out any crumbs to
prevent smoking.) Dip in hot syrup; drain.

Combine grated nuts, sugar and cinnamon; sprinkle over each
rosette. Store in plastic containers. Will keep several weeks in
a cool place. Freezes well. Makes 3 to 4 dozen.

<u>Syrup:</u>
  2 cups sugar   1 cup honey
  1 1/2 cups water

Bring all ingredients to a boil, reduce heat and simmer uncovered 10 minutes.

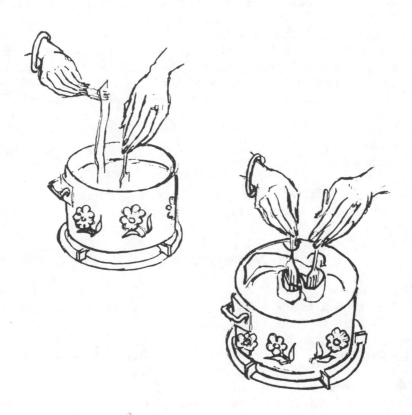

LOUKOUMATHES I
Fritter Puffs
A deep-fried pastry similar to the American donut.

2 eggs
1 teaspoon vanilla
2 cups bread flour
2 teaspoons baking powder
1/4 teaspoon salt

1 1/4 cups buttermilk
Vegetable oil for frying
Syrup (below)
Ground cinnamon

Beat eggs and vanilla slightly. Combine dry ingredients and add to eggs alternately with buttermilk. Beat until batter is the consistency of thick pancake batter. Drop by teaspoon into hot oil in deep fryer (360 degrees), using a spatula to push off dough. Fry 3 to 5 minutes, turning puffs with slotted spoon until golden brown on all sides. Drain on paper towels. Drizzle with syrup and sprinkle with cinnamon. Makes about 3 dozen. Serve immediately.

Syrup:
2 cups sugar
1 cup water

1 tablespoon lemon juice
1 tablespoon honey

Boil sugar, water and lemon juice 10 minutes, stirring at first to dissolve sugar. Stir in honey; simmer 1 minute.

LOUKOUMATHES II

1 pkg. active dry yeast
1 1/4 cups warm water or milk
  (110 degrees)
2 cups all-purpose flour
1/4 teaspoon salt

1/2 to 1 teaspoon finely-
  grated orange peel
1 teaspoon vanilla
Honey (optional)
Ground cinnamon

Dissolve yeast in 1/4 cup warm wter. Sift flour and salt into a large bowl. Mix in orange peel. Add remaining water, vanilla and yeast mixture; mix well with a spoon to make a sticky batter. (Batter is right when dough pulled up by fingers holds together without breaking off.) Cover dough with a clean cloth, set aside in warm place to rise for 2 hours or until batter bubbles.

Heat oil in deep fryer to 375 degrees. Proceed as directed in second paragraph of preceding recipe. Drizzle puffs with honey or with syrup (recipe above), and sprinkle with ground cinnamon. Serve immediately. Makes about 3 dozen.

PUDDINGS

GALAKTOPITA
Baked Custard

3 eggs
1/2 cup sugar
1 teaspoon vanilla extract
1/4 teaspoon salt

2 1/2 cups scalded milk
(180 degrees)
Dash of nutmeg

Combine eggs, sugar, vanilla and salt. Add milk and mix well.
Pour into 6 custard cups or 1 1/2-quart baking dish. Sprinkle top
with nutmeg. Place in a 13 x 9-inch pan filled one inch deep with
hot water. Bake at 350 degrees for 35 to 40 minutes, or until a
knife inserted in center comes out clean. Serve warm or chilled.
Serves 6.

KREMA KARAMELLA
Cream Caramel

1 1/2 cups sugar
1/4 cup water
6 eggs
Dash of salt

2 teaspoons vanilla
3 3/4 cups scalded milk
(180 degrees)

To caramelize, combine 1 cup sugar and water in a heavy saucepan;
bring to a boil, slowing swirling pan to dissolve the sugar. Boil
2 to 3 minutes, swirling pan frequently, until the syrup has turned
a caramel brown. Immediately pour hot caramel into 9-inch baking
dish and turn in all directions to cover bottom and sides.

Beat eggs slightly. Add remaining 1/2 cup sugar, salt and vanilla.
Gradually add milk. Blend well. Pour over caramelized sugar.
Place in 14 x 11-inch pan filled one inch deep with hot water.
Bake at 350 degrees about 1 1/4 hours, or until knife inserted in
center comes out clean. Serve warm or chilled. Serves 6 to 8.

RIZOGALO I
Rice Pudding

3/4 cup long-grain rice
2 to 2 1/2 cups water
Pinch of salt
1 quart milk
3/4 cup sugar

2 teaspoons cornstarch
2 tablespoons cold milk
2 eggs, well beaten
1 1/2 teaspoons vanilla

In a large saucepan, add rice to boiling, salted water; cook over low heat until all the water is absorbed and rice is very soft and fluffy. (Add more water if necessary.) Stirring constantly with wooden spoon, add milk and sugar; cook 25 to 30 minutes. Dissolve cornstarch in 2 tablespoons cold milk. Add to well-beaten eggs. Remove milk mixture from heat and slowly pour in the eggs, stirring until well blended. Return to heat and simmer over low heat for 2 minutes, stirring constantly until slightly thickened. Cool; add vanilla. Pour into individual dishes or a large bowl. Serves 10.

RIZOGALO II
Rice Pudding

8 cups water
1 cup long-grain rice
1 can condensed milk
1 can warm water

2/3 cup sugar
2 eggs well beaten
1 teaspoon vanilla
Ground cinnamon

Boil water and add rice. Reduce heat; simmer, stirring frequently, until all the water has been absorbed and rice is very soft, about 1 hour. Add the condensed milk, water, sugar, eggs and vanilla. Stir well, cooking until thickened. Pour into individual cups or a large bowl. Chill. Sprinkle top with cinnamon. Serves 8.

PEACH COBBLER

4 cups fresh or drained, canned
   peaches, sliced
1 tablespoon lemon juice
1 cup sifted all-purpose flour
1 cup sugar

1/2 teaspoon salt
1 teaspoon baking powder
1 egg, beaten
6 tablespoons butter, melted

Place peaches in bottom of greased 10 x 6-inch baking dish. Sprinkle with lemon juice. Sift together dry ingredients. Add egg and blend in with fork until crumbly. Sprinkle over peaches. Drizzle with butter. Bake at 375 degrees for 35 minutes. Serve with vanilla ice cream. Serves 6.

Variation: Fresh blueberries can be substituted for the peaches.

MOUSSE AU CHOCOLATE
An easy and elegant dessert.

6 squares semi-sweet chocolate
2 tablespoons instant coffee
3 tablespoons water
5 eggs, separated

1/4 cup sugar
1 tablespoon brandy
Whipped cream

Melt chocolate, coffee and water in top of a double boiler over hot, not boiling water, or place in microwave for 60 seconds on full power. Blend egg yolks into chocolate mixture, one at a time. Add brandy. Beat egg whites until frothy; gradually add sugar and beat until stiff. Gently fold chocolate mixture into egg whites. Spoon into sherbert glasses. Refrigerate at least 4 hours or overnight. Garnish with whipped cream. Serves 6.

GLYKA TOU KOUTALIOU

Spoon Sweet Preserves

Glyka tou koutaliou (spoon sweets) served with a glass of ice water are the Greek expressions of traditional hospitality to visitors. Fragrant and spicy fruits, vegetables and nuts cooked in a smooth syrup are an ancient art in Greece dating back to the fourth century B.C. Lemon juice is added to the syrup to avoid crystallization of the sugar.

VISSINO GLYKO[†]
Cherry Preserves

2 (16-oz.) cans tart cherries   Juice of 1/2 lemon
3 cups sugar

Combine cherries, sugar and lemon juice; bring to a boil. Reduce heat and gently boil until syrup slightly thickens, about 30 to 45 minutes. Cool slightly and pour into sterilized jars and seal. Makes 1 1/2 pints.

AHLATHI GLYKO[†]
Pear Preserves

6 cups sliced pears   1 1/2 cups water
4 cups sugar   1/2 cup slivered almonds,
Juice of 1 lemon   blanched

Combine pears, sugar and lemon juice in a kettle; let stand 1 hour. Add water; simmer gently 30 minutes. Remove pears; continue cooking syrup until thickened, about 1 1/2 hours. Return the pears to the kettle; continue cooking 10 minutes longer. Add the almonds. Pack in sterilized jars and seal. Makes 1 quart.

FRAPA GLYKO[†]
Grapefruit Rind Preserves

4 large thick-skinned grapefruit   Juice of 1 grapefruit
6 cups sugar   Juice of 1 lemon
2 cups water

Using the fine side of a grater, scrape off the yellow peel of the grapefruit. Cut the rind away from the grapefruit into 6 or 8 pieces. Roll each piece tightly and thread with a heavy needle and thread (see sketch). Continue until 15 to 20 rolls are threaded; tie ends together. Soak overnight in lightly salted water, changing water once. The next day, drain the grapefruit rind and cover with fresh water. Bring to a boil for several minutes. Drain; repeat procedure 2 more times. During the last boiling, boil grapefruit rind until tender. Drain well.

Combine sugar and water; gently boil for 30 minutes. Add the tied grapefruit rind, grapefruit juice and lemon juice. Boil slowly for 1 to 1 1/2 hours. Cool. Pull the thread out and pack grapefruit rind into sterilized jars, covering with syrup.

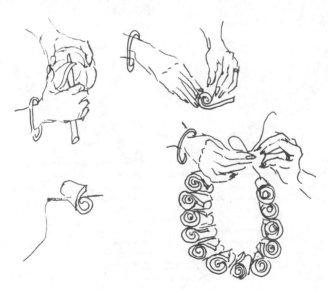

ON THE LIGHT SIDE

ON THE LIGHT SIDE
or
(Dieting without Deprivation)

This chapter may not be what you expected — it is not another new miracle diet with prescribed menus and recipes, no magic formulas to mix. The reason it is not is precisely the reason you are looking for another diet — because the ones you've tried probably didn't work, at least not permanently, and the reasons they didn't work are two:

1) They were a temporary solution you couldn't imagine living with for the rest of your life - they didn't permanently restructure your habits.

2) They were somebody else's diet — it wasn't your diet planned around your personal schedule and lifestyle and the foods you like.

The word "diet" derives from the Greek meaning "manner of living."

Many recipes passed down through the generations were created for the different "manner of living" of yesteryear. Having enough to eat was a measure of wealth and a plump figure a standard of beauty. On the other hand, consumption of considerable amounts of calorie-laden foods was necessary to produce the energy needed for hard physical work.

Our modern "manner of living," less active with all its labor-saving devices and less physically strenuous jobs (along with modern medical discoveries that plumper is not necessarily better), gives rise to a need for a total reevaluation of our eating habits.

This chapter outlines the basic principles of diet moderation and should serve to ignite your own creative ideas for streamlining favorite family recipes. These principles are illustrated by traditional Greek recipes which have been altered to eliminate approximately 1/3 of the calories (by reducing fats, starches and sugars) while preserving the wonderful taste, texture and nutritional quality so characteristic of Greek cookery.

177

A word about **DIETS FOR SPECIAL PROBLEMS...**

There are certain diet needs for specific health problems — be
sure to consult your physician for guidelines. This chapter deals
basically with the principles of moderation in the traditional
balanced diet, but the same general principles can be applied to
special needs as well.

SALT

Since it is necessary to replenish salt lost through perspiration,
those who engage regularly in athletics and other strenuous outdoor
physical activities need to consume more salt. For most of us
whose physical activity generally falls in a moderate range, the
amount of salt found naturally in foods is fairly adequate.
Therefore, we need to cut down on salt as an added seasoning.

Reduction of salt intake relates not only to good health but also
directly to weight loss, since too much salt can cause water
retention. A low-sodium commercial salt substitute helps, but try
to wean yourself gradually to like the taste of less salt on foods.

LOW CALORIE PRODUCTS AVAILABLE

There are many diet products on the market to help in the
preparation of reduced calorie dishes. For instance, Butter Buds
can be spooned over vegetables to add most of the taste of melted
butter with almost none of the calories. Other examples are diet
whipped toppings, "light" varieties of cottage cheese and milk,
reduced calorie salad dressings, fruit canned or frozen in its own
juice, gelatin, custard and pudding mixes and artificial
sweeteners. If you prefer not to use artificial sweeteners,
fructose is a naturally low-calorie sugar, or you can sweeten with
natural fruit juices.

UTENSILS

A few special utensils make preparation of low-calorie dishes easier. Nonstick coated saute pans and skillets cut down on the amount of butter or oil needed to keep food from sticking — be sure to use nonmetal spatulas, cooking forks and spoons to prevent scratching the smooth nonstick surface. For smooth lump-free sauces and gravies made with very little fat or butter, a spring-whisk gravy stirrer is very helpful.

In the beginning, measuring spoons, measuring cups and a small scale for measuring ounces are helpful in gauging food amounts; but soon your eyes will gauge the approximate measurements.

Similarly, a good calorie book which includes brand name listings helps in the learning process.

CALORIES: TO COUNT OR NOT TO COUNT

Being knowledgeable about the general number of calories in foods you eat is important, but it is not necessary to burden yourself with accounting for every mouthful. Simply cutting out excessive fats and starches and monitoring your dessert and snack consumption will automatically reduce your calorie count sufficiently for long term success, even if you don't count calories.

However, once you familiarize yourself with the basic number of calories and nutritional content of foods, it is easier to devise your own altered versions of recipes and to plan daily menus for a balanced diet.

ON THE LIGHT SIDE

GOALS

A range of 1,200 to 1,500 calories per day can give you plenty of nutrition and energy and keep you from feeling deprived — and not feeling deprived is one of the secrets of dieting with long-lasting results.

Each person's metabolism is different; consequently, rate of weight loss will also vary, but even if it takes a year to reach your ideal weight, consider how many years you've been fighting the "battle of the bulge." After losing the desired weight, you can gradually increase daily calorie intake until you've established your "break-even" point. A few people may require a lower daily calorie intake to achieve desired weight level, but it is wise to consult your doctor before embarking on a diet below 1,200 calories per day.

QUICK WEIGHT LOSS DIETS

If you feel you really need the morale boost that comes from seeing an immediate loss of 5 to 10 pounds, any of the quick weight loss diets popularly advertised would probably work; and unless you have a particular health problem, two weeks on such a diet would probably not do your body any real harm. However, consider the following reasons for choosing a more moderate alternative:

1) <u>Negative attitude toward dieting</u>: Inevitably, after two weeks on a diet that is too boring or too troublesome to prepare or that leaves a constant "raw" feeling in your stomach, that feeling of "deprivation" starts creeping in, setting you up for a desire to compensate by overeating. In short, you can't wait to get off that diet.

2) <u>Plateau of discouragement</u>: Since it takes approximately 3,500 calories to make a pound, you can't continue to lose at the rate of two pounds a day on any diet unless you were previously eating over 7,000 calories per day. You will not see further permanent weight loss until your body has "caught up" with that initial quick loss, most of which was water loss that can be put back on immediately.

3) <u>Lowered energy level</u>: A drastic diet may leave you feeling listless and irritable and you will actually use up fewer calories due to reduced level of activity.

4) And most important, <u>not a single step forward has been made toward restructuring permanent habits.</u>

The aim of diet restructure is never to have to go on another harsh diet again and never to have to resort to a feeling of "deprivation" in order to achieve the attractiveness and health you desire.

COPING WITH PERSONAL PITFALLS

Most diets ignore or make us feel guilty about our weakness in eating habits. First of all, there is nothing <u>wrong</u> with enjoying good food! However, we can overdo a good thing. It works far better to honestly identify these weaknesses without guilt; and instead of pretending you'll never indulge in them again, incorporate them into your diet, such as:

A. Don't tell yourself you'll never have chocolate again — allow for a certain number of calories of it per week. Then assess your habits to determine if you would rather have a mini portion of it every day at a certain time, or go out for a large portion at a prescribed time twice a week. Look at this number of calories as your splurge allotment in your "bank account" — you can use up a certain number per day, or any you don't use daily can be banked for Saturday night or for a whole festive weekend next month, as long as you don't depart <u>too</u> much from your desired daily calorie intake. (No accrued "interest" is permitted and no installment plan; you must save them up first. "Eat now and pay later" does <u>not</u> work!)

B. If the call of the refrigerator makes the call of the wild seem tame, prepare for it by keeping low-calorie "munchies" available.

You will be pleasantly surprised after you have been on your new regime for several months that even a real "off the wagon" holiday splurge will not be as much as you would have consumed before. It's not the once-in-a-great-while splurge that does you in (especially if you don't feel guilty about having done it), but not getting right back to good daily habits will.

ON THE LIGHT SIDE

EXERCISE

Exercise is as essential to good health and successful weight loss as the food you eat, and it doesn't have to be extreme — a brisk walk around your neighborhood for 30 minutes every day (or an hour every other day) will go a long way toward achieving tangible results. That half hour every day may be the best investment of time you'll ever make. Exercise:

1) relieves nervousness and irritability,
2) develops good muscle tone to "firm" as you lose,
3) improves all bodily functions from heart to gastrointestinal tract,
4) promotes better quality sleep,
5) burns more calories, and
6) generates more "pep," thereby using up more calories just by doing daily tasks with more enthusiasm and energy.

This leads to a "good" circle of events — the more you exercise, the more you feel like doing, the quicker you lose weight, to say nothing of the psychological "high" experienced from feeling good about yourself. Thus the circle is completed, creating a positive attitude toward dieting, permitting you to take part without self-consciousness in activities that keep weight down and your mind away from eating out of sheer boredom and frustration.

Note: If you begin a diet the same time you begin a strenuous exercise routine, don't be discouraged if weight loss is not as great as you had expected. First, we tend to try to reform all at once and sometimes overdo the exercise regime right away instead of gradually building up muscle condition. When this happens and our muscles are mildly injured (indicated by a feeling of soreness), they temporarily retain additional water to promote healing — when this water is released, its additional weight and bulk will be gone. Also with regular exercise, lighter weight fatty tissue is lost and denser firmer muscle tissue is built up. Therefore, your actual weight loss may not be as great, but the loss of flabby inches is the mark of success.

One last word about exercise: the same philosophy holds true that is the key to successful dieting — select a moderate level of something you like to do that can become a part of the rest of your life.

SLEEP

You may feel the need for more sleep in the very beginning of a diet program, but you can use that to advantage — going to bed a bit earlier avoids that treacherous period of late-night snacking temptation. Soon regular exercise and the moderate 1200 to 1500 calorie-per-day range will generate more energy than ever felt before.

SCHEDULING MEALS

Plan meals to fit your schedule. The most important key to a successful diet is never to allow yourself to get too hungry. It may help to divide the daily allotment into four meals if your schedule permits. Eat more during the earlier part of your day to keep your energy level up and to burn calories more efficiently. Starving all day can set you up for overeating at night, but neither is it good to go to bed hungry and dreaming of food.

BREAKFAST

On a reduced-calorie diet, you may wake up hungrier than before due to cutting back on dinner and late-night snacking. It is easier, particularly if you have a busy schedule, to make breakfast a meal that is: 1) pre-planned, 2) easily available, and 3) something you like, even if it is not a traditional "breakfast food."

The people in Greece, as in other European countries, eat a light continental breakfast, consume a large mid-day meal followed by a restful period and then enjoy a resurgence of daily activities into the late evening hours, concluding with a light dinner. Here our standard schedule is different and menu planning for a well-balanced breakfast to provide for a full day of alertness and high energy demands is important. Dietary planning for breakfast needs to include a good dose of protein as well as carbohydrates. The conversion time for morning protein comes in the afternoon to eliminate that saggy feeling.

MENU PLANNING

A. Plan meals to divide your daily allotment of calories evenly over the waking hours.

B. Plan meals to satisfy the desire for volume as well as taste. If you plan a relatively high-calorie entree, serve a small portion of it and balance it with generous servings of low-calorie salad and water-based vegetables such as green beans, okra, asparagus, squash, tomatoes and broccoli. Similarly, serve a low-calorie entree when accompanied by potatoes, corn, pasta or other starchy vegetables.

C. Be sure to include plenty of liquids and fiber.

D. Try to cook planned amounts to avoid the temptation of "cleaning up" leftovers. Plan enough to allow larger portions for growing family members, prepared according to the same principles of moderation outlined for weight control — it is never too early to begin developing good habits.

E. If you're invited to a special dinner party, cut back a little on other meals but not so much that it will lower your will power for refusing seconds. It's harder to maintain good diet habits when dining out; but if social engagements are a large part of your lifestyle, you _can_ apply the principles of moderation to those occasions, too, by planning ahead what to allow yourself. It isn't easy; it _is_ worth it.

BREAD

Whether dining out or at home, control of bread portions is important. The choice is between a full portion of low-calorie bread or a half portion of your favorite bread. Remember, rice, pasta or other cereal products can take the place of a portion of bread.

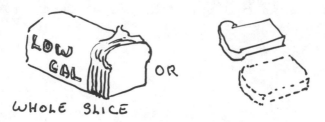

WHOLE SLICE

EXPENSE

Don't say, "I can't go on a diet that has expensive foods like shrimp and tenderloin." If you add up the money you won't be spending on junk food, desserts and the former larger portions of everything else, you will have saved enough to buy small quantities of almost any taste-tempting food that will help you feel that dieting is a gourmet experience instead of a deprivation.

PRESENTATION OF MEALS

A little extra time and attention spent in the attractive presentation of food can help turn a plain diet meal into a gourmet dining experience.

We need to satisfy the eye in terms of quantity as well as desirability. Even if you eat alone, arrange all food attractively on one plate or place setting. Sometimes it is surprising how much we can consume standing in front of the refrigerator without ever feeling satisifed, which, if arranged attractively on a single plate, would be completely satisfying with less actual quantity.

Serving a plate of food (without entertaining the thought of second helpings) is better than putting the food on the table in serving dishes; and cooking casseroles in individual ramekins, for instance, adds a gourmet touch while defining the serving portion.

A little flair makes the everyday meal an occasion to look forward to — and adds a little romance.

APPETIZERS (Mezethakia)

A delectable Greek tray of assorted "mezethakia" is a good example of the art of presentation. A tray of low-calorie nutritious foods along with a few bites of higher-calorie morsels served about 30 minutes before your meal can help to curb the appetite, especially if you have let yourself get too hungry by mealtime.

A 4-ounce glass of dry white or red wine only adds 75 calories; but be careful of its tendency to heighten appetite and lower resistance to overeating, especially in the initial stages of your diet.

MEZETHAKIA
Assorted Hors d'Oeuvres
Festive enough for party fare.

8 medium shrimp, boiled and
  peeled
1 ounce kasseri cheese, cut
  into 4 cubes
12 celery sticks
12 carrot sticks
8 radishes

8 small cucumber spears
2 ounces crusty bread sticks
8 Greek black olives
8 cherry tomatoes, halved
1 ounce feta cheese, crumbled
Lettuce leaves to line plate
Tzadziki dip (below)

Arrange all, except feta cheese, on bed of lettuce lining a large
tray or 4 individual plates. Sprinkle feta cheese on tomato
halves. Serve with toothpicks for dunking bites into tzadziki dip.
Serves 4.

Tzadziki Dip:
  1 cup plain yogurt
  1 clove garlic, minced
  1 1/2 teaspoons olive oil

1 1/2 teaspoons white vinegar
1 teaspoon dill (optional)
Dash of salt

Mix all ingredients in small bowl. If possible, make dip the night
before and refrigerate until serving to enhance blending of
flavors.

PIPERIES TOURSI[†]
Pickled Roasted Green Peppers

4 large green peppers
1/3 cup vinegar
1 small onion, finely chopped
2 tablespoons olive or vegetable oil
1 bay leaf, crumbled

1/2 teaspoon basil
1/2 teaspoon salt
1/4 teaspoon pepper
1/4 teaspoon garlic powder

Bake peppers at 400 degrees for 15 to 20 minutes, or until skins
puff and blister. Place in paper bag; close tightly. Let stand 15
minutes. Remove seeds and stems and peel. Cut lengthwise in 1/2-
inch strips, then in half crosswise. In small bowl, mix remaining
ingredients. Add peppers, stir to coat, cover and refrigerate
overnight. Serve on picks or on crackers. Makes 30 (1-inch)
strips.

SOUPS

Except for cream soups, almost any recipe for basic soup stock can be used in a reduced calorie diet if you skim fat off top first. (This applies to stews, also.) Allow pot to cool and then refrigerate until fat or oil has congealed on top. Remove the more solid form of fat before reheating. Remember to reduce the amounts of fat or oil used in the preparation of a recipe other than that which comes from the meat, chicken skin, etc.

AVGOLEMONO SOUP
Egg-Lemon Soup
A rich, thick soup prepared without fat or flour.

3 quarts boiling water	3 celery tops
Salt and pepper	1/2 cup long grain rice
1 whole chicken, cut up	2 eggs
1 small onion, studded with cloves	Juice of 2 lemons

Measure 2 quarts water into pot to mark that amount for later, then add third quart, salt and pepper; bring to a boil. Add chicken, onion and celery; bring to a boil again and reduce heat. Cover and simmer about 2 hours until chicken is done, skimming top occasionally to keep broth clear.

Remove chicken for later use as desired. Skim top again for any oil or fat. Strain broth and boil until reduced to 2 quarts. Add rice; cook for 20 minutes or until tender. Remove from heat.

In medium bowl, beat eggs with wire whisk; gradually add lemon juice while continuing to beat. Slowly add in thin stream 1 cup hot broth to egg-lemon mixture, stirring constantly. Pour back into pot and stir vigorously over very low heat until thickened. Do not boil or it will curdle.

187

SALADS

Salads are great low-calorie fillers for diet meals.

TZADZIKI WITH CUCUMBER

1 1/2 cups plain yogurt
2 teaspoons olive oil
2 teaspoons white vinegar
1 teaspoon dried mint

2 medium cucumbers, peeled
  and diced
4 lettuce leaves

Mix first 4 ingredients in small bowl, add cucumber. Line 4 plates with lettuce leaves; top with salad. Serves 4.

CABBAGE, TOMATOES AND CUCUMBER
A standard on village tables.

2 cups shredded raw cabbage
2 small cucumbers, sliced
2 tablespoons wine vinegar
3 tomatoes

2 teaspoons olive oil
Salt and pepper
1 ounce feta cheese, crumbled

Arrange bed of cabbage on each of 4 salad plates, with a circle of cucumber slices around outside. Sprinkle with vinegar. In separate bowl, cut tomatoes into wedges so juice that escapes can be mixed with the olive oil. Arrange tomatoes in center of cabbage, sprinkle with salt, pepper, olive oil and tomato juice. Garnish with feta cheese. Serves 4.

ELLINIKI SALATA
Traditional Greek Salad

Alter traditional recipe in Salads Chapter to reduce higher-calorie items like cheese, olives and especially oil; increase amounts of lower-calorie greens, cucumbers and tomatoes.

A generous portion, with 1 1/2 ounces feta cheese per person, makes a good lunch served with low-calorie bread.

VEGETABLES

Plan larger than usual servings of vegetables to provide fiber and satisfy the desire for volume in a low-calorie food.

DOMATES PSITES
Broiled Tomatoes

2 large tomatoes, halved
1 1/2 teaspoons olive oil
1 teaspoon basil
1/2 teaspoon dried oregano

Salt and pepper
2 tablespoons crumbled feta cheese

Place tomatoes on baking tray. Brush tops with olive oil; sprinkle with basil, oregano, salt and pepper. Place under broiler until hot. Sprinkle cheese on tops, return to broiler until cheese just melts.

Variation: Use diet Italian dressing instead of olive oil, basil and oregano.

FASOLIA YIAHNI
Green Beans with Limas

Yiahni Sauce:
  1 medium onion, chopped
  2 teaspoons butter or olive oil
  2 tomatoes, cut up
  Salt and pepper

1 (10-oz.) pkg. frozen baby lima beans
1 (10-oz.) pkg. frozen french-cut green beans

Saute onion in butter or oil until tender. Add tomatoes, salt and pepper; simmer 5 minutes. Add limas and enough water to cover. Bring to boiling and cook 10 minutes. Add green beans and continue to cook about 10 to 15 minutes or until tender.

Variation: Substitute yellow squash, fresh green beans or okra for frozen beans.

KOUNOUPITHI MEH SALTSA TIRI
Cauliflower with Diet Cheese Sauce

1 whole head cauliflower, steamed or boiled

Cheese Sauce:
   3/4 cup skim milk   1/3 cup grated kasseri or
   1 tablespoon cornstarch   Cheddar cheese
   Salt and pepper

Keep cauliflower hot while preparing cheese sauce. Mix 1/4 cup milk with cornstarch in cup. In small nonstick skillet, heat remaining milk over medium heat. Add cornstarch mixture, stirring until thickened. Add salt, pepper and cheese, stirring until cheese has melted.

Divide cauliflower into serving portions and spoon sauce over each. Garnish with paprika or a few bacon bits, if desired. Serves 4.

Variation: Substitute cooked broccoli or yellow squash for cauliflower.

SAUTEED ZUCCHINI STRIPS

2 teaspoons butter or olive oil   2 tomatoes, peeled and cut up
2 medium zucchini   Salt and pepper
1 medium onion, chopped   Dash of dried oregano
1 clove garlic, minced

Cut zucchini into 1/4-inch thick strips about 2 to 3 inches long. In nonstick skillet, melt butter and saute zucchini, onion and garlic, stirring constantly. Add tomatoes, salt, pepper and oregano. Simmer until tender. Serves 4.

SEAFOOD

Seafood <u>can</u> be deliciously low calorie when not batter-fried.

PSARI MEH LEMONI
Fish with Lemon
Simple and elegant, with absolutely no guilt.

1 1/2 pounds flounder or other white fish fillets	Salt and pepper
Juice of 1 lemon	1 tablespoon butter

In shallow baking pan, arrange fish fillets in single layer. Sprinkle with lemon juice, salt, pepper and dot with butter. Add a little water to cover bottom half-way up sides of fish. Bake at 350 degrees about 10 minutes, turn once, and continue to bake for about 20 minutes or until flaky. Serves 4.

Variation I: Substitute 5 large shrimp per person, peeled and deveined. Add 1 clove garlic, minced, in water surrounding shrimp.

Variation II: This method works well for calves' liver. Instead of dotting with butter, saute sliced onion rings in the butter and place on liver while baking.

GARITHES MEH KARITHIA
Shrimp with Walnuts
An unusually good combination.

1 tablespoon butter	Juice of 1/2 lemon
20 large shrimp, peeled and deveined	Salt and pepper
	4 tablespoons chopped walnuts

Melt butter in shallow baking dish or in 4 individual small baking dishes. Arrange shrimp in single layer and turn to coat both sides with butter. Sprinkle with lemon juice, salt and pepper. Pack chopped walnuts around and on top of shrimp. Bake at 350 degrees for 10 to 20 minutes, depending upon desired firmness of shrimp. Serves 4.

COMPANY FISH CASSEROLE
Your family is your own best company.

2 (10-oz.) pkgs. frozen spinach
1/4 teaspoon nutmeg
1 1/2 pounds flounder fillets
1 tablespoon butter
Salt and pepper

Juice of 1 lemon
1 tablespoon mayonnaise
2 tablespoons grated
Parmesan cheese
1/4 cup dry white wine

Cook spinach according to package directions, adding nutmeg while cooking. Drain and set aside. Saute flounder fillets in butter in nonstick skillet, or bake in oven according to instructions in first recipe of this seafood section. Add salt, pepper and lemon juice while cooking. Arrange spinach in bottom of lightly buttered casserole; place fish on top. Spread top of fish fillets evenly with mayonnaise. Sprinkle with Parmesan cheese. Pour wine over casserole. Bake at 400 degrees for 10 minutes or until lightly browned on top. If desired, place briefly under broiler to brown, watching carefully. Serves 4.

MEATS AND POULTRY

Lean cuts of meat and poultry are excellent low-calorie sources of high protein.

ARNI MEH SPANAKI
Lamb with Spinach
Good served with broiled tomatoes and plain rice.

1 pound lean lamb (shoulder or leg),
    cut into 1/2-inch cubes
1 medium onion, chopped
1 clove garlic, minced

1 tablespoon butter
Salt and pepper
2 (10-oz.) pkgs. frozen
    whole leaf spinach

Trim lamb meat of any fat. In Dutch oven, saute onion and garlic in butter over medium heat. Add lamb to brown, stirring constantly, adding a few drops of water to prevent sticking. Add salt, pepper and enough water to cover lamb; simmer covered until tender, about 1 1/2 hours, adding a little water if necessary. Add spinach and 1/4 cup water. Cook until spinach has thawed, stir and continue to cook until spinach is done, about 10 minutes. Serves 4.

VOTHINO STIFATHO
Beef with Onions

1 pound very lean beef, cut into
   1/2-inch cubes
1 tablespoon olive oil
1 clove garlic, minced
Salt and pepper
1 teaspoon sugar
1/8 teaspoon ground cloves

1/8 teaspoon ground cinnamon
1 tablespoon red wine vinegar
2 tablespoons red wine
1 tomato, peeled and chopped
1 bay leaf
1 pound tiny white onions,
   peeled

In nonstick skillet, brown beef in olive oil over high heat, stirring constantly, adding a few drops of water to prevent sticking. Add garlic, salt and pepper; stir well. Remove meat to lightly greased 2-quart casserole, reserving oil mixture left in pan. Mix sugar with clove and cinnamon. Add to meat in casserole and stir. Add vinegar, wine, tomato, bay leaf and just enough water to cover beef. Add onions on top; sprinkle with reserved oil mixture, toss lightly to mix onions in, cover and bake at 300 degrees for 2 to 2 1/2 hours or until tender. Discard bay leaf before serving. Serves 4.

KOTA MEH BAMIES
Chicken with Okra

By the time you count the weight of skin, fat and bones, you'll find that skinned, boned chicken is not that expensive.

3 cups small fresh okra
Salt
Lemon juice
1 tablespoon olive oil or butter
1 medium onion, chopped
1 clove garlic, minced

1 pound boned, skinned chicken
   breasts or thighs, cut into
   1-inch square pieces
3 medium tomatoes, peeled and
   quartered
Salt and pepper

Wash okra and trim stems. Dip stems in salt and place in deep bowl. Sprinkle lemon juice over okra and let stand. In nonstick skillet, heat oil or butter; brown onion and chicken over high heat, stirring constantly, adding a few drops of water if necessary to prevent sticking. Reduce heat and add garlic, tomatoes, salt and pepper; mix well. Layer chicken mixture and okra in Dutch oven; add enough water to barely cover. Gently cook covered for 45 minutes, or until okra is tender. Serves 4.

193

YIOUVARLAKIA
"Porcupines"

1 pound extra lean ground beef
Juice and pulp of 2 large
  tomatoes, finely chopped
1 egg, slightly beaten
1 tablespoon dried mint
1 teaspoon dried parsley
2/3 cup long grain rice, uncooked

Salt and pepper
1 medium onion, finely
  chopped
1 teaspoon butter
1 cup beef bouillon (made
  from 1 bouillon cube)
1 cup tomato juice

Put first 7 ingredients in medium bowl and blend well. In nonstick
saucepan, saute onion until tender; add to meat mixture. Form into
balls 2 inches in diameter and arrange in single layer in bottom of
Dutch oven. Combine bouillon and tomato juice and add to pot until
about 1/2-inch deep. Simmer covered 15 to 20 minutes, checking to
be sure there's at least 1/4-inch liquid in pan. (Add more liquid
as needed.) Gently turn meatballs, cover and continue to simmer
about 20 minutes. Uncover and raise heat to medium to evaporate
liquid about 10 mintues, or until rice and meat are cooked. Serves
4 to 5.

Variation: If juicy tomatoes are not in season, substitute 2/3 cup
tomato sauce or tomato puree.

Note: This meat mixture can be used to stuff tomatoes, peppers,
squash, eggplant, etc. (See Ground Beef section of Entrees.)

SOUVLAKIA
Shish-Kebab

Almost any recipe for souvlakia can be made dietetic without much
sacrifice of taste simply by reducing the amount of oil called for
in the marinade or in basting. Marinating lean meat is a good way
to tenderize and flavor it, and a quick low-calorie marinade can be
made from equal portions of diet Italian dressing and dry red wine.
The meat and vegetables on the skewer, served over a bed of plain
rice and accompanied by a salad, make a diet meal fit for a party.

TRADITIONAL PASTA AND PHYLLO FAVORITES

Greek recipes are known for their many steps — and for their extraordinary delectability as a reward — but remember that the calorie-reduction principles work just as well on foods that can be quickly assembled. You can cook larger quantities of the time-consuming portions of recipes and freeze in portioned containers enough for other meals. Two examples are the "yiahni" sauce for cooking vegetables and the meat sauce for spaghetti or pastitsio. If you are cooking for two, you can make a regular-size recipe and freeze half for another time.

BASIC SAUCES

MEAT SAUCE

1 medium onion, chopped
1 clove garlic, minced
2 teaspoons butter
3/4 pound lean ground beef

Salt and pepper
1/4 teaspoon ground cinnamon
1 (6-oz.) can tomato paste
1/8 cup water

In a large nonstick skillet, saute onion and garlic in butter until tender. Add crumbled ground beef to brown. Tilt pan and drain off excess oil. Add salt, pepper, cinnamon, tomato paste and water. Stir and cook over low heat for 15 minutes.

CREAM SAUCE

1 tablespoon butter
2 tablespoons all-purpose flour
2 cups warm lowfat milk

Salt and pepper
2 large eggs

In medium saucepan, melt butter. With gravy stirrer (spring whisk), blend in flour and cook, stirring constantly over low heat for 2 to 3 minutes. Slowly add milk, stirring to blend until mixture thickens. Add salt and pepper. Remove from heat. Beat eggs in medium bowl; slowly pour milk mixture in thin stream, stirring constantly until fully mixed.

CHEESE SAUCE

1 tablespoon butter
2 tablespoons all-purpose flour
1 cup warm skim milk

1/2 cup grated Graviera or
  Parmesan cheese
Salt and pepper

In nonstick saucepan, melt butter, blend in flour with gravy stirrer (spring whisk) and cook, stirring constantly for 2 minutes over low heat. Slowly add milk in thin stream, stirring constantly to prevent lumping. Add cheese, salt and pepper; stir over low heat until cheese has melted.

PASTITSIO
Ground Beef and Macaroni Casserole

6 ounces macaroni, ziti, or
  other pasta, uncooked
1/2 cup grated kasseri or
  Parmesan cheese (2 ounces)

1 recipe meat sauce
  (see beginning of section)
1 recipe cream sauce
  (see beginning of section)

Cook pasta until almost done in boiling, salted water. Drain and spread on bottom of lightly buttered 8-inch square casserole. Sprinkle with grated cheese, cover evenly with meat sauce. Slowly pour cream sauce over top. Bake uncovered at 400 degrees for 20 minutes, reduce heat to 350 degrees and continue to bake for 30 minutes, or until cream sauce is set. Serves 5 to 6.

Note: If cream sauce forms "skin" while baking, scratch in several places with tines of fork to allow steam to escape.

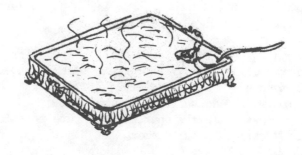

MAKARONIA
Spaghetti

1 recipe meat sauce (see beginning
  of section)
6 ounces thin spaghetti, uncooked

3/4 cup grated kasseri
  cheese (3 ounces)

Heat meat sauce over low heat while boiling spaghetti in salted
water to desired doneness. Drain spaghetti in colander. Put 1/3
of the meat sauce in bottom of spaghetti pan and cover with 1/3 of
spaghetti; stir gently to mix. Sprinkle 1/3 of the cheese over
layer, add second 1/3 meat sauce, second 1/3 spaghetti, mix gently,
and add second 1/3 of cheese. Repeat procedure for 1 more layer,
cover pan to allow cheese to melt. Serve immediately. Serves 4.

Note: If kasseri cheese is unavailable, use 1/2 cup grated Romano
or Parmesan cheese.

KOTA MEH PASTA
Chicken with Pasta

1 tablespoon butter
1 pound boned, skinned chicken
  breasts, cut into bite-size pieces
1 clove garlic, minced
1/4 pound loukanika sausage,
  pepperoni or ham, slivered*

6 ounces linguine or
  fettuccine, uncooked
1 recipe cheese sauce
  (see beginning of
  section)

In large nonstick skillet, melt butter and brown chicken over high
heat, stirring constantly, adding a few drops of water to prevent
sticking. Reduce heat, add garlic, sausage and saute 5 minutes.
Set aside, covered. Cook pasta to desired degree of doneness in
boiling, salted water; drain, add to chicken mixture. Add cheese
sauce; mixing well to coat. Serve immediately. Serves 4.

Company version: For a quick and elegant dish for a dinner party,
use 4 large boned, skinned breast fillets and 4 slices ham instead
of bite-size chicken pieces and sausage. Saute as directed above.
Arrange each chicken breast topped with ham slice on bed of pasta,
and pour cheese sauce over top but do not mix in. Garnish with
toasted almonds, if desired.

---

* See Appetizer Chapter for Loukanika recipe.

197

SPANAKOPITA
Spinach Pita
Entree Casserole.

2 (10-oz.) pkgs. frozen whole leaf
spinach, or 1 pound fresh spinach
2 eggs
1 (12-oz.) lowfat cottage cheese
3 ounces feta cheese, crumbled
Salt and pepper

1 medium onion, chopped
1 teaspoon butter
6 ounces macaroni or
linguine, uncooked
1 recipe cream sauce
(see beginning of section)

Cook spinach according to package directions, or steam boil fresh spinach until cooked. Drain, reserving spinach water for cooking pasta. Beat eggs in medium bowl, add cheeses, salt and pepper. In a nonstick saucepan, saute onion in butter until tender. Add spinach and cheese-egg mixture; mix well.

Cook pasta until almost done in boiling, salted water to which the reserved spinach water has been added. Drain and spread on bottom of lightly buttered 8-inch square casserole. Spread spinach mixture evenly over pasta, gently pour cream sauce over top. Bake at 350 degrees for 45 minutes, or until cream sauce is set. Serves 4 to 5.

Note: Mixing feta cheese and cottage cheese overnight enhances flavor. If cream sauce forms "skin" while baking, scratch with tines of fork in several places to allow steam to escape.

Variation: With phyllo, traditional-style

First 7 ingredients above to make basic spinach mixture as
directed in first paragraph above
4 to 5 whole phyllo sheets, cut into 48 individual circles to
fit ramekin top
6 individual ramekins, lightly buttered
3 to 4 tablespoons butter, melted

Place 1 circle sheet of phyllo in bottom of each ramekin, brushing very lightly with melted butter. Place second phyllo sheet on top. Divide spinach mixture among the ramekins. Place 6 phyllo sheets over spinach, brushing each very lightly with butter. Bake at 350 degrees for 30 minutes, or until phyllo is puffed and golden. Serves 6.

DESSERTS

Although Greece is famous for its delicious pastries, they are not served for dessert immediately following a dinner. In fact, their traditional dessert to end a meal is the perfect answer to dieting — fruit. Again, presentation is important, and it only takes an extra minute.

FRUIT DESSERT

Allow 3/4 cup sliced fruit per person, fresh, frozen (without sugar) or canned (in its own juice), such as: apples, bananas, strawberries, blueberries, pineapple, melon, peaches, etc. If prepared ahead, sprinkle with lemon juice to eliminate discoloration.

<u>Topping</u>:
Choose any two of the following per person:

2 tablespoons plain yogurt	2 teaspoons honey
1 tablespoon diet-whipped topping	2 teaspoons toasted
1 tablespoon liqueur	almond slivers
1 tablespoon shredded coconut	

Arrange fruit in sherbet glass or small bowl. Garnish with topping.

A lunch of "fast" food can break your calorie bank. Typically, a deluxe cheeseburger with a large order of fries tops 1,000 calories. A standard boxed 3-piece chicken dinner has about 950 calories.

YIAOURTI
Yogurt for Dieters
Good with fruit or by itself.

1 quart lowfat milk
2 tablespoons yogurt starter (mayia)
  from previous batch, or commercial
  plain yogurt

8 drops peppermint extract
  (optional)
Artificial sweetener to
  equal 8 teaspoons sugar

Boil milk until it comes to a "pouf." Immediately remove from heat and let cool until you can keep a finger in the milk and count to 20. Spoon yogurt starter into a cup and stir in a little milk until well blended. Pour back into pot. Add sweetener and peppermint extract. Pour milk through a strainer into 5 (6-oz.) cups; cover cups with plastic lids or similar. Place yogurt in a draft-free spot and let sit about 4 to 6 hours, or until it has thickened.* Refrigerate. Serves 5.

Variation: Make yogurt as directed, omitting peppermint. Mix 2 cups yogurt with 2 cups fruit-flavored diet gelatin prepared according to package instructions. Refrigerate. Garnish with fresh fruit or diet whipped topping. The gelatin mixture can also be made from one envelope plain gelatin and 1 1/2 cups natural fruit juice; see package directions on gelatin box.

-----

* You may use a commercial yogurt maker or this old-fashioned method: place a wash cloth in a baking pan that will hold the cups; place cups in pan and cover with a hand towel.

DESSERT ALTERNATIVES

A. One small (1/4 normal serving) piece of your favorite rich dessert each day.

B. Forego daily desserts and "bank" them for a splurge of one large serving of your favorite dessert once a week. When you reach your desired weight and are ready for a maintenance diet, increase the frequency to twice a week. This eliminates the feeling of "deprivation" that comes from diets that decree that you can "never have those rich foods again."

YOGURT MILKSHAKE
A refreshing tart drink on a hot day.

1 cup cold dieter's yogurt
   (see previous page)
1 cup cold lowfat milk
2 tablespoons sugar or
   artificial sweetener

1 cup or more mashed fruit (fresh
   or canned, drained) of either
   strawberries, peaches, apricots,
   pineapple, blueberries,
   mandarins, or bananas

Blend all ingredients in a blender until smooth. Serves 2.

MISCELLANEOUS

MISCELLANEOUS

    A few special Greek recipes that do not fit into other chapters are included here, such as Greek coffee, yogurt and <u>trahana</u>. Also recipes for homemade phyllo and pastry dough are given as well as an in-depth explanation of "How to Work with Commercial Phyllo." Detailed instructions for the dyeing of Easter eggs and the making of <u>Kolliva</u> are also included along with a brief explanation of the history and symbolism behind the recipes. How to freeze fresh grapeleaves, prepare chestnuts, blanch almonds, make soft and dry bread crumbs are other hints invaluable to the novice and to the accomplished cook.

YIAOURTI

Homemade Yogurt

Yogurt dates back to the ninth century when the Bulgars crossed over the border in northern Greece and taught the Greek mountaineers the secret of making yogurt. Today, yogurt is found in grocery stores everywhere in the United States although it did not make its way to this country until 1930. The Greeks claim many benefits from yogurt, including longevity and a cure for stomach ailments.

* * * * * * * * *

3/4 cup instant, nonfat
   dry milk
1 quart whole milk

2 tablespoons yogurt (starter
   [mayia] from previous batch,
   or commercial type)

In top of double boiler, dissolve dry milk and whole milk. Heat until milk mixture comes almost to a boil, stirring occasionally. Remove pan; cool about 30 minutes or to 115 to 120 degrees. (A sure way to test is to stick a finger in the hot milk until you can count to 20.) Do not allow milk to get any cooler. Stir starter yogurt until creamy; blend in 1/4 cup of warm milk and pour back into the pan of milk, blending thoroughly. Pour into containers of a commercial yogurt maker and incubate for 12 hours; or pour into a bowl, cover with a heavy towel and place in a warm place about 6 to 8 hours. (A gas oven with pilot is often just right, or place a saucepan of hot water in the oven to raise the temperature.) When thickened, place 3 or 4 thicknesses of paper towels on top of yogurt to absorb the water. Cover bowl with aluminum foil and refrigerate. Replace paper towels as needed. Yogurt will keep up to 7 days. Makes 8 cups.

Variation: If thicker yogurt is preferred, empty chilled yogurt into a muslin bag, suspend and drain. Thickened yogurt can be thinned with half and half cream.

Note: If using this yogurt as a starter (mayia) for a new batch, starter should be used within 3 days.

TRAHANA
Homemade Sourdough Pasta
Trahana, a nutritious pasta that can be substituted
for orzo or rice in soup.

2 cups whole milk
2 cups buttermilk
2 eggs, well beaten
1 tablespoon salt

4 cups semolina or farina
7 1/2 to 8 1/2 cups all-purpose
flour

In a large bowl, blend well the milk, buttermilk and eggs. Add salt, semolina and 6 cups of flour; mix thoroughly. Begin adding flour, 1/2 cup at a time, until dough is stiff and comes cleanly away from sides of pan. With floured hands, pinch dough off into little pieces (the size of a quarter) and place on greased baking sheets. Slightly flatten dough with palm of hand. Bake at 200 degrees for 2 hours, removing from oven after first hour to turn dough pieces over with a spatula. When finished baking, turn oven off and leave trahana in for several hours. Grind in blender until trahana resembles coarse meal. Spread on cookie sheets to air dry overnight. Store in air-tight containers; will keep several months. Makes 3 quarts.

Variation I: If a more tart taste is desired, substitute plain yogurt for the milk and buttermilk.

Variation II: Trahana makes a delicious hot breakfast cereal. Bring to a boil 2 cups water, 2 cups milk and 1 cup trahana. Reduce heat and simmer 25 to 30 minutes, stirring frequently. Salt to taste. For a creamier consistency, use 3 cups milk and 1 cup water.

KOUFETA

Candy-coated almonds called koufeta are presented as tokens of joy, fertility, and good wishes to guests at a Greek Orthodox wedding and baptism.. This custom was first recorded in 177 B.C. when a patrician Roman family used honeyed almonds at the marriage of their daughter. Elaborate koufeta can be purchased at specialty stores, or can be simply made by placing an odd number (5 or 7) white Jordan almonds in a 6-inch square of white netting material and tied with a 12-inch length of white satin ribbon. If desired, 2 or 3 sprigs of artificial lily of the valley flowers can be anchored to the bow.

PASCALIATIKA AVGA
Easter Eggs

One of the most popular Easter traditions of Orthodox Christians is the "cracking" of eggs. The egg is held tightly in the hand, pointed end up. The other person who's challenging holds his egg pointed end down. Each tries to crack the other's egg, all the while proclaiming "Christos Anesti" (Christ is Risen) and replying "Alithos Anesti" (Truly, He is Risen). The winner is the lucky one who successfully escapes having his egg cracked.

The custom is said to have originated with Mary Magdalene, who after having learned of Christ's Resurrection went to the Emperor of Rome to give him a red egg. The Easter egg represents the sealed Tomb of Christ, while the red color symbolizes the blood of Christ.

The eggs are usually dyed on Holy Thursday or Holy Saturday. For best results, use imported red dye (see Shopper's Guide in Appendix).

* * * * * * * * * *

1 package of red dye	1 tablespoon salt
1/2 cup white vinegar	18 white eggs, room temperature

Dilute dye in vinegar; add enough warm water to cover the eggs. Stir in salt. Gently boil 5 minutes, stirring occasionally to completely dissolve the dye. Remove from heat; add eggs. Return to heat and simmer eggs for 15 minutes or until done. Remove eggs and cool slightly. Polish each egg with an oiled cloth.

Variation: A package of Scarlet Rit dye (No. 5) may also be used. Combine dye and 1/4 cup vinegar in 2 quarts boiling water. Stir to dissolve dye. Add hard-boiled eggs, 2 or 3 at a time, making sure none are cracked. Keep eggs in dye until desired color is achieved. Remove eggs with slotted spoon, dry on rack and polish with an oiled cloth.

KAFETHAKI
Greek Coffee

Greek coffee is made in a longhandled, cylindrical pot known as briki. Briki pots come in 2, 4 or 6 demitasse cup sizes. Greek coffee is never served with milk or cream or made in larger quantities because the kaimaki, the rich frothy topping, tends to lose its proper consistency. Before enjoying a kafethaki, let coffee stand a few seconds to allow the grounds to settle to the bottom of the cup. The coffee is carefully sipped without disturbing grounds. Serve with a glass of cold water to cleanse and prepare the palate to taste only the coffee!

* * * * * * * *

Greek coffee is served the following ways:
1. Sketos, plain (no sugar)
2. Metrios, medium sweet (1 teaspoon sugar per cup)
3. Glykos, sweet (2 teaspoons sugar per cup)

For each demitasse cup of coffee, add to the briki 1 demitasse cup water, 1 rounded teaspoon Greek coffee and sugar according to taste. Stir well. Place over medium heat, stirring frequently, while waiting for coffee to come to boil. As soon as coffee starts rising to rim of briki, remove from heat and pour a little into a demitasse cup. This first rising forms the kaimaki, the essence of the coffee. Return briki to heat and allow coffee to rise a second time. Fill demitasse cup to the brim, being careful not to disturb the kaimaki. Briki pots and Greek coffee are available in Greek specialty stores (see Shopper's Guide in Appendix).

Note: A kafetzou is a "fortune teller" who specializes in the age-old custom of reading the future from coffee grounds left in a cup. When coffee is finished, quickly invert cup onto a saucer and let stand a minute. Lift the cup and examine the pattern of grounds; the future is clearly revealed. If the grounds are separated by wide spaces, a long voyage is indicated; smaller spaces, a short trip. A large blob means money, small blobs mean trouble, and so on.

207

TSAI TOU VOUNOU
Mountain Tea

The Greeks have brewed various kinds of sweet smelling leaves for many centuries. Hippocrates, the Greek physician, used <u>tsai</u> (tea) as a prescription for curing colds, fevers and stomach ailments. One such tea recipe is still in use today.

4 cups boiling water
1/2 teaspoon dried hamomilo
  (camomile), faskomilo (sage)
  leaves, or thiosmo (mint) leaves

2 teaspoons honey
1 lemon slice
Dash of ground cinnamon
  (optional)

Bring water to a boil and add leaves. Steep 3 to 5 minutes; strain. Add honey, lemon and cinnamon. Makes 4 servings.

KOLLIVA

A memorial service (mnemosinon) is traditionally offered in the Orthodox Church in remembrance of the departed 40 days after death and again one year after death. Family members of the deceased prepare a tray of Kolliva consisting of boiled wheat kernels, raisins, almonds, spices and powdered sugar to be blessed during the service and distributed to the congregation. The offering of Kolliva is an ancient custom and signifies that the dead will rise again just as the wheat when planted in the earth sprouts and bears fruit. The various sweets added to the Kolliva signify that after Resurrection, life will be sweet and blissful.

The preparation of Kolliva begins three days before the memorial service and is a time-consuming process. The wheat should be kept in a cool place during the preparation to prevent spoilage. The entire tray of Kolliva is assembled the morning of the service.

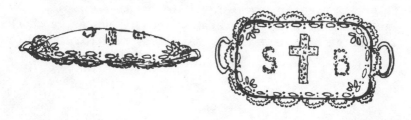

KOLLIVA

5 pounds sitari (whole wheat, unpeeled)
1 1/2 teaspoons salt
1 1/2 pounds walnuts, finely chopped
1 pound slivered almonds, blanched, lightly toasted
1 cup white raisins
1 1/2 to 2 tablespoons ground cinnamon
2 cups sesame seeds, lightly toasted (optional)
2 (6-oz.) boxes zwieback, ground
1 (1-pound) box powdered sugar
Silver dragees
White Jordan almonds
5-ounce paper cups
Plastic spoons

Late in Day of First Day: Inspect sitari for any foreign matter. Place in a large strainer or colander and wash well under warm running water. Place in a large kettle, cover with water and soak overnight.

Second Day: The next morning, drain sitari and cover with fresh water. Add salt, bring to a boil, lower heat and gently simmer 2 to 3 hours, stirring often, or until tender and wheat splits in two. **Watch carefully to prevent scorching.** Skim off any froth on top. Drain, reserving stock for making kollivozoumi, if desired (see following recipe). Place in a colander and rinse thoroughly under cold running water to remove starch. Drain thoroughly. Air dry sitari about 8 to 12 hours in a single layer on a double thickness of linens placed on a large table.

Morning of Services: In a large bowl, mix well the dried sitari, walnuts, almonds, raisins, ground cinnamon and sesame seeds. Line a medium-size serving tray with plastic wrap, and edge with paper doilies, if desired. Mound sitari mixture on the tray; pack and shape with hands. Cover top with an even layer of ground zwieback, pressing and patting down with a piece of waxed paper to form a smooth compact top. Sift powdered sugar over zwieback at least 1/4-inch thick; repeat pressing and patting down of sugar as with zwieback. To decorate, cut out a large cardboard cross and make an impression on the sugar; fill in with silver dragees. On either side of the cross, form initials of deceased, using dragees or Jordan almonds. Further designs for border and corners may be made with remaining dragees and Jordan almonds as desired. After memorial service, carefully transfer sitari into a large bowl; mix sitari well to blend the layers of zwieback and powdered sugar. Spoon into cups. Serves about 100.

KOLLIVOZOUMI
Wheat Pudding

The reserved broth of the strained wheat used in the preparation of kolliva makes a unique and nutritious pudding-like dessert. Add sugar to taste, raisins, chopped almonds and ground cinnamon. Dilute a little flour in 1 cup wheat broth and add to mixture. Boil until slightly thickened. Pour into individual dishes and cool. Sprinkle top with ground cinnamon.

HOW TO WORK WITH COMMERCIAL PHYLLO

Commercial phyllo is an unique, versatile pastry dough that's a basis for dozens of popular Greek dishes from appetizers to desserts and can be readily found in supermarkets and specialty stores across the country (see Shopper's Guide in Appendix).

Phyllo (feelo) is the Greek word for leaf. The phyllo dough is made from flour and water and is stretched either by hand or machine until it becomes as thin as tissue paper. Making phyllo is one of the pastry arts of the world. The origin for this ancient recipe is still unknown for Indians, Persians, Syrians, Yugoslavs, Turks and Greeks all claim it as their own, as do the Germans who call their phyllo strudel.

Commercial phyllo is found in the frozen food section in 1-pound boxes. Each contains approximately 22 (14 x 18-inch) pastry sheets that have been folded over, put into plastic bags and packed in long, flat narrow boxes. An unopened box of phyllo can be kept in the refrigerator up to 5 weeks, or in the freezer for several months. For best results thaw frozen phyllo in refrigerator overnight, then at room temperature for 2 hours before using.

Phyllo, once exposed to air, dries out quickly; therefore, always lay out all ingredients (filling, melted butter) and cooking utensils (pan, pastry brush) before opening phyllo. Work with the number of sheets necessary, keeping remaining phyllo covered with plastic wrap. Leftover phyllo should be placed in original bag, sealed tightly and refrigerated up to one week. Do not refreeze.

When a recipe requires phyllo to be cut into portions, cut through the entire stack at one time, using a sharp knife. If using whole sheets of phyllo for a pan pita or dessert pastry, carefully lift the sheets, one at a time. Should a sheet tear, use it between whole sheets. Usually the pastry sheets in the middle of the stack are the best, so try to reserve those sheets for the top layers where appearance is important.

The secret to crispy, flaky phyllo is butter; do not skimp or skip. Using a good pastry brush, generously brush each sheet with melted, clarified butter (see How to Clarify Butter in this chapter), beginning at the edges and working inward, using broad strokes.

Generally, when making a pan of dessert pastry, the sheets are trimmed to pan size. For a pita with a filling, however, the bottom layers of phyllo are overlapped to extend over the sides of the pan to enclose the filling. (See sketch in Phyllo Entrees Chapter.) The overhang is then folded over the filling and brushed with butter. The top layers of phyllo are trimmed to one inch beyond pan size. The excess phyllo is then tucked down the sides of the pan, using the edge of a pastry brush to seal in the filling. A few drops of cold water sprinkled over the top will help prevent phyllo from curling during baking. Score top with a sharp knife according to recipe directions.

PHYLLO TOU SPETIOU
Homemade Phyllo

4 cups all-purpose flour, sifted
1 teaspoon salt
1 1/3 cups warm water
(110 to 115 degrees)

1/4 cup olive oil
Cornstarch (used throughout
rolling process)

In a large bowl, combine 3 cups flour, salt, water and oil; stir to make a dough. With oiled hands, knead in enough of the remaining flour to make a moderately soft dough. Turn out onto an unfloured surface. Continue kneading 8 to 10 minutes or until smooth and satiny. Divide dough into 10 equal portions, shaping into balls the size of a lemon and dusting with cornstarch. Place in a bowl; sprinkle with more cornstarch. Cover with a clean cloth; let rest at room temperature several hours or overnight. If all the dough is not to be used, wrap unused portion in plastic wrap and store in refrigerator for up to 1 week. Bring to room temperature before rolling out.

On a flat surface dusted with cornstarch, slightly flatten 1 ball of dough; sprinkle with more cornstarch. Using a dowel 25 inches long and 7/8 inch in diameter, roll out to a 10-inch diameter. Place dowel at bottom of circle and fold over the dough. Lightly roll up dough, moving your hands from center to edges of dowel in a continuous motion to stretch the dough as it is being rolled. Unroll from dowel stretching slightly and repeat process, rotating dough each time a quarter turn before rolling. To finish stretching, pick up dough on one end with both hands and briefly suspend while rotating around circumference with finger tips. Phyllo sheet should be about 20 to 24 inches in diameter when finished. Do not be concerned if phyllo sheet tears during stretching. Tears may be mended as phyllo is being used. Place on a clean surface and allow to dry until slightly stiff. Use immediately, trimming where necessary. Store by laying sheets on top of each other with waxed paper in between, folding and wrapping tightly in plastic wrap. Can refrigerate up to 3 days or freeze up to three months. Bring to room temperature before using. Makes 10 phyllo sheets.

PASTRY DOUGH FOR TURNOVERS

Either of these pastry dough recipes can be used with your favorite filling as a dessert or as an appetizer. Both freeze well. Prepare dough and place in air-tight container. Thaw at room temperature before using.

PASTRY DOUGH I

3 cups all-purpose flour   Pinch of baking soda
1/2 cup boiling water   1 cup margarine, softened

Mix flour, water and soda thoroughly. Cut in margarine with a fork or pastry blender. Work dough with hands until it holds together. Divide into 2 balls. Cover and refrigerate a few hours or overnight.

On floured surface, roll out 1 dough ball at a time to 1/8-inch thickness. Cut into 3-inch or 4-inch rounds. Place a teaspoon of filling of choice in the center and fold over dough. Press edges together to seal or crimp with fork. Place on greased cookie sheets. Bake at 425 degrees for 15 minutes or until golden brown.

PASTRY DOUGH II

1 (8-oz.) pkg. cream cheese,   2 cups all-purpose flour,
  softened   sifted
1 cup butter or margarine, softened

Combine cheese and butter; cut flour in with pastry blender. Work dough with hands until it holds together. Divide into 2 balls. Cover and refrigerate a few hours or overnight.

Proceed as directed in previous recipe.

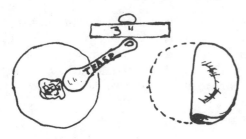

FRESH GRAPELEAVES

The recipes in this book call for canned grapevine leaves which can be purchased in 12-ounce or 16-ounce jars at specialty stores (see Shoppper's Guide in Appendix). However, if available, fresh grapeleaves are preferred. Select young, tender grapeleaves. Trim the stems and wash thoroughly in cold water. In a Dutch oven, parboil for 5 minutes in boiling water. Drain; rinse in cold water and drain again. Use right away as directed in recipe or freeze.

To freeze, thoroughly drain grapeleaves, then stack about 30 to 35 leaves dull-side down on a large square of waxed paper. Roll up leaves and waxed paper jelly-roll fashion, squeezing out any remaining water as you roll. Secure with string. Seal in plastic bags and freeze. Thaw frozen leaves in warm water. Fresh leaves can stay in freezer indefinitely and can be refrozen.

COOKING FRESH CHESTNUTS

Cut an "X" in the flat side of each chestnut shell with a small, sharp knife. Cover the nuts with water, bring to a boil and simmer covered 45 minutes to 1 hour. Cool slightly in water before removing and peeling.

BLANCHED ALMONDS

Plunge whole almonds with skins into boiling water for 2 minutes. Remove skins by rubbing off with fingers.

MAKING BRINE FOR FETA CHEESE

Put feta cheese in a wide-mouthed jar and fill with salted water (1 teaspoon salt for each cup of water). A piece of cheese will float when proportions of salt and water are correct. Tighten top on jar and refrigerate; it will stay fresh for months. Always remember to rinse feta before using to rid it of excessive saltiness.

MAKING MARINADE FOR OLIVES

1 pound olives
3/4 cup olive oil
1/4 cup wine vinegar
Salt

1 clove garlic, finely minced
1 teaspoon dried oregano
1 bay leaf

Cut a slit in each olive. Fill a jar with olives; combine remaining ingredients, pour over olives and refrigerate. Shake jar to redistribute contents before taking out olives.

CLARIFIED BUTTER

Clarified butter produces a better flavor and texture in phyllo pastries, cookies and cakes.

Melt 1 pound butter over low heat until it foams. Be careful not to brown or burn. Remove from heat; let stand 2 minutes to settle. Skim off salt crystals from top. Slowly pour butter in a small bowl, being careful not to disturb the milk solids which have settled to the bottom. Store in the refrigerator until needed. One pound butter equals 1 7/8 cups clarified butter.

MAKING SOFT BREAD CRUMBS

Cut off crusts of stale white bread and tear into 1-inch pieces. Grind for a few seconds in a blender or crumble it lightly with your fingers. To measure soft bread crumbs, always pile lightly into a measuring cup and do not compress.

MAKING DRY BREAD CRUMBS

Bake several slices of bread at 375 degrees until hard and golden. Crush with rolling pin or put into blender.

MAKING CROUTONS

Plain: Fry small squares of bread in hot butter until crisp.

Garlic-Flavored: Use stale Greek bread; saute small squares in garlic butter, dry in slow oven and store in glass jar.

APPENDIX

SPICES, HERBS AND FLAVORINGS

Olive oil, onion, garlic, lemon, honey, cheese, wine and a wide variety of Greek spices, herbs and flavorings are the basic essentials that give Greek food its character. One of the pleasures of preparing food is to find one's own combination of seasonings; results should be distinctive but not overpowering. Experiment with the following to flavor your favorite recipes in the Greek tradition:

ANISE SEED (Glykániso) – a licorice-flavored seed that spices holiday breads, cakes, pastries and the popular ouzo liqueur.

BASIL (Vasilikós) – the "herb of royalty," a popular herb used to flavor soups, stews and salads.

BAY LEAF, LAUREL (Dáphne) – adds a distinct flavor to soups and stock, fish, stews and spaghetti sauce.

CINNAMON (Kanélla) – stick and ground, used in the flavoring of poultry and meat stews, moussaka, pastitsio, turkey dressing, kolliva, rice pudding, cream caramel, finikia and in most phyllo pastry desserts.

CLOVES (Garíphallo) – whole cloves are used to stud kourambiethes and baklava. Ground cloves are generally used in phyllo pastry desserts, cakes and cookies.

CORIANDER (Koliantro) – aromatic seeds, commonly used by the Cypriots to flavor their sausages.

CUMIN (Kimíno) – used to flavor meat by those Greeks who come from Smyrna, now Izmir.

DILL (Anítho) – flavors many vegetable dishes, salads and soups.

FENNEL (Máratho) – adds a sweet licorice flavor to soups, stews and vegetables.

GARLIC (Skórtho) – a faint garlic taste laces many Greek stews and meat dishes; particularly used with roast lamb and in salad dressings. Also the basis of skorthalia, a pungent garlic sauce.

LEMON (Lemóni) - the most widely used citrus fruit in Greece: added to the syrup in Greek desserts; the key ingredient of the egg and lemon sauce, avgolemono; mated with oregano to flavor fish, lamb and poultry; squeezed over boiled vegetables and over meats to season and tenderize.

MAHLEPI - an unusual spice originating from Persia; must be ground before using. Adds a distinct flavor to holiday breads, cakes and cookies. Purchased in specialty shops.

MARJORAM (Matzouràna) - used as frequently as basil or oregano to flavor meats, fish and stews.

MASTIC (Mastíha) - a unique Greek flavoring derived from the sap of the mastic tree grown exclusively on the Island of Chios. Used in the flavoring of chewing gum, holiday breads, cakes, cookies, candies and liqueurs.

MINT (Thiósmos) - used with lamb and in vegetables, salads and soups. Dried mint leaves make a flavorful tea said to aid digestion.

OLIVE OIL (Láthi) - a leading export of Greece; the most essential ingredient in Greek cooking. The first pressing of the olives produces a strong-flavored virgin oil, dark green in color. Second pressings have a lighter flavor, color and aroma and is most commonly used. Meats and vegetables are often sauteed first in olive oil. Also used over fresh salads and cooked greens.

OREGANO (Rígani) - a popular pungent herb used in the preparation of most roast meats, stews, fish, salad dressings and vegetable dishes.

ORANGE (Portakáli) - the rind and juice of oranges flavor sausages, stews, phyllo pastry desserts, cakes and cookies.

PARSLEY (Maïdanós) - used generously in meat and vegetable combinations, salads and vegetables.

ROSEMARY (Thentrolivano) – a strong herb with tiny needle-like leaves used to sparingly flavor meat, fish and sauces.

ROSEWATER (Triantáphyllo) – this distinctive yet delicate flavoring is primarily used in desserts, syrups and candies.

SAGE (Faskomília) – used to flavor poultry, pork, sausages and stuffings. A tea can be made from the dried leaves of one variety found in the mountains.

SAVORY (Thrumbí) – a green herb, similar to sage, and used over poultry, pork or in sausages.

SESAME SEEDS (Sousáme) – a nutritious, nut-like seed grown on the Island of Kos; used as a topping for breads and cookies. Also the basis of the popular Greek candies halva and pastelle.

THYME (Thimári) – a popular pungent herb used to flavor fish, poultry and lamb.

VINEGAR (Xíthi) – Greeks generally use wine vinegar to flavor salads, marinades, vegetables and lentil soup.

WINES AND LIQUEURS

The following are a few of the more popular and accessible Greek wines and liqueuers:

DEMESTICA - a dry light wine that comes in red and white. A good inexpensive table wine; served chilled.

HYMETTUS - a dry light wine made from the grapes grown on Mount Hymettus; served chilled.

KOKINELLI - a full-bodied rosé with a resin flavor; served chilled.

MASTIHA - an anise-flavored liqueur served as an aperitif, favored by women.

MAVRODAPHNE - a heavy sweet, ruby-red wine served with fruit at end of meal or over cracked ice as an aperitif.

METAXA - a smooth liqueur brandy, rated with the best in the world.

OUZO - an anise-flavored colorless distillation from grape mash, running as high as 100 proof. Served as an aperitif poured over ice and sipped very slowly.

PENDELI - a light fruity red wine served at room temperature.

RETSINA - the popular resin-flavored white, red or rosé wine made in all parts of Greece. Best served chilled as an aperitif or as a table wine.

RODITYS - a good, popular all-purpose rosé served chilled or at room temperature.

ZITSA - a golden champagne-like wine made in Epirus.

CHEESES

Greek cheeses possess distinctive and unique flavors of their own. Most of the following cheeses can now be purchased in American supermarkets and all can be found in specialty stores listed in the Shopper's Guide in the Appendix:

FETA – a salty white, moist cheese made from goat's milk. Considered the favorite of Greek cheeses, it is an integral ingredient of many recipes and is served as an appetizer as well as a table cheese. (See "Making Brine for Feta Cheese" in Miscellaneous Chapter.)

KASSERI – a firm aged cheese, mildly-flavored, sliced as a table cheese. Kasseri cubes can be fried and served as an appetizer.

KEFALOTIRI – a hard, cream-colored, aged cheese with a strong flavor, often grated over vegetables, meat and pasta dishes.

MIZITHRA – a mild, semi-soft grating cheese that is excellent over pasta.

OLIVES

The following varieties of olives, sold in jars or by the pound, are ready to be eaten just as they are, but a marinade does add to their flavor (see "Making Marinade for Olives" in Miscellaneous Chapter):

CALAMATA OLIVES – oblong, semi-soft olives with a smooth, purple skin. Considered the most delicious and come from the city of Kalamata in Messinia.

BLACK OLIVES – oily small and round olives, slightly bitter and salty.

AMPHISSA OLIVES – big, black juicy olives that come from Amphissa in the Parnassus region.

GREEN OLIVES – an oblong-shaped olive with firm flesh, smooth skin and a tart flavor; picked unripe.

SUBSTITUTIONS

Self-rising flour equals
  1 cup plain flour
  1 teaspoon baking powder
  1/2 teaspoon salt

1 square of baking chocolate equals
  3 tablespoons cocoa
  1 tablespoon shortening

1 cup cake flour equals
  7/8 cup all-purpose flour (1 cup minus 2 tablespoons)
  +2 tablespoons cornstarch

1 teaspoon baking powder equals
  1/4 teaspoon soda plus 1/2 teaspoon cream of tartar

1 clove of garlic equals
  1/8 teaspoon granulated or minced garlic

1 cup whole milk equals
  1 cup reconstituted nonfat dry milk plus 1 tablespoon butter or
  1/2 cup evaporated milk plus 1/2 cup water

1 teaspoon dry mustard equals
  1 tablespoon prepared mustard

1 tablespoon fresh herbs equals
  1 teaspoon dried herbs

1 cup honey equals
  1 1/4 cups sugar plus 1 cup liquid

2 small eggs may be used instead of 1 large egg

1 cup buttermilk or sour milk may be used instead of 1 cup yogurt

1 (15-oz.) can tomato sauce equals
  1 (6-oz.) can of tomato paste plus 1 cup water

2 cups whipped cream equals
  1/2 cup dry milk plus 1/2 cup ice water

SHOPPER'S GUIDE

The following stores in the area have been contacted and stock most of the Greek wines, grocery and delicatessen items found in this cookbook:

CHAPEL HILL — Fowler's Food Store
 306 W. Franklin Street

 *Mariakakis' Restaurant & Bakery
 15-501 By-Pass (across from
 Holiday Inn near
 Eastgate Shopping Center)

 Southern Seasons
 Eastgate Shopping Center

CARRBORO — Harris-Teeter Super Market
 Carr-Mill Shopping Village

DURHAM — *Fowler's Gourmet
 Brightleaf Square

 Wellspring Grocery
 1002 9th Street

_____

* Carry a complete selection of all specialty items.

MENU PLANNING

    Whatever the occasion, there are appropriate and distinctive dishes in the Greek cuisine that adapt well to entertaining and will establish your reputation as a creative hostess and a good cook. The following menus suggest dishes that are in this cookbook. Any specialty items can be purchased in stores listed in the Shopper's Guide of the Appendix.

COCKTAIL PARTY

Calamata Olives, Kasseri Cheese

* * *

Artichoke Dip with Crackers

* * *

Dolmathakia Yialadji
(Stuffed Grape Leaves with Rice)

* * *

Spanakopitakia
(Spinach Triangles)

* * *

Souzoukakia
(Cocktail Meatballs)

* * *

Chicken Roll-ups with Phyllo

* * *

Retsina, Greek Red and White Wines,
Ouzo, Mixed Drinks

FORMAL DINNER

Kotosoupa Avgolemono
(Chicken Egg-Lemon Soup)

* * *

Taramosalata
(Caviar Spread)

* * *

Astakos a la Skyros
(Lobster a la Skyros Island)

* * *

Rizi Pilafi
(Rice Pilaf)

* * *

Spanaki meh Krema
(Spinach Quiche)

* * *

Manitaria meh Voutero
(Sauteed Mushrooms)

* * *

Greek Dry White Wine

* * *

Kopenhaghi
(Copenhagen)

* * *

Kafethaki
(Greek Coffee)

<u>NAME DAY OR SPECIAL EVENT DINNER</u>
<u>Buffet Style</u>

MEZETHAKIA (APPETIZERS)

Feta Cheese   Calamata Olives
Salonika Peppers   Stuffed Baby Eggplant
        Taramosalata (Caviar Spread)
Dolmathakia Yialadji (Rice-Stuffed Grapeleaves)

* * *

Arni Bouti Yemisto
(Stuffed Leg of Lamb with Veal)

* * *

Domates Yemistes meh Rizi
(Stuffed Tomatoes with Rice)

* * *

Spanakopita
(Spinach Pita)

* * *

Psomi
(Greek Bread)

* * *

Greek Red Wine

* * *

Kataife and Lemon Koulourakia

* * *

Coffee

EASTER DINNER

Pascaliatika Avga
(Easter Eggs)

* * *

Kasseri Cheese, Calamata Olives and Relishes

* * *

Mayeritsa Apli
(Easter Soup Simplified)

* * *

Arni Psito meh Patates
(Roast Leg of Lamb with Potatoes)

* * *

Spanaki meh Kritharaki
(Spinach Casserole with Orzo)

* * *

Elliniki Salata
(Greek Salad)

* * *

Lambropsomo Tsoureki
(Braided Easter Bread)

* * *

Retsina Wine

* * *

Galaktoboureko and Koulourakia

* * *

Kafethaki
(Greek Coffee)

* * *

Freska Frouta
(Bowl of Fresh Fruit)

CHRISTMAS DINNER

MEZETHAKIA (APPETIZERS)

Tiropitakia (Cheese Triangles)
Marinated Sausage Meatballs
Eggplant Dip with Crackers

* * *

Soupa Hristouyeniatiki
(Christmas Soup)

* * *

Galopoula Psiti meh Yemisi
(Roast Turkey with Greek Stuffing)
Giblet Sauce

* * *

Patates tou Fournou
(Oven-Baked Potatoes)

* * *

Fasolia Yiahni
(Green Beans in Tomato Sauce)

* * *

Spanakopita
(Spinach Pita)

* * *

Christopsomo Tsoureki
(Holiday Bread)

* * *

Greek Dry White Wine

* * *

Kourambiethes
Finikia
Baklava

* * *

Coffee

SUMMER PARTY (Buffet Style)

MEZETHAKIA (APPETIZERS)

Celery Sticks   Carrot Sticks
Cucumber Spears   Tomato Wedges
Boiled Shrimp   Radishes
        Crusty Bread Sticks
     (Served with Tzadziki Sauce)

* * *

Souvlakia
(Shish-kebab)

* * *

Rizi Pilafi
(Rice Pilaf)

* * *

Marinated Broccoli and Squash

* * *

Zimaropita
(Squash Corn Bread)

* * *

Retsina, Greek Red Wine

* * *

Karithopita
(Nut Cake)

Baklavas meh Mela
(Baklava with Apples)

Freska Frouta
(Fresh Fruit)

* * *

Coffee

FAMILY DINNERS

MENU I

Fresh Spinach Salad

Moussaka
(Eggplant and Beef Casserole)

Psomi
(Greek White Bread)

Rizogalo
(Rice Pudding)

MENU II

Psari Plaki
(Baked Fish)

Rizi keh Kritharaki Pilafi
(Rice and Orzo Pilaf)

Aginares Lathoxitho
(Marinated Artichoke Hearts)

Eliopsomakia
(Olive Muffins)

Pantespani
(Lemon Sponge Cake)

Freska Frouta
(Fresh Fruit)

MENU III

Kota Riganati
(Chicken with Oregano)

Patates tou Fournou
(Oven-Baked Potatoes)

Kolokithia Yiahni
(Squash with Tomato Sauce)

Psomi
(Greek White Bread)

Pasta Flora II
(Latticed Jam Squares)

MENU IV

Keftethes meh Rizi Avgolemono
(Meatballs with Rice and Egg-Lemon Sauce)

Pantzaria Freska Vrasta
(Fresh Beet Salad)

Psomi
(Greek White Bread)

Krema Karamella
(Cream Caramel)

LENTEN DINNER

Calamata Olives

* * *

Fasolatha (Bean Soup)
or
Fakies (Lentil Soup)

* * *

Lahanika Plaki
(Baked Vegetables)

* * *

Paxemathia Apla
(Toasted Biscuits)

* * *

Koulourakia Nistisima
(Lenten Koulourakia)

AFTERNOON TEA OR COFFEE

Tiropitakia
(Cheese Triangles)

Domatitses meh Kavouri
(Crab-Stuffed Cherry Tomatoes)

* * *

Saragli   Kourambiethes

Poura   Halsema
(Nut Fingers)   (Yogurt Cake)

Paxemathia meh Amigthala
(Almond Tea Biscuits)

* * *

Tea or Coffee

GREEK-ENGLISH GLOSSARY

A

a la: (ah-lah) after, or according to
aginares: (ah-ghe-nah-rehs) artichokes
agouria: (ah-ghoo-re-ah) cucumbers
ahlathi: (ach-lah-the) pear
amigthala: (ah-meg-thah-lah) almonds
antithia: (an-te-the-ah) endive
apli: (ah-plee) plain
arni: (ahr-nee) lamb

Artoclasia: (ahr-to-klah-see-ah) five loaves of sweet bread
    signifying the miracle of the "Feeding of Five Thousand,"
    blessed and distributed to the congregation after a brief
    prayer service
astakos: (ah-stah-kos) lobster
avga: (ahv-ghah) eggs
avgolemono: (ahv-gho-leh-mo-no) egg and lemon

B

bakaliaros: (bah-kah-le-ah-ros) codfish
baklava: (bah-klah-vah) the famous layered nut and phyllo pastry
    dessert
bamies: (bahm-yes) okra
bourekakia: (boo-reh-kah-ke-ah) small phyllo triangles or rolls
    made with a variety of fillings
bouti: (boo-tee) leg, such as leg of lamb
breezoles: (bree-zo-lehs) meat chops
briki: (bree-kee) a special coffeepot used for making Greek coffee
brokola: (bro-ko-lah) broccoli
bulgur: (boul-gour) a whole-wheat grain, served like rice, popular
    in the Middle East

C

celino: (seh-lee-no) celery
Christopsomo: (hre-sto-pso-mo) a sweet bread baked at
    Christmastime

D

demitasse: (dehm-e-tas') a small coffee cup

dolmathakia yialadji: (dol-mah-thah'-ke-ah yiah-lah-dgee') rice-
stuffed grapeleaves served cold

dolmathes: (dol-mah'-thehs) cabbage or grape leaves stuffed with
either rice or meat

domates: (do-mah'-tehs) tomatoes

domatitses: (do-mah-tee'-tsehs) cherry or small tomatoes

E

elies: (eh-lyes') olives

Elliniki; Ellinko: (eh-le-nee-kee', ko') Greek, Grecian, Hellenic

F

faki; fakies: (fah-kee', fah-kyes') lentils

faskomilo: (fah-sko'-me-lo) sage leaves used in brewing an herbal
tea

fasolatha: (fah-so-lah'-thah) bean soup

fasolia: (fah-so'-le-ah) green or string beans

fava beans: (fah'-vah) also known as koukia or broad beans

feta cheese: (feh'-tah) a popular Greek semi-soft white cheese,
made from goat's milk

finikia: (fe-nee'-ke-ah) also known as melomakarona; cookies dipped
in a honey syrup and sprinkled with nuts

fistikia: (fe-stee'-ke-ah) pistachios

forma: (for'-mah) to make into a mold or form

frapa: (frah'-pah) grapefruit

freska: (freh'-skah) fresh

frouta: (froo'-tah) fruit

G

galaktoboureko: (ghah-lahk-to-boo'-re-ko) a baked custard dessert
with phyllo

galaktopita: (ghah-lahk-to'-pe-tah) a milk or custard pie

galopoula: (ghah-lo-poo'-lah) turkey

garithopitakia: (ghah'-re-tho-pe-tah'-ke-ah) small phyllo triangles
with a shrimp filling

glyka; glyko; glykos: (ghlee-kah', ko', kos') meaning sweets (noun)
or sweet (adjective)

H

halva: (hal-vah) a farina-based dessert served hot or cold and flavored with cinnamon

hamomilo: (hah-mó-mee-lo) camomile, an herbal tea

hirino: (hee-ree-nó) pork

horta: (hor-tah) vegetable greens

Hristouyeniatiki soupa: (hres-too-yeh-niah-tee-kee soó-pah) Christmas soup

I

Imam Baildi: (e-mahm bahl-deé) a meatless eggplant casserole made with tomatoes, onions, olive oil and herbs; named after a Turkish Imam (priest) who, as legend has it, swooned when he tasted this delicious dish

K

kafethaki: (kah-feh-thah-kee) Greek coffee

kafetzou: (kah-feh-tzoó) a fortune teller reading the future from coffee ground designs left in an inverted coffee cup

kaimaki: (ky-mah-kee) froth on top of the Greek coffee

kalamarakia; kalamaria: (kah-lah-mah-rah-ke-ah, kah-lah-mah-re-ah) baby squid, squid

kalamboki: (kah-lahm-bo-kee) corn

kali orexi: (kah-leé o-reh-xee) hearty appetite

karamella: (kah-rah-meh-lah) caramel

karithia: (kah-reé-the-ah) nuts

karithopita: (kah-ree-thó-pe-tah) nut cake

karota: (kah-ró-tah) carrots

kasseri: (kah-seh-ree) a creamy semi-firm cheese similar to Romano cheese

kataife: (kah-ty-eé-fee) shredded phyllo dough

kavouri: (kah-voó-ree) crab

kavouropitakia: (kah-voo-ró-pe-tah-ke-ah) small phyllo triangles with a crab filling

kavourosalata: (kah-voo-ro-sah-lah-tah) crab salad

kavourthismeno: (kah-voor-the-smeh-no) braised or fried

kefalotiri: (keh-fah-lo-teé-ree) a salty firm cheese used for grating

keftethes: (keh-fteh-thehs) meatballs

kema: (kee-mah) ground beef

kolliva: (kó-lee-vah) boiled wheat combined with raisins, spices and sugar; offered at a special prayer service for the deceased

kollivozoumi: (ko-lee-vo-zoó-mee) a pudding-like dessert made from the broth of the kolliva wheat

235

kolokithia: (ko-lo-kee-the-ah) squash or zucchini

kolokithopita: (ko-lo-kee-tho-pe-tah) squash or zucchini pie

kolokithopsomo: (ko-lo-ke-tho-pso-mo) squash or zucchini bread

kopanisto: (ko-pah-ne-stó) pounded or well beaten

Kopenhaghi: (ko-pen-hah-ghe) Copenhagen, a rich pastry cake named
    to honor the Danish King, George I, upon his coronation as
    King of Greece

kota: (ko-tah) chicken

kotopita: (ko-to-pe-tah) chicken pie

kotosoupa: (ko-to-soo-pah) chicken soup

koufeta: (koo-feh-tah) candy-coated Jordan almonds

koukia: (koo-ke-ah) fava beans or broad beans

koulourakia: (koo-loo-rah-ke-ah) crisp butter cookies made in
    various shapes

kouneli: (koo-neh-lee) rabbit

kounoupithi: (koo-noo-pee-thee) cauliflower

kourambiethes: (koo-rahm-bieh-thehs) butter cookies dusted with
    confectionary sugar

krasi: (krah-seé) wine

kreas: (kreh-as) meat

kreatopita: (kreh-ah-to-pe-tah) meat pie

kreatopitakia: (kreh-ah-to-pe-tah-ke-ah) small phyllo triangles
    with a meat stuffing

krema: (kreh-mah) cream

kremmithia: (kreh-mee-the-ah) onions

kritharaki: (kree-thah-rah-kee) orzo

Kritika: (kree-tee-kah) Cretan

kroketes: (kro-keh-tehs) croquettes, a ball made of minced meat,
    vegetable, rice or the like, coated with egg and bread crumbs
    and fried in deep fat

ktenia: (kteh-ne-ah) scallops

L

lahanika: (lah-hah-nee-kah) vegetables

lahano: (lah-hah-no) cabbage

lahanodolmathes: (lah-hah-no-dol-mah-thehs) cabbage leaves stuffed
    with rice and meat

Lambropsomo: (lahm-bro-pso-mo) sweet Easter bread

lathera; latheres: (lah-theh-rah, rehs) meatless dishes made with
    olive oil

lathoxitho: (lah-tho-xee-tho) with olive oil and vinegar

lekani: (leh-kah-nee) a large mixing bowl or basin

lemonata; lemoni: (leh-mo-nah-tah, leh-mo-nee) lemony, lemon

loukanika; loukaniko: (loo-kah-nee-kah, ko) Greek sausage
loukoumathes: (loo-koo-mah-thehs) deep-fried pastry puffs dipped
    in a honey syrup and sprinkled with grated nuts and cinnamon

M

mahlepi: (mah-leh-pee) an unusual flavoring added to holiday
    breads and cakes
makaronia: (mah-kah-ro-ne-ah) macaroni
manestra: (mah-neh-strah) orzo pasta
manitaria: (mah-nee-tah-re-ah) mushrooms
marinata: (mah-ree-nah-tah) marinated
mastiha: (mah-stee-hah) an anise-flavored resin from the mastic
    tree finely ground and used as a flavoring in holiday breads
    and cakes
Mavrodaphne: (mah-vro-dah-fnee) a sweet dessert wine
mayeritsa: (mah-yeh-ree-tsah) Easter soup, traditionally served
    after the midnight liturgy of the Resurrection
mayia: (mah-yiah) yogurt starter
mayioneza: (mah-yio-neh-zah) mayonnaise
mela; melo: (me-lah, lo) apples, apple
melitzana; melitzanes: (meh-lee-tzah-nah, nehs) eggplant,
    eggplants
melitzanosalata: (meh-lee-tzah-no-sah-lah-tah) eggplant salad
melomakarona: (meh-lo-mah-kah-ro-nah) also known as finikia
mezethakia: (meh-zeh-thah-ke-ah) appetizers
mizithra: (me-ze-thrah) a white, mild table cheese
mnemosinon: (mnee-mo-see-nun) a memorial service
moussaka: (moo-sah-kah) a popular meat and eggplant casserole
    topped with a rich cream sauce
msg: monosodium glutamate

N

nameday: an Orthodox Christian at his baptism generally receives
    the name of a Christian Saint who becomes his patron. On the
    day of the Saint's commemoration, the namesake also celebrates
nistisima: (nee-stee-see-mah) Lenten

O

oktapothi: (och-tah-po-thee) octopus
orektika: (o-rehk-tee-kah) appetizers
orzo: (or-zo) an oval-shaped pasta
ospria: (o-spree-ah) legumes, beans
ouzo: (oo-zo) a potent anise-flavored liqueur

P

pantespani: (pah-teh-spah-nee) sponge cake

pantzaria: (pahn-tzah-re-ah) beets

pantzorophylla: (pahn-tzo-ro-fee-lah) beet greens

papoutsakia: (pah-poo-tsah-ke-ah) literally means "little shoes"; stuffed eggplant or zucchini resemble little shoes

Pascaliatika avga: (pahs-kah-le-ah-te-kah ahv-gha) Easter eggs

pasta: (pah-stah) pastry; macaroni products

pasta flora: (pah-stah flo-rah) a lattice-topped dessert with a cookie base spread with fruit preserves

pastitsio: (pah-stee-tse-o) the popular macaroni and ground beef casserole topped with a rich cream sauce

patates: (pah-tah-tehs) potatoes

paxemathia: (pah-xee-mah-the-ah) semi-sweet cookies; dough is baked in narrow loaves, then sliced and toasted in oven

phyllo: (fee-lo) paper-thin pastry sheets; the basic ingredient to many appetizer, entree and dessert recipes

pignolia nuts: (pig-no-le-ah) pine nuts from tree native to the Mediterranean region

pilafi: (pe-lah-fee) pilaf or rice sauteed in butter and simmered in chicken, meat or fish stock until fluffy

piperies: (pe-peh-ryes) peppers

pita; pites: (pe-tah, tehs) a Greek pie or pies; a phyllo pastry entree with a cheese, vegetable or meat filling

plaki: (plah-kee) baked vegetables and/or fish in tomatoes, onions and olive oil

poura: (poo-rah) literally means "cigars"; nut mixture rolled in phyllo resembling a cigar

prasa: (prah-sah) leeks

prasines elies: (prah-se-nehs eh-lyes) green olives

prasopita: (prah-so-pe-tah) leek pie

Prosphoron: (pro-sfo-ron) Bread of Oblation, used in Greek Orthodox Church services

psari: (psah-re) fish

psarosoupa: (psah-ro-soo-pah) fish soup

psites; psito: (pse-tehs, to) baked

psomi: (pso-mee) bread

R

ramekin: (ram-eh-kin) a small ovenproof dish for individual servings

rathikia: (rah-the-ke-ah) dandelion greens

Retsina: (reh-tse-nah) a resin-flavored wine popular in Greece

238

revani: (reh-vah-neé) a fine-textured cake made with farina and
    moistened with syrup
revithia: (reh-veé-the-ah) chick peas
riganati; riganato: (ree-ghah-nah-tee, to) with oregano
rizi: (reé-zee) rice
rizogalo: (ree-zo-ghah-lo) rice pudding
rolo: (ro-ló) roll or loaf

S

saganaki: (sah-ghah-nah-kee) fried kasseri cheese cubes
salata: (sah-lah-tah) salad
Salonika peppers: (sah-ló-ne-kah) small pickled peppers
saltsa: (sahl-tsah) sauce
saragli: (sah-rah-gleé) a rolled pastry version of baklava
semolina: (se-mo-leé-nah) a granular durum wheat flour used in the
    baking of certain cakes and custards
sikotakia: (see-ko-tah-ke-ah) chicken livers
silver dragees: silver-coated candy used in decorating kolliva for
    memorial services
sinapia: (se-nah-pe-ah) mustard greens
sitari: (se-tah-ree) whole wheat kernels used in making kolliva
    for memorial services
skaltsounia: (skahl-tsoo-ne-ah) small turnovers with a fruit,
    cheese or vegetable filling, baked or fried; a Cretan specialty
skorthalia: (skor-thah-le-ah) a pungent garlic sauce served with
    fish or certain fried vegetables
Skyros: (skeé-ros) a Greek island famous for its tasty lobsters
Smyrna: (smear-nah) an old city of Turkey once populated by the
    Greek majority and known for its superb cuisine
soupa: (soo-pah) soup
souvlakia: (soo-vlah-ke-ah) shish-kebab; small cubes of marinated
    meat skewered with vegetables and broiled or grilled
souzoukakia: (soo-zoo-kah-ke-ah) small spicy meatballs in tomato
    sauce
spanaki: (spah-nah-kee) spinach
spanakopita: (spah-nah-ko-pe-tah) spinach pie
spanakopitakia: (spah-nah-ko-pe-tah-ke-ah) small phyllo triangles
    with a spinach filling
spanakorizo: (spah-nah-ko-ree-zo) spinach and rice
stifatho: (stee-fah-tho) an aromatic stew of either chicken, beef,
    lamb or rabbit simmered in a wine-flavored tomato sauce
    containing many small whole onions

tarama: (tah-rah-mah) carp roe, used in making the popular caviar dip, taramosalata

taramokeftethes: (tah-rah-mo-keh-fteh-thehs) fried patties of mashed potatoes and tarama

taverna: (tah-vehr-nah) neighborhood tavern

thamaskina: (thah-mah-skee-nah) prunes

thiosmos: (thio-smos) fresh mint

thiples: (the-plehs) delicate deep-fried pastry shaped into a rosette, dipped in syrup and sprinkled with grated nuts and cinnamon

tiganita; tiganitos: (te-ghah-nee-tah, tos) fried

tiri: (tee-ree) cheese

tirobiskotakia: (tee-ro-bees-ko-tah-ke-ah) cheese squares

tiropita: (tee-ro-pe-tah) cheese pie

tiropitakia: (tee-ro-pe-tah-ke-ah) small phyllo triangles with a cheese filling

tou fournou: (too foor-noo) a dish baked in the oven

tou koutaliou: (too koo-tah-lioo) literally means "a spoon sweet"; fruit preserves served with a spoon

tourlou: (toor-loo) a medley of vegetables and/or meat baked in a casserole

toursi: (toor-see) pickled

tou spetiou: (too spe-tioo) homemade

tou vounou: (too voo-noo) from or of the mountain, such as mountain tea

trahana: (trah-hah-nah) a nutritious homemade pasta used in soups and stews and in making a hot breakfast cereal

tsai: (tsah-e) tea

tsakistes: (tsah-kee-stehs) Greek green olives packed in a vinegar-flavored brine

tsoureki: (tsoo-reh-kee) the general term for sweet holiday bread

tzadziki: (tzah-dzee-kee) a garlic-flavored cucumber and yogurt sauce used as a dip or topping on a "gyro" sandwich

V

Vasilopita: (vah-see-lo-pe-tah) a cake bread baked for New Year's Day

vissino: (vee-see-no) sour cherry preserves

vothino: (vo-the-no) beef

voutero: (voo-tee-ro) butter

vrasta: (vrah-stah) boiled

yemista; yemistes; yemisto: (yeh-me-stah, stehs, stó) stuffed
   vegetables
yiahni: (yiah-neé) foods simmered in tomato sauce and olive oil
yialadji: (yiah-lah-djeé) a dish without meat, served cold or room
   temperature
yiaourti: (yiah-oor-tee) yogurt
yiouvarlakia: (yiou-vahr-lah-ke-ah) small rice-meatballs simmered
   in stock and usually topped with an egg-lemon sauce
yiouvetsi: (yiou-veh-tsee) a dish cooked in the oven

Z

zaharoplastion: (zah-hah-ro-plah-stee-on) a pastry or sweet shop
zimaropita: (zee-mah-ro-pe-tah) a type of pita or pie

Index I

243

Index II

248

NOTES

HELLENIC LADIES SOCIETY
ST. BARBARA GREEK ORTHODOX CHURCH
P.O. BOX 1149
DURHAM, NORTH CAROLINA 277002

Please send me _____ copies of **The Grecian Plate** at
$9.95 per copy plus $1.55 for postage and handling.

Enclosed you will find $_____ for this order.
Name_____

Address_____

City_____State_____Zip_____
North Carolina Residents please add 4% sales tax.

- -

HELLENIC LADIES SOCIETY
ST. BARBARA GREEK ORTHODOX CHURCH
P.O. BOX 1149
DURHAM, NORTH CAROLINA 277002

Please send me _____ copies of **The Grecian Plate** at
$9.95 per copy plus $1.55 for postage and handling.

Enclosed you will find $_____ for this order.
Name_____

Address_____

City_____State_____Zip_____
North Carolina Residents please add 4% sales tax.

- -

HELLENIC LADIES SOCIETY
ST. BARBARA GREEK ORTHODOX CHURCH
P.O. BOX 1149
DURHAM, NORTH CAROLINA 277002

Please send me _____ copies of **The Grecian Plate** at
$9.95 per copy plus $1.55 for postage and handling.

Enclosed you will find $_____ for this order.
Name_____

Address_____

City_____State_____Zip_____
North Carolina Residents please add 4% sales tax.

Re-order Additional Copies